ROOSEVELT IN THE BAD LANDS

BY
HERMANN HAGEDORN

ISBN 0-9601652-4-X

Published by the Theodore Roosevelt Nature &
    History Association
P.O. Box 167
Medora, North Dakota 58645

Cover Illustrations: Lili Stewart

It was still the Wild West in those days, the Far West, the West of Owen Wister's stories and Frederic Remington's drawings, the West of the Indian and the buffalo-hunter, the soldier and the cow-puncher. That land of the West has gone now, "gone, gone with lost Atlantis," gone to the isle of ghosts and of strange dead memories. It was a land of vast silent spaces, of lonely rivers, and of plains where the wild game stared at the passing horseman. It was a land of scattered ranches, of herds of long-horned cattle, and of reckless riders who unmoved looked in the eyes of life or death. In that land we led a free and hardy life, with horse and with rifle. We worked under the scorching midsummer sun, when the wide plains shimmered and wavered in the heat; and we knew the freezing misery of riding night guard round the cattle in the late fall round-up. In the soft springtime the stars were glorious in our eyes each night before we fell asleep; and in the winter we rode through blinding blizzards, when the driven snow-dust burnt our faces. There were monotonous days, as we guided the trail cattle or the beef herds, hour after hour, at the slowest of walks; and minutes or hours teeming with excitement as we stopped stampedes or swam the herds across rivers treacherous with quicksands or brimmed with running ice. We knew toil and hardship and hunger and thirst; and we saw men die violent deaths as they worked among the horses and cattle, or fought in evil feuds with one another; but we felt the beat of hardy life in our veins, and ours was the glory of work and the joy of living.

THEODORE ROOSEVELT
(*Autobiography*)

PREFACE

To write any book is an adventure, but to write this book has been the kind of gay and romantic experience that makes any man who has partaken of it a debtor forever to the Giver of Delights. Historical research, contrary to popular opinion, is one of the most thrilling of occupations, but I question whether any biographer has ever had a better time gathering his material than I have had. Amid the old scenes, the old epic life of the frontier has been re-created for me by the men who were the leading actors in it. But my contact with it has not been only vicarious. In the course of this most grateful of labors I have myself come to know something of the life that Roosevelt knew thirty-five years ago — the hot desolation of noon in the scarred butte country; the magic of dawn and dusk when the long shadows crept across the coulees and woke them to unexpected beauty; the solitude of the prairies, that have the vastness without the malignancy of the sea. I have come to know the thrill and the dust and the cattle-odors of the round-up; the warm companionship of the ranchman's dinner-table; such profanity as I never expect to hear again; singing and yarns and hints of the tragedy of prairie women; and, at the height of a barbecue, the appalling intrusion of death. I have felt in all its potency the spell which the "short-grass country" cast over Theodore Roosevelt; and I cannot hear the word Dakota without feeling a stirring in my blood.

It was Mr. Roosevelt himself who gave me the impulse to write this book, and it was the letters of introduction which he wrote early in 1918 which made it possible for me to secure the friendly interest of the men who knew most about his life on the ranch and the range. "If you want to know what I was like when I had bark on," he said, "you ought to talk to Bill Sewall and Merrifield and Sylvane Ferris and his brother Joe." I was writing a book about him for boys at the time, and again and again he said, "I want you to go out to Dakota!" On one occasion I referred to his life in the Bad Lands as "a kind of idyl." "That's it!" he exclaimed. "That's it ! That's exactly what it was !"

The wish he had expressed, living, became in a sense a command after he was dead. The letters he had given me unsealed the lips of the men who, for thirty-five years, had steadily refused to reveal to "newspaper fellers" the intimate story of the romantic life they had shared with the man who became President of the United States. From Dickinson, North Dakota, came Sylvane Ferris; from Terry, Montana, came "Joe" Ferris; from Somers, Montana, came "Bill" Merrifield, and, on their old stamping-ground along the Little Missouri, unfolded, bit by bit, the story of the four years of Roosevelt's active ranching life. In the deserted barroom of the old "Metropolitan Hotel" at

Medora (rechristened the "Rough Riders"); on the ruins of the Maltese Cross cabin and under the murmuring cottonwoods at Elkhorn, they spun their joyous yarns. Apart from what they had to tell, it was worth traveling two thirds across the Continent to come to know these figures of an heroic age; and to sit at Sylvane Ferris's side as he drove his Overland along the trails of the Bad Lands and through the quicksands of the Little Missouri, was in itself not an insignificant adventure. Mrs. Margaret Roberts, at Dickinson, had her own stories to tell; and in the wilderness forty miles west of Lake McDonald, on the Idaho border, John Reuter, known to Roosevelt as "Dutch Wannigan," told, as no one else could, of the time he was nearly killed by the Marquis de Mores. A year later it was Schuyler Lebo who guided me in a further search for material, fifty miles south from Medora by buckboard through the wild, fantastic beauty of the Bad Lands. I doubt if there is any one I missed who had anything to tell of Roosevelt.

So far as any facts relating to Roosevelt or to the Western frontier can ever be described as "cold," it is a narrative of cold facts which I have attempted to tell in this book. The truth, in this case, is romantic enough and needs no embellishment. I have made every effort to verify my narrative, but, to some extent, I have had to depend, inevitably, on the character of the men and women who gave me my data, as every historical writer must who deals not with documents (which may, of course, themselves be mendacious), but with what is, in a sense, "raw material." One highly dramatic story, dealing with Roosevelt's defiance of a certain desperate character, which has at different times during the past twenty-five years been printed in leading newspapers and periodicals, told always by the same writer, I have had to reject because I could find no verification of it, though I think it may well be true.

In weaving my material into a connected narrative I have consciously departed from fact in only one respect. Certain names — a half-dozen or so in all — are fictitious. In certain cases, in which the story I had to tell might give needless offense to the actors in it still surviving, or to their children, and in which I was consequently confronted by the alternative of rejecting the story in question or changing the names, I chose the latter course without hesitation. It is quite unessential, for instance, what the real name was of the lady known in this book as "Mrs. Cummins"; but her story is an important element in the narrative. To those who may recognize themselves under the light veil I have thrown over their portraits, and may feel grieved, I can only say that, inasmuch as they were inhabitants of the Bad Lands when Theodore Roosevelt and the Marquis de Mores shaped their destinies there for good or ill, they became historical figures and must take their chances at the judgment seat of posterity with Nebuchadnezzar and Cæsar and St. Augustine and Calamity Jane.

The Northwestern newspapers of the middle

eighties contain much valuable material, not only about the Marquis and his romantic enterprises, which greatly interested the public, but about Roosevelt himself. The files of the *Press* of Dickinson, North Dakota, and the *Pioneer* of Mandan, have proved especially useful, though scarcely more useful than those of the Bismarck *Tribune*, the Minneapolis *Journal*, and the *Dispatch* and *Pioneer Press* of St. Paul. The cut of Roosevelt's cattle-brands, printed on the jacket, is reproduced from the *Stockgrowers' Journal* of Miles City. I have sought high and low for copies of the *Bad Lands Cowboy*, published in Medora, but only one copy — Joe Ferris's — has come to light. "'Bad-man' Finnegan," it relates among other things, "is serving time in the Bismarck penitentiary for stealing Theodore Roosevelt's boat." But that is a part of the story; and this is only a Preface.

Colonel Roosevelt's own books, notably "Hunting Trips of a Ranchman," "Ranch Life and the Hunting Trail," "The Wilderness Hunter," and the "Autobiography," have furnished me an important part of my material, giving me minute details of his hunting experiences which I could have secured nowhere else; and I am indebted to the publishers, Messrs. G. P. Putnam's Sons, Messrs. Charles Scribner's Sons, and the Century Company, for permission to use them. I am indebted to the following publishers, likewise, for permission to reprint certain verses as chapter headings: Messrs. Houghton Mifflin Company ("Riders of the Stars," by Henry

Herbert Knibbs, and "Songs of Men," edited by
Robert Frothingham); the Macmillan Company
("Cowboy Songs," edited by Professor John A.
Lomax); and Mr. Richard G. Badger ("Sun and
Saddle Leather," by Badger Clark). I am espe-
cially indebted to Mr. Roosevelt's sisters, Mrs. W.
S. Cowles and Mrs. Douglas Robinson, and to the
Honorable Henry Cabot Lodge for the opportunity
to examine the unpublished letters of Colonel Roose-
velt in their possession and to reprint excerpts from
them. Through the courtesy of Mr. Clarence L. Hay
I have been able to print a part of an extraordinary
letter written by President Roosevelt to Secretary
Hay in 1903; through the courtesy of Messrs. Har-
per and Brothers I have been permitted to make
use of material in "Bill Sewall's story of T. R.," by
William W. Sewall, and in "The Boys' Life of
Theodore Roosevelt."

Partly from books and letters, partly from documents and old newspapers, I have gathered bit by
bit the story of Roosevelt's life as a ranchman; but
my main sources of material have been the men
and women (scattered now literally from Maine to
the State of Washington) who were Roosevelt's
companions and friends. It is difficult to express
adequately my gratitude to them for their unfailing
helpfulness; their willingness to let themselves be
quizzed, hour after hour, and to answer, in some cases,
a very drumfire of importunate letters; above all
for their resistance, to what must at times have been
an almost overpowering temptation, to "string the

tenderfoot." They took my inquisition with grave seriousness and gave me what they had without reserve and without elaboration.

There are five men to whom I am peculiarly indebted: to Mr. Sylvanus M. Ferris and Mr. A. W. Merrifield, who were Roosevelt's ranch-partners at the Maltese Cross Ranch, and to Mr. William W. Sewall, of Island Falls, Maine, who was his foreman at Elkhorn; to Mr. Lincoln A. Lang, of Philadelphia, who, having the seeing eye, has helped me more than any one else to visualize the men and women who played the prominent parts in the life of Medora; and to Mr. A. T. Packard, of Chicago, founder and editor of the *Bad Lands Cowboy*, who told me much of the efforts to bring law and order into Billings County. To Mr. Joseph A. Ferris and Mrs. Ferris; to Mr. William T. Dantz, of Vineland, New Jersey; to Mrs. Margaret Roberts and Dr. Victor H. Stickney, both of Dickinson, North Dakota; to Mr. George Myers, of Townsend, Montana; to Mr. John Reuter, to Mr. John C. Fisher, of Vancouver, British Columbia, and to Mr. John Willis, of Glasgow, Montana, Roosevelt's companion of many hunts, I am indebted to a scarcely less degree. Others who gave me important assistance were Mr. Howard Eaton, of Wolf, Wyoming, and Mr. "Pete" Pellessier of Sheridan, Wyoming; Mr. James Harmon, Mr. Oren Kendley, Mr. Schuyler Lebo, and Mr. William McCarty, of Medora, North Dakota; Mr. William G. Lang, of Baker, Montana; Mr. W. H. Fortier, of Spokane, Washington; Mr. Edward

A. Allen and Mr. George F. Will, of Bismarck, North Dakota; Mr. J. B. Brubaker, of Terry; Mr. Laton A. Huffman and Mr. C. W. Butler, of Miles City, Montana; Dr. Alexander Lambert, of New York City; Dr. Herman Haupt, of Setauket, New York; the Reverend Edgar Haupt, of St. Paul, Minnesota; Mr. Alfred White, of Dickinson; Mr. Dwight Smith, of Chicago; Mrs. Granville Stuart, of Grantsdale, Montana; Mr. Frank B. Linderman, of Somers, Montana; Mr. C. R. Greer, of Hamilton, Ohio; Mrs. George Sarchet, of New England, South Dakota; and especially, my secretary, Miss Gisela Westhoff.

I have enjoyed the writing-man's rarest privilege — the assistance of wise and friendly critics, notably Professor Albert Bushnell Hart, of Harvard; President John Grier Hibben, of Princeton; and Professor William A. Dunning, of Columbia, who generously consented to serve as a committee of the Roosevelt Memorial Association to examine my manuscript; and Dr. John A. Lester, of the Hill School, who has read the proof and given me valuable suggestions.

To all these friendly helpers my gratitude is deep. My warmest thanks, however, are due Mr. William Boyce Thompson, President of the Roosevelt Memorial Association, whose quick imagination and effective interest made possible the collection of the material under the auspices of the Association.

H. H.

FAIRFIELD, CONNECTICUT
June 20, 1921

CONTENTS

INTRODUCTION   XXV

CHAPTER I. Arrival — Little Missouri — A game country — Joe Ferris — The trail to Chimney Butte — The three Canadians — The buckskin mare   3

CHAPTER II. Gregor Lang — The Vine family — The buffalo hunt — The argonauts — Politics — The passing of the buffalo — Pursuit — The charge of the buffalo — Broken slumbers — Failure — "It's dogged that does it" — Roosevelt makes a decision — He acquires two partners — He kills his buffalo   18

CHAPTER III. Jake Maunders — The "bad men" — Archie the precocious — County organization — The graces of the wicked   47

CHAPTER IV. Marquis de Mores — Founding of Medora — The machinations of Maunders result in bloodshed — The boom begins — The Marquis in business — Roosevelt returns East — The Marquis's idea — Packard — Frank Vine's little joke — Medora blossoms forth — The Marquis has a new dream — Joe Ferris acquires a store — Roosevelt meets disaster — Invasion — Roosevelt turns West   58

CHAPTER V. "I will not be dictated to!" — George Myers — Mrs. Maddox — The Maltese Cross — On the round-up — "Hasten forward quickly there!" — Trying out the tenderfoot — A letter to "Bamie" — The emerald biscuits   89

CHAPTER VI. The neighbors — Mrs. Roberts — Hell-Roaring Bill Jones — A good man for "sassing" — The master of Medora — The Marquis's stage-line — The road to Deadwood — The Marquis finds a manager   108

CHAPTER VII. The gayety of Medora — Holocaust — Influence of the cowboy — Moulding public opinion — The "Bastile" — The mass meeting — The thieves — The underground railway — Helplessness of the righteous — Granville Stuart — The three argonauts　　123

CHAPTER VIII. The new ranch — The bully at Mingusville — The end of the bully — Dakota discovers Roosevelt — Stuart's vigilantes — Sewall and Dow — Mrs. Lang — Sewall speaks his mind — Enter the Marquis　　148

CHAPTER IX. "Dutch Wannigan" — Political sirens — "Able to face anything"　　167

CHAPTER X. The start for the Big Horns — Roosevelt writes home — A letter to Lodge — Indians — Camp in the mountains — Roosevelt gets his bear　　175

CHAPTER XI. Rumblings from the Marquis — The "stranglers" — The band of "Flopping Bill" — Fifteen marked men — Maunders the discreet — Sewall receives callers　　189

CHAPTER XII. "Medicine Buttes" — Roosevelt returns to Elkhorn — Maunders threatens Roosevelt — Packard's stage-line — The dress rehearsal — Another bubble bursts　　202

CHAPTER XIII. Bleak camping — Roosevelt "starts a reform" — The deputy marshal — Winter activities — Breaking broncos — A tenderfoot holds his own — Wild country — Mountain sheep — The stockmen's association　　215

CHAPTER XIV. Winter misery — Return to Medora — Illness and recovery — Mingusville — "He's drunk and on the shoot" — The seizure of Bill　　235

CHAPTER XV. The spring of 1885 — Swimming the Little Missouri — Ranching companions — Golden expectations — The boss of the Maltese Cross — The buttermilk — Hospitality at Yule — Lang's love of debate — Nitch comes to dine 248

CHAPTER XVI. Cattle torture — Trailing cattle — Roosevelt's horsemanship — Gentling the Devil — The spring round-up — The first encampment — The day's work — Diversions — Profanity — "Fight or be friends" 266

CHAPTER XVII. The "mean" horse — Ben Butler — Dr. Stickney — Dinner with Mrs. Cummins — The stampede — Roping an earl's son — A letter to Lodge — Sylvane's adventure — Law 286

CHAPTER XVIII. Sewall's skepticism — Interview at St. Paul — The women-folks — The Elkhorn "Outfit" — The Wadsworths' dog 305

CHAPTER XIX. Medora — "Styles in the Bad Lands" — The coming of law — The preachers — Packard's parson — Johnny O'Hara 318

CHAPTER XX. De Mores the undaunted — Genealogy of the Marquis — Roosevelt and the Marquis — Hostility — The first clash — Indictment of the Marquis — The Marquis's trial — The Marquis sees red — Peace 331

CHAPTER XXI. Red man and white — Roosevelt's adventure — Good Indian, dead Indian — Prairie fires — Sewall delivers a lecture — The testing of Mrs. Joe — Mrs. Joe takes hold 350

CHAPTER XXII. The theft of the boat — Redhead Finnegan — Preparations for pursuit — Departure — "Hands up!" — Capture of the thieves — Marooned — Cross country to jail — Arrival in Dickinson — "The only damn fool" 365

CHAPTER XXIII. Medora's first election — The celebration — Miles City meeting — Roosevelt's cattle prospects — "His upper lip is stiff" — Completing "Benton" — The summer of 1886 — Influence over cowboys — "A Big Day" — Oratory — Roosevelt on Americanism — "You will be President"   387

CHAPTER XXIV. A troop of Rough Riders — Premonitions of trouble — The hold-up — The Cœur d'Alênes — Hunting white goats — John Willis — Elkhorn breaks up — Facing east   412

CHAPTER XXV. The bad winter — The first blizzard — Destruction of the cattle — The spring flood — The boneyard   429

CHAPTER XXVI. Roosevelt's losses — Morrill vs. Myers — Roosevelt takes a hand — A country of ruins — New schemes of the Marquis — The fading of Medora   440

CHAPTER XXVII. Bill Jones — Old friends — Seth Bullock — Death of the Marquis — Roosevelt's progress — Return as Governor — Medora celebrates — The "cowboy bunch" — Return as President — Death of Bill Jones — The Bad Lands to-day   453

INTRODUCTION

Theodore Roosevelt Nature and History Association is proud to offer this re-publication of Hermann Hagedorn's classic *Roosevelt in the Badlands*. It is an important book among the literature of a great conservationist and President of the United States, Theodore Roosevelt. Mr. Roosevelt was profoundly influenced by his experiences as a ranchman in Dakota and later remarked that it was "the most important educational asset of all my life." In 1910, during a return trip to North Dakota, Roosevelt told a crowd in Fargo, "If it had not been for what I learned during these years...here in North Dakota, I would never in the world have been president of the United States."

It was Theodore Roosevelt himself who encouraged Hermann Hagedorn to write this story; and Mr. Hagedorn did his job admirably. He drew upon Roosevelt's extensive writings and private papers, newspapers of the time, and most importantly upon the interviews he conducted with men and women who had lived and worked alongside Mr. Roosevelt in the badlands.

Mr. Hagedorn admitted to using fictitious names "in certain cases, in which the story...might give needless offense to the actors...or their children." While historian at Theodore Roosevelt National Park, Ray H. Mattison researched the identities of these "actors" and published his findings in a 1950 report entitled *Roosevelt's Contemporaries along the Little Missouri*. He concluded that

Hagedorn's character Frank Vine was really Frank Moore, Jake Maunders was E.G. ("Gerry") Paddock, Mr. and Mrs. Cummins were in fact Mr. and Mrs. D.K. Wade, and that Van Zander was J.A. Van Eeghan.

Mr. Hagedorn wrote eloquently about situations, issues, and experiences that molded the rugged individualism of Theodore Roosevelt and his friends along the Little Missouri River. In writing this book Mr. Hagedorn unwittingly added a unique portion to the regional history of western North Dakota and eastern Montana.

Our sincere gratitude is extended to Mrs. Mary H. Kershner and Mrs. Eric Parfit, who have granted their permission to reprint this important work, and to the staff of Theodore Roosevelt National Park for their encouragement and support of this project. *Roosevelt in the Badlands* is once again available to scholars, history buffs, and to those who admire Theodore Roosevelt, the man.

Tim McLaughlin
President,
Theodore Roosevelt Nature
   & History Association
May 21, 1987

ROOSEVELT IN THE BAD LANDS

MY FRIENDS, I never can sufficiently express the obligations I am under to the territory of Dakota, for it was here that I lived a number of years in a ranch house in the cattle country, and I regard my experience during those years, when I lived and worked with my own fellow ranchmen on what was then the frontier, as the most important educational asset of all my life. It is a mighty good thing to know men, not from looking at them, but from having been one of them. When you have worked with them, when you have lived with them, you do not have to wonder how they feel, because you feel it yourself. Every now and then I am amused when newspapers in the East — perhaps, I may say, not always friendly to me — having prophesied that I was dead wrong on a certain issue, and then finding out that I am right, express acid wonder how I am able to divine how people are thinking. Well, sometimes I don't and sometimes I do; but when I do, it comes simply from the fact that this is the way I am thinking myself. I know how the man that works with his hands and the man on the ranch are thinking, because I have been there and I am thinking that way myself. It is not that I divine the way they are thinking, but that I think the same way.

THEODORE ROOSEVELT
Speech at Sioux Falls
September 3, 1910.

ROOSEVELT IN THE
BAD LANDS

I

Rainy dark or firelight, bacon rind or pie,
Livin' is a luxury that don't come high;
Oh, be happy and onruly while our years and luck allow,
For we all must die or marry less than forty years from now!
BADGER CLARK

THE train rumbled across three hundred feet of
trestle and came to a stop. A young man, slender, not over-tall, with spectacles and a moustache,
descended the steps. If he expected that his foot,
groping below the bottom step in the blackness for
something to land on, would find a platform, he
was doomed to disappointment. The " depot " at
Little Missouri did not boast a platform. The
young man pulled his duffle-bag and gun-case down
the steps; somebody waved a lantern; the train
stirred, gained momentum, and was gone, having accomplished its immediate mission, which was to de-
posit a New York " dude," politician and would-be
hunter, named Theodore Roosevelt, in the Bad
Lands of Dakota.

The time was three o'clock of a cool, September
morning, and the place, in the language of the Bad
Lands, was " dark as the inside of a caow." If
the traveler from afar had desired illumination and
a reception committee, he should have set his arrival

not for September 7th, but for September 6th. Twenty-four hours previous, it happened, the citizens of Little Missouri had, in honor of a distinguished party which was on its way westward to celebrate the completion of the road, amply anticipated any passion for entertainment which the passengers on the Overland might have possessed. As the engine came to a stop, a deafening yell pierced the night, punctuated with pistol-shots. Cautious investigation revealed figures dancing wildly around a bonfire; and the passengers remembered the worst they had ever heard about Indians. The flames shot upward, setting the shadows fantastically leaping up the precipitous bluffs and among the weird petrifactions of a devil's nightmare that rimmed the circle of flaring light. A man with a gun in his hand climbed aboard the train and made his way to the dining-car, yelling for " cow-grease," and demanding, at the least, a ham-bone. It took the burliest of his comrades to transport the obstreperous one back to solid earth just as the train moved out.

There was nothing so theatrical awaiting Theodore Roosevelt. The " depot " was deserted. Roosevelt dragged his belongings through the sagebrush toward a huge black building looming northeastward through the night, and hammered on the door until the proprietor appeared, muttering curses.

The face that Roosevelt saw, in the light of a smoky lantern, was not one to inspire confidence in a tenderfoot on a dark night. The features were those of a man who might have been drinking, with inconsiderable interruptions, for a very long time. He was short and stout and choleric, with a wiry moustache under a red nose; and seemed to be distinctly under the impression that Roosevelt had done something for which he should apologize.

He led the way upstairs. Fourteen beds were scattered about the loft which was the second story of the Pyramid Park Hotel, and which, Roosevelt heard subsequently, was known as the " bull-pen." One was unoccupied. He accepted it without a murmur.

What the thirteen hardened characters who were his roommates said next morning, when they discovered the " Eastern punkin-lily " which had blossomed in their midst, is lost to history. It was unquestionably frank, profane, and unwashed. He was, in fact, not a sight to awaken sympathy in the minds of such inhabitants as Little Missouri possessed. He had just recovered from an attack of cholera morbus, and though he had written his mother from Chicago that he was already " feeling like a fighting-cock," the marks of his illness were still on his face. Besides, he wore glasses, which, as he later discovered, were considered in the Bad Lands as a sign of a " defective moral character."

It was a world of strange and awful beauty into which Roosevelt stepped as he emerged from the dinginess of the ramshackle hotel into the crisp autumn morning. Before him lay a dusty, sagebrush flat walled in on three sides by scarred and precipitous clay buttes. A trickle of sluggish water in a wide bed, partly sand and partly baked gumbo, oozed beneath steep banks at his back, swung sharply westward, and gave the flat on the north a fringe of dusty-looking cottonwoods, thirstily drinking the only source of moisture the country seemed to afford. Directly across the river, beyond another oval-shaped piece of bottom-land, rose a steep bluff, deeply shadowed against the east, and south of it stretched in endless succession the seamed ranges and fantastic turrets and cupolas and flying buttresses of the Bad Lands.

It was a region of weird shapes garbed in barbaric colors, gray-olive striped with brown, lavender striped with black, chalk pinnacles capped with flaming scarlet. French-Canadian *voyageurs*, a century previous, finding the weather-washed ravines wicked to travel through, spoke of them as *mauvaises terres pour traverser*, and the name clung. The whole region, it was said, had once been the bed of a great lake, holding in its lap the rich clays and loams which the rains carried down into it. The passing of ages brought vegetation, and the passing of other ages turned that vegetation into coal. Other deposits settled over the coal. At last this vast lake found an outlet in the Missouri. The wear and wash of the waters cut in time through the clay, the coal, and the friable limestone of succeeding deposits, creating ten thousand watercourses bordered by precipitous bluffs and buttes,

which every storm gashed and furrowed anew. On
the tops of the flat buttes was rich soil and in countless pleasant valleys were green pastures, but
there were regions where for miles only sagebrush
and stunted cedars lived a starved existence. Bad
lands they were, for man or beast, and Bad Lands
they remained.

The " town " of Little Missouri consisted of a
group of primitive buildings scattered about the
shack which did duty as a railroad station. The
Pyramid Park Hotel stood immediately north of
the tracks; beside it stood the one-story palace of sin
of which one, who shall, for the purposes of this
story, be known as Bill Williams, was the owner,
and one who shall be known as Jess Hogue, the evil
genius. South of the track a comical, naïve Swede
named Johnny Nelson kept a store when he was not
courting Katie, the hired girl in Mrs. McGeeney's
boarding-house next door, or gambling away his
receipts under Hogue's crafty guidance. Directly
to the east, on the brink of the river, the railroad
section-foreman, Fitzgerald, had a shack and a
wife who quarreled unceasingly with her neighbor,
Mrs. McGeeney. At a corresponding place on the
other side of the track, a villainous gun-fighter
named Maunders lived (as far as possible) by his
neighbors' toil. A quarter of a mile west of him,
in a grove of cottonwood trees, stood a group of
gray, log buildings known as the " cantonment,"
where a handful of soldiers had been quartered
under a major named Coomba, to guard the con-

struction crews on the railroad from the attacks of
predatory Indians seeking game in their ancient
hunting-grounds. A few huts in the sagebrush, a
half-dozen miners' shacks under the butte to the
south, and one or two rather pretentious frame
houses in process of construction completed what
was Little Missouri; but Little Missouri was not
the only outpost of civilization at this junction of
the railroad and the winding, treacherous river. On
the eastern bank, on the flat under the bluff that
six months previous had been a paradise for jackrabbits, a few houses and a few men were attempting to prove to the world, amid a chorus of hammers,
that they constituted a town and had a future.
The settlement called itself Medora. The air was
full of vague but wonderful stories of a French
marquis who was building it and who owned it,
body and soul.

Roosevelt had originally been turned in the
direction of the Bad Lands by a letter in one of the
New York papers by a man from Pittsburgh named
Howard Eaton and the corroborative enthusiasm
of a high-spirited naval officer named Gorringe,
whose appeals for an adequate navy brought
Roosevelt exuberantly to his side. Gorringe was a
man of wide interests and abilities, who managed, to
a degree mysterious to a layman, to combine his
naval activities with the work of a consulting engineer, the promotion of a shipyard, and the formation of a syndicate to carry on a cattle business in
Dakota. He had gained international notice by

his skill in bringing the obelisk known as " Cleo-patra's Needle " from Alexandria to New York, and had six months previous flared before the public in front-page headlines by reason of a sharp controversy with the Secretary of the Navy, which had resulted in Gorringe's resignation.

Roosevelt had said that he wanted to shoot buffalo while there were still buffalo left to shoot, and Gorringe had suggested that he go to Little Missouri. That villainous gateway to the Bad Lands was, it seems, the headquarters for a motley collection of guides and hunters, some of them experts,[1] the majority of them frauds, who were accustomed to take tourists and sportsmen for a fat price into the heart of the fantastic and savage country. The region was noted for game. It had been a great winter range for buffalo; and elk, mountain-sheep, blacktail and whitetail deer, antelope and beaver were plentiful; now and then even an occasional bear strayed to the river's edge from God knows whence. Jake Maunders, with his sinister face, was the center of information for tourists, steering the visitor in the direction of game by day and of Bill Williams, Jess Hogue, and their crew of gamblers and confidence men by night. Gorringe had planned to go with Roosevelt himself, but at the last moment had been forced to give up the trip. He advised Roosevelt to let one of the men representing his own

[1] Roosevelt tells, in his *Hunting Trips of a Ranchman*, of the most notable of these, a former scout and Indian fighter named " Vic " Smith, whose exploits were prodigious.

interests find him a guide, especially the Vines, father and son.

Roosevelt found that Vine, the father, was none other than the crusty old party who had reluctantly admitted him at three o'clock that morning to the Pyramid Park Hotel. The Captain, as he was called, refused to admit that he knew any one who would undertake the ungrateful business of " trundling a tenderfoot " on a buffalo hunt; and suggested that Roosevelt consult his son Frank.

Frank Vine turned out to be far less savage than his father, but quite as bibulous, a rotund hail-fellow-well-met, oily as an Esquimau, with round, twinkling eyes and a reservoir of questionable stories which he tapped on the slightest provocation. The guidebook called him " the innkeeper," which has a romantic connotation not altogether true to the hard facts of Frank's hostelry, and spoke of him as " a jolly, fat, rosy-cheeked young man, brimming over with animal spirits." He habitually wore a bright crimson mackinaw shirt, tied at the neck with a gaudy silk handkerchief, and fringed buckskin trousers, which Roosevelt, who had a weakness for " dressing up," no doubt envied him. He was, it seemed, the most obliging soul in the world, being perfectly willing to do anything for anybody at any time except to be honest, to be sober, or to work; and agreed to find Roosevelt a guide, suggesting that Joe Ferris, who was barn superintendent for him at the Cantonment and occasionally served as a guide for tourists who came to see " Pyramid Park," might be persuaded to find him a buffalo.

Frank guided his " tenderfoot " to the Post store, of which he was manager. It was a long log building, one fourth used for trading and the rest for storage. Single window lights, set into the wall here and there, gave the place the air of perpetual dusk which, it was rumored, was altogether necessary to cloak Frank's peculiar business methods.

They found Joe Ferris in the store. That individual turned out to be as harmless a looking being as any " down-East " farmer — a short, stockily built young fellow of Roosevelt's own age, with a moustache that drooped and a friendly pair of eyes. He did not accept the suggestion that he take Roosevelt on a buffalo hunt, without debate. The " dude " from the East did not, in fact, look at first sight as though he would be of much comfort on a hunt. His large, round glasses gave him a studious look that to a frontiersman was ominous. Joe Ferris agreed at last to help the tenderfoot find a buffalo, but he agreed with reluctance and the deepest misgivings.

Ferris and Frank Vine, talking the matter over, decided that the camp of Gregor Lang on Little Cannonball Creek fifty miles up the river, was the logical place to use as headquarters for the hunt. Gregor Lang, it happened, had just left town homeward bound with a wagon-load of supplies. He was a Scotchman, who had been a prosperous distiller in Ireland, until in a luckless moment the wife of his employer had come to the conclusion that it was wicked to manufacture a product which, when taken in sufficient quantities, was instrumental in sending people to hell; and had prevailed on her husband to close the distillery. What Frank Vine said in describing Gregor Lang to Roosevelt is lost to history. Frank had his own reason for not loving Lang.

Ferris had a brother Sylvane, who was living with his partner, A. W. Merrifield, in a cabin seven or eight miles south of Little Missouri, and suggested that they spend the night with him. Late that afternoon, Joe and his buckboard, laden to overflowing, picked Roosevelt up at the hotel and started for the ford a hundred yards north of the trestle. On the brink of the bluff they stopped. The hammer of Roosevelt's Winchester was broken. In Ferris's opinion, moreover, the Winchester itself was too light for buffalo, and Joe thought it might be a good scheme to borrow a hammer and a buffalo-gun from Jake Maunders.

Jake was at home. He was not a reassuring person to meet, nor one of whom a cautious man would care to ask many favors. His face was villainous and did not pretend to be anything else. He was glad to lend the hammer and the gun, he said.

September days had a way of being baking hot along the Little Missouri, and even in the late afternoon the air was usually like a blast from a

furnace. But the country which appeared stark
and dreadful under the straight noon sun, at dusk
took on a magic more enticing, it seemed, because
it grew out of such forbidding desolation. The
buttes, protruding like buttresses from the ranges
that bordered the river, threw lengthening shadows
across the grassy draws. Each gnarled cedar in
the ravines took on color and personality. The
blue of the sky grew soft and deep.

They climbed to the top of a butte where the road
passed between gray cliffs, then steeply down on the
other side into the cool greenness of a timbered
bottom where the grass was high underfoot and the
cottonwoods murmured and twinkled overhead.
They passed a log ranch-house known as the
" Custer Trail," in memory of the ill-fated expedition which had camped in the adjacent flat seven
years before. Howard Eaton and his brothers lived
there and kept open house for a continuous stream of
Eastern sportsmen. A mile beyond, they forded the
river; a quarter-mile farther on, they forded it
again, passed through a belt of cottonwoods into
a level valley where the buttes receded, leaving a
wide stretch of bottom-lands dominated by a solitary peak known as Chimney Butte, and drew up·
in front of a log cabin.

Sylvane Ferris and Bill Merrifield were there and
greeted Roosevelt without noticeable enthusiasm.
They admitted later that they thought he was
"just another Easterner," and they did not like his
glasses at all. They were both lithe, slender young

fellows, wiry and burnt by the sun, Sylvane twenty-four or thereabouts, Merrifield four years his senior. Sylvane was shy with a boyish shyness that had a way of slipping into good-natured grins; Merrifield, the shrewder and more mature of the two, was by nature reserved and reticent. They did not have much to say to the " dude " from NewYork until supper in the dingy, one-room cabin of cotton-wood logs, set on end, gave way to cards, and in the excitement of " Old Sledge " the ice began to break. A sudden fierce squawking from the direction of the chicken-shed, abutting the cabin on the west, broke up the game and whatever restraint remained; for they all piled out of the house together, hunting the bobcat which had raided the roost. They did not find the bobcat, but all sense of strangeness was gone when they returned to the house, and settling down on bunks and boxes opened their lives to each other.

The Ferrises and Merrifield were Canadians who had drifted west from their home in New Brunswick and, coming out to the Dakota frontier two years previous because the Northern Pacific Railroad carried emigrants westward for nothing, had re-mained there because the return journey cost five cents a mile. They worked the first summer as section hands. Then, in the autumn, being back-woodsmen, they took a contract to cut cordwood, and all that winter worked together up the river at Sawmill Bottom, cutting timber. But Merrifield was an inveterate and skillful hunter, and while

Joe took to doing odd jobs, and Sylvane took to driving mules at the Cantonment, Merrifield scoured the prairie for buffalo and antelope and crept through the underbrush of countless coulees for deer. For two years he furnished the Northern Pacific dining-cars with venison at five cents a pound. He was a sure shot, absolutely fearless, and with a debonair gayety that found occasional expression in odd pranks. Once, riding through the prairie near the railroad, and being thirsty and not relishing a drink of the alkali water of the Little Missouri, he flagged an express with his red handkerchief, stepped aboard, helped himself to ice-water, and rode off again, to the speechless indignation of the conductor.

The three men had prospered in a small way, and while Joe turned banker and recklessly loaned the attractive but unstable Johnny Nelson a hundred dollars to help him to his feet, Sylvane and Merrifield bought a few horses and a few head of cattle, took on shares a hundred and fifty more, belonging to an old reprobate of a ranchman named Wadsworth and a partner of his named Halley, and, under the shadow of the bold peak that was a landmark for miles around, started a ranch which they called the " Chimney Butte," and every one else called, after their brand, the " Maltese Cross." A man named Bly who had kept a hotel in Bismarck, at a time when Bismarck was wild, and had drifted west with the railroad, was, that season, cutting logs for ties a hundred and fifty miles south in the

Short Pine Hills. He attempted to float the timber down the river, with results disastrous to his enterprise, but beneficial to the boys at Chimney Butte. A quantity of logs perfectly adapted for building purposes stacked themselves at a bend not an eighth of a mile from the center of their range. The boys set them on end, stockade-fashion, packed the chinks, threw on a mud roof, and called it " home."

Lang's cow-camp, which was to be the starting-point for the buffalo hunt, was situated some forty-five miles to the south, in the neighborhood of Pretty Buttes. Merrifield and the Ferrises had spent some months there the previous winter, staying with a half-breed named O'Donald and a German named Jack Reuter, known to the countryside as " Dutch Wannigan," who had built the rough log cabin and used it as their headquarters. Buffalo at that time had been plentiful there, and the three Canadians had shot them afoot and on horseback, now and then teasing one of the lumbering hulks into charging, for the excitement of the " close shave " the maddened beast would provide. If there were buffalo anywhere, there would be buffalo somewhere near Pretty Buttes.

Joe, who was of a sedentary disposition, decided that they would make the long trip south in the buckboard, but Roosevelt protested. He saw the need of the buckboard to carry the supplies, but he saw no reason why he should sit in it all day. He asked for an extra saddle horse.

The three declared they did not have an extra saddle horse.

Roosevelt pleaded. The three Canadians thereupon became suspicious and announced more firmly than before that they did not have an extra saddle horse.

Roosevelt protested fervidly that he could not possibly sit still in a buckboard, driving fifty miles.

" By gosh, he wanted that saddle horse so bad," said Joe a long time after, " that we were afraid to let him have it. Why, we didn't know him from Job's off ox. We didn't know but what he'd ride away with it. But, say, he wanted that horse so blamed bad, that when he see we weren't going to let him have it, he offered to buy it for cash."

That proposal sounded reasonable to three cautious frontiersmen, and, before they all turned into their bunks that night, Roosevelt had acquired a buckskin mare named Nell, and therewith his first physical hold on the Bad Lands.

II

It rains here when it rains an' it's hot here when it's hot,
The real folks is real folks which city folks is not.
The dark is as the dark was before the stars was made;
The sun is as the sun was before God thought of shade;
An' the prairie an' the butte-tops an' the long winds, when they blow,
Is like the things what Adam knew on his birthday, long ago.

From *Medora Nights*

JOE in the buckboard and Roosevelt on his new acquisition started south at dawn.

The road to Lang's — or the trail rather, for it consisted of two wheel-tracks scarcely discernible on the prairie grass and only to be guessed at in the sagebrush — lay straight south across a succession of flats, now wide, now narrow, cut at frequent intervals by the winding, wood-fringed Little Missouri; a region of green slopes and rocky walls and stately pinnacles and luxuriant acres. Twenty miles south of the Maltese Cross, they topped a ridge of buttes and suddenly came upon what might well have seemed, in the hot mist of noonday, a billowy ocean, held by some magic in suspension. From the trail, which wound along a red slope of baked clay falling at a sharp angle into a witch's cauldron of clefts and savage abysses, the Bad Lands stretched southward to the uncertain horizon. The nearer slopes were like yellow shores jutting into lavender waters.

West of Middle Butte, that loomed like a purple island on their left, they took a short cut across the big Ox Bow from the mouth of Bullion Creek on the one side to the mouth of Spring Creek on the other, then followed the course of the Little Missouri southward once more. They met the old Fort Keogh trail where it crossed the river by the ruins of the stage station, and for three or four miles followed its deep ruts westward, then turned south again. They came at last to a crossing where the sunset glowed bright in their faces along the bed of a shallow creek that emptied into the Little Missouri. The creek was the Little Cannonball. In a cluster of hoary cottonwoods, fifty yards from the point where creek and river met, they found Lang's cabin.

Lang turned out to be stocky, blue-eyed, and aggressively Scotch, wearing spectacles and a pair of " mutton-chop " whiskers. He had himself just arrived, having come from town by the longer trail over the prairie to the west in order to avoid the uncertain river crossings which had a way of proving fatal to a heavily laden wagon. His welcome was hearty. With him was a boy of sixteen, fair-haired and blue-eyed, whom he introduced as his son Lincoln. The boy remembered ever after the earnestness of the tenderfoot's "Delighted to meet you."

Roosevelt talked with Gregor Lang until midnight. The Scotchman was a man of education with views of his own on life and politics, and if he was more than a little dogmatic, he was unquestionably sincere.

He had an interesting story to tell. A year or

less ago Henry Gorringe, Abram S. Hewitt, of New York, and a noted London financier named Sir John Pender, who had been instrumental in laying the first successful Atlantic cable, had, in the course of a journey through the Northwest, become interested in the cattle business and, in May, 1883, bought the Cantonment buildings at Little Missouri with the object of making them the headquarters of a trading corporation which they called the Little Missouri Land and Stock Company. The details they left to the enterprising naval officer who had proposed the scheme. Gorringe had meanwhile struck up a friendship with Frank Vine. This was not unnatural, for Frank was the social center of Little Missouri and was immensely popular. What is almost incredible, however, is that, blinded evidently by Frank's social graces, he took the genial and slippery post-trader into the syndicate, and appointed him superintendent. It was possibly because he did not concur altogether in this selection that Pender sent Gregor Lang, who, owing to Lady Pender's scruples, was without employment, to report to Gorringe in New York and then proceed to Little Missouri.

What a somewhat precise Scotch Presbyterian thought of that gathering-place of the wicked, the Presbyterian himself did not see fit to divulge. He established himself at the Cantonment, set to work with European thoroughness to find out all there was to find out about the cattle business, and quietly studied the ways of Frank Vine. Those ways were altogether extraordinary. Where he had originally come from no one exactly knew. His father, whom the new superintendent promptly established as manager of the Pyramid Park Hotel, had been a Missouri steamboat captain and was regarded far and wide as a terror. He was, in fact, a walking arsenal. He had a way of collecting his bills with a cavalry saber, and once, during the course of a " spree," hearing that a great Irishman named Jack Sawyer had beaten up his son Frank, was seen emerging from the hotel in search of the oppressor of his offspring with a butcher-knife in his boot, a six-shooter at his belt, and a rifle in his hand. Frank himself was less of a buccaneer and was conspicuous because he was practically the only man in Little Missouri who did not carry arms. He was big-hearted and not without charm in his nonchalant disregard of the moralities, but there was no truth in him, and he was so foul-mouthed that he became the model for the youth of Little Missouri, the ideal of what a foul-mouthed reprobate should be.

" Frank was the darndest liar you ever knew," remarked, long after, a man who had authority on his side. " And, by jinx, if he wouldn't preface his worst lies with ' Now this is God's truth!' "

He had an older brother named Darius who was famous as " the champion beer-drinker of the West," having the engaging gift of being able to consume untold quantities without ever becoming drunk. In their way they were a notable family.

Gregor Lang, with the fortunes of his employer at heart, watched Frank's activities as storekeeper with interest. During the military régime, Frank had been post-trader, a berth which was an eminent article of barter on the shelves of congressional politicians and for which fitness seemed to consist in the ability to fill lonely soldiers with untold quantities of bad whiskey. Frank's " fitness," as the term was understood, was above question, but his bookkeeping, Lang found, was largely in his mind. When he received a shipment of goods he set the selling-price by multiplying the cost by two and adding the freight; which saved much calculating. Frank's notions of " mine " and " thine," Lang discovered, moreover, were elastic. His depredations were particularly heavy against a certain shipment of patent medicine called " Tolu Tonic," which he ordered in huge quantities at the company's expense and drank up himself. The secret was that Frank, who had inherited his father's proclivities, did not like the " Forty-Mile Red Eye " brand which Bill Williams concocted of sulphuric acid and cigar stumps mixed with evil gin and worse rum; and had found that " Tolu Tonic " was eighty per cent alcohol.

Seeing these matters, and other matters for which the term " irregularity " would have been only mildly descriptive, Gregor Lang sent Sir John a report which was not favorable to Frank Vine's régime. Sir John withdrew from the syndicate in disgust and ordered Lang to start a separate ranch for him; and Gorringe himself began to investigate the interesting ways of his superintendent. Why Lang was not murdered, he himself was unable to say.

Lang had made it his business to acquire all the information he could secure on every phase of the cattle industry, for Sir John was avid of statistics. Roosevelt asked question after question. The Scotchman answered them. Joe Ferris, Lincoln, and a bony Scotch Highlander named MacRossie, who lived with the Langs, had been asleep and snoring for three hours before Gregor Lang and his guest finally sought their bunks.

It was raining when they awoke next morning. Joe Ferris, who was willing to suffer discomfort in a good cause, but saw no reason for unnecessarily courting misery, suggested to Roosevelt that they wait until the weather cleared. Roosevelt insisted that they start the hunt. Joe recognized that he was dealing with a man who meant business, and made no further protest.

They left Lang's at six, crossing the Little Missouri and threading their way, mile after mile, eastward through narrow defiles and along tortuous divides. It was a wild region, bleak and terrible, where fantastic devil-carvings reared themselves from the sallow gray of eroded slopes, and the only green things were gnarled cedars that looked as though they had been born in horror and had grown up in whirlwinds.

The ground underfoot was wet and sticky; the

rain continued all day long. Once, at a distance, they saw two or three blacktail deer, and a little later they came upon a single buck. They crept to within two hundred yards. Roosevelt fired, and missed. There was every reason why he should miss, for the distance was great and the rain made a clear aim impossible; but it happened that, as the deer bounded away, Joe Ferris fired at a venture, and brought him down. It was a shot in a thousand.

Roosevelt flung his gun on the ground. " By Godfrey! " he exclaimed. " I'd give anything in the world if I could shoot like that! "

His rage at himself was so evident that Joe, being tender-hearted, was almost sorry that he had shot so well.

They found no buffalo that day; and returned to Lang's after dusk, gumbo mud to the eyes.

Of the two, Ferris was the one, it happened, who wrapped himself in his buffalo robe immediately after supper and went to sleep. Roosevelt, apparently as fresh and vigorous as he had been when he started out in the morning, promptly set Gregor Lang to talking about cattle.

Lang, who had been starved for intellectual companionship, was glad to talk; and there was much to tell. It was a new country for cattle. Less than five years before, the Indians had still roamed free and unmolested over it. A few daring white hunters (carrying each his vial of poison with which to cheat the torture-stake, in case of capture) had invaded their hunting-grounds; then a few surveyors; then grading crews under military guard with their retinue of saloon-keepers and professional gamblers; then the gleaming rails; then the thundering and shrieking engines. Eastern sportsmen, finding game plentiful in the Bad Lands, came to the conclusion that where game could survive in winter and thrive in summer, cattle could do likewise, and began to send short-horned stock west over the railroad. A man named Wadsworth from Minnesota settled twenty miles down the river from Little Missouri; another named Simpson from Texas established the " Hash-Knife " brand sixty or seventy miles above. The Eatons and A. D. Huidekoper, all from Pittsburgh, Sir John Pender from England, Lord Nugent from Ireland, H. H. Gorringe from New York, came to hunt and remained in person or by proxy to raise cattle in the new-won prairies of western Dakota and eastern Montana. These were the first wave. Henry Boice from New Mexico, Gregor Lang from Scotland, Antoine de Vallombrosa, Marquis de Mores (very much from France) — these were the second; young men all, most under thirty, some under twenty-five, dare-devil adventurers with hot blood, seeing visions.

Roosevelt and Lang talked well into the night. The next morning it was still raining. Roosevelt declared that he would hunt, anyway. Joe protested, almost pathetically. Roosevelt was obdurate, and Joe, admiring the " tenderfoot " in spite of himself, submitted. They hunted all day and shot nothing, returning to the cabin after dark, covered with Dakota mud.

Again it was Joe who tumbled into his corner, and the " tenderfoot " who, after supper, fresh as a daisy, engaged his host in conversation. They talked cattle and America and politics; and again, cattle. The emphatic Scotchman was very much of an individual. The eyes behind the oval glasses were alert, intelligent, and not without a touch of defiance.

Gregor Lang was one of those Europeans to whom America comes as a great dream, long before they set foot on its soil. He felt sharply the appeal of free institutions, and had proved ready to fight and to suffer for his convictions. He had had considerable opportunity to do both, for he had been an enthusiastic liberal in an arch-conservative family, frankly expressing his distaste for any form of government, including the British, which admitted class distinctions and gave to the few at the expense of the many. His insistence on naming his son after the man who had been indirectly responsible for the closing of England's cotton-mills had almost disrupted his household.

He enjoyed talking politics, and found in Roosevelt, who was up to his eyes in politics in his own State, a companion to delight his soul. Lang was himself a good talker and not given as a rule to patient listening; but he listened to Theodore Roosevelt, somewhat because he wanted to, and somewhat because it was difficult for any one to do anything else in those days when Roosevelt once took the floor. Gregor Lang had known many reformers in his time, and some had been precise and meticulous and some had been fiery and eloquent, but none had possessed the overwhelming passion for public service that seemed to burn in this amazingly vigorous and gay-spirited American of twenty-four. Roosevelt denounced " boss rule " until the rafters rang, coupling his denunciation of corrupt politicians with denunciations of those " fireside moralists " who were forever crying against bad government yet raising not a finger to correct it. The honest were always in a majority, he contended, and, under the American Constitution, held in their hands the power to overcome the dishonest minority. It was the solemn duty of every American citizen, he declared, not only to vote, but to fight, if need be, for good government.

It was two in the morning before Gregor Lang and Theodore Roosevelt reluctantly retired to their bunks.

Roosevelt was up and about at dawn. It was still raining. Joe Ferris suggested mildly that they wait for better weather before plunging again into the sea of gumbo mud, but Roosevelt, who had not come to Dakota to twiddle his thumbs, insisted that they resume their hunt. They went and found nothing. The rain continued for a week.

" He nearly killed poor Joe," Lincoln remarked afterwards. " He would not stop for anything."

Every morning Joe entered his protest and

Roosevelt overruled it, and every evening Joe rolled, nigh dead, into his buffalo robe and Roosevelt talked cattle and politics with Gregor Lang until one and two in the morning. Joe and the Highlander sawed wood, but the boy Lincoln in his bunk lay with wide eyes.

" It was in listening to those talks after supper in the old shack on the Cannonball," he said, a long time after, " that I first came to understand that the Lord made the earth for all of us and not for a chosen few."

Roosevelt, too, received inspiration from these nocturnal discussions, but it was an inspiration of another sort.

" Mr. Lang," he said suddenly one evening, " I am thinking seriously of going into the cattle business. Would you advise me to go into it? "

Gregor Lang was cautious. " I don't like to advise you in a matter of that kind," he answered. " I myself am prepared to follow it out to the end. I have every faith in it. If it's a question of my faith, I have full faith. As a business proposition, it is the best there is."

They said no more about the matter that night.

The weather cleared at last. Joe Ferris, who had started on the hunt with misgivings, had no misgivings whatever now. He confided in Lincoln, not without a touch of pride in his new acquaintance, that this was a new variety of tenderfoot, altogether a " plumb good sort."

They started out with new zest under the clear

sky. They had, in their week's hunting, come across the fresh tracks of numerous buffalo, but had in no case secured a shot. The last great herd had, in fact, been exterminated six months before, and though the Ferrises and Merrifield had killed a half-dozen within a quarter-mile of the Maltese Cross early that summer, these had been merely a straggling remnant. The days when a hunter could stand and bombard a dull, panic-stricken herd, slaughtering hundreds without changing his position, were gone. In the spring of 1883 the buffalo had still roamed the prairies east and west of the Bad Lands in huge herds, but moving in herds they were as easy to shoot as a family cow and the profits even at three dollars a pelt were great. Game-butchers swarmed forth from Little Missouri and fifty other frontier " towns," slaughtering buffalo for their skins or for their tongues or for the mere lust of killing. The hides were piled high at every shipping point; the carcasses rotted in the sun. Three hundred thousand buffalo, driven north from the more settled plains of western Nebraska, and huddled in a territory covering not more than a hundred and fifty square miles, perished like cattle in a stockyard, almost overnight. It was one of the most stupendous and dramatic obliterations in history of a species betrayed by the sudden change of its environment.

Hunting buffalo on horseback had, even in the days of the great herds, been an altogether different matter from the methodical slaughter from a

" stand," where a robe for every cartridge was not
an unusual " bag," and where an experienced game-
butcher could, without recourse to Baron Munch-
ausen, boast an average of eighty per cent of
" kills." There was always the possibility that the
bison, driven to bay, might charge the sportsman
who drove his horse close in for a sure shot. With
the great herds destroyed, there was added to
the danger and the privations of the wild country
where the few remaining stragglers might be found,
the zest and the arduousness of long searching.
Roosevelt and Joe Ferris had had their full share of
the latter.

They came on the fresh track of a buffalo two
hours after their departure, that clear warm morning, from Lang's hospitable cabin. It was, for a
time, easy to follow, where it crossed and recrossed
a narrow creek-bottom, but became almost un-
discernible as it struck off up the side of a winding
coulee, where the soil, soaked as it had been by a
week of September drizzle, was already baked hard
by the hot sun. They rode for an hour cautiously
up the ravine. Suddenly, as they passed the mouth
of a side coulee, there was a plunge and crackle
through the bushes at its head, and a shabby-
looking old bull bison galloped out of it and plunged
over a steep bank into a patch of broken ground
which led around the base of a high butte. The
bison was out of sight before they had time to fire.
At the risk of their necks they sped their horses over
the broken ground only to see the buffalo emerge

from it at the farther end and with amazing agility climb up the side of a butte over a quarter of a mile away. With his shaggy mane and huge forequarters he had some of the impressiveness of a lion as he stood for an instant looking back at his pursuers. They followed him for miles, but caught no glimpse of him again.

They were now on the prairie far to the east of the river, a steaming, treeless region stretching in faint undulations north, east, and south, until it met the sky in the blurred distance. Here and there it was broken by a sunken water-course, dry in spite of a week of wet weather, or a low bluff or a cluster of small, round-topped buttes. The grass was burnt brown; the air was hot and still. The country had the monotony and the melancholy and more than a little of the beauty and the fascination of the sea.

They ate their meager lunch beside a miry pool, where a clump of cedars under a bluff gave a few square feet of shadow.

All afternoon they rode over the dreary prairie, but it was late before they caught another glimpse of game. Then, far off in the middle of a large plain, they saw three black specks.

The horses were slow beasts, and were tired besides and in no condition for running. Roosevelt and his mentor picketed them in a hollow, half a mile from the game, and started off on their hands and knees. Roosevelt blundered into a bed of cactus and filled his hands with the spines; but he came within a hundred and fifty feet or less of the buffalo. He drew up and fired. The bullet made the dust fly from the hide as it hit the body with a loud crack, but apparently did no particular harm. The three buffalo made off over a low rise with their tails in the air.

The hunters returned to their horses in disgust, and for seven or eight miles loped the jaded animals along at a brisk pace. Now and again they saw the quarry far ahead. Finally, when the sun had just set, they saw that all three had come to a stand in a gentle hollow. There was no cover anywhere. They determined, as a last desperate resort, to try to run them on their worn-out ponies.

The bison faced them for an instant, then turned and made off. With spurs and quirt, Roosevelt urged his tired pony forward. Night closed in and the full moon rose out of the black haze on the horizon. The pony plunged to within sixty or seventy yards of the wounded bull, and could gain no more. Joe Ferris, better mounted, forged ahead. The bull, seeing him coming, swerved. Roosevelt cut across and came almost up to him. The ground over which they were running was broken into holes and ditches, and the fagged horses floundered and pitched forward at every step.

At twenty feet, Roosevelt fired, but the pony was pitching like a launch in a storm, and he missed. He dashed in closer.

The bull's tail went up and he wheeled suddenly and charged with lowered horns.

The pony, panic-stricken, spun round and tossed up his head, striking the rifle which Roosevelt was holding in both hands and knocking it violently against his forehead, cutting a deep gash. The blood poured into Roosevelt's eyes.

Ferris reined in his pony. " All right? " he called, evidently frightened.

" Don't mind me! " Roosevelt shouted, without turning an instant from the business in hand. " I'm all right."

For an instant it was a question whether Roosevelt would get the buffalo or the buffalo would get Roosevelt. But he swerved his horse, and the buffalo, plunging past, charged Ferris and followed him as he made off over the broken ground, uncomfortably close to the tired pony's tail. Roosevelt, half-blinded, tried to run in on him again, but his pony stopped, dead beat; and by no spurring could he force him out of a slow trot. Ferris, swerving suddenly and dismounting, fired, but the dim moonlight made accurate aim impossible, and the buffalo, to the utter chagrin of the hunters, lumbered off and vanished into the darkness. Roosevelt followed him for a short space afoot in hopeless and helpless wrath.

There was no possibility of returning to Lang's that night. They were not at all certain where they were, but they knew they were a long way from the mouth of the Little Cannonball. They determined to camp near by for the night.

They did not mount the exhausted horses, but

led them, stumbling, foaming and sweating, while they hunted for water. It was an hour before they found a little mud-pool in a reedy hollow. They had drunk nothing for twelve hours and were parched with thirst, but the water of the pool was like thin jelly, slimy and nauseating, and they could drink only a mouthful. Supper consisted of a dry biscuit, previously baked by Lincoln under direction of his father, who insisted that the use of a certain kind of grease whose name is lost to history would keep the biscuits soft. They were hard as horn.[1] There was not a twig with which to make a fire, nor a bush to which they could fasten their horses. When they lay down to sleep, thirsty and famished, they had to tie their horses with the lariat to the saddles which were their pillows.

They did not go quickly to sleep. The horses were nervous, restless, alert, in spite of their fatigue, continually snorting or standing with their ears forward, peering out into the night, as though conscious of the presence of danger. Roosevelt remembered some half-breed Crees they had encountered the day before. It was quite possible that some roving bucks might come for their horses,

---

[1] "I would start to make biscuits and as usual go about putting shortening into them, which father didn't like. We'd argue over it a little, and I would say, 'Good biscuits can't be made without grease.' Then he'd say, 'Well, use elbow grease.' I'd say then, 'Well, all right, I'll try it.' Then I'd go to work and knead the dough *hard* (on purpose), understanding, of course, that kneading utterly spoils biscuit dough, whether there is shortening in it or not. The result is a pan of adamantine biscuits which, of course, I blame on him." — *Lincoln Lang.*

and perhaps their scalps, for the Indians, who were still unsettled on their reservations, had a way of stealing off whenever they found a chance and doing what damage they could. Stories he had heard of various bands of horse-thieves that operated in the region between the Little Missouri and the Black Hills likewise returned to mind to plague him. The wilderness in which Roosevelt and Ferris had pitched their meager camp was in the very heart of the region infested by the bandits. They dozed fitfully, waking with a start whenever the sound of the grazing of the horses ceased for a moment, and they knew that the nervous animals were watching for the approach of a foe. It was late when at last they fell asleep.

They were rudely wakened at midnight by having their pillows whipped out from under their heads. They leapt to their feet. In the bright moonlight they saw the horses madly galloping off, with the saddles bounding and trailing behind them. Their first thought was that the horses had been stampeded by horse-thieves, and they threw themselves on the ground, crouching in the long grass with rifles ready.

There was no stir. At last, in the hollow they made out a shadowy, four-footed shape. It was a wolf who strode noiselessly to the low crest and disappeared.

They rose and went after the horses, taking the broad trail made by the saddles through the dewy grass.

Once Joe Ferris stopped. "Say, I ain't ever committed any crime deservin' that anything like this should happen!" he exclaimed plaintively. Then, turning straight to Roosevelt, evidently suspecting that he had a Jonah on his hands, he cried, in a voice in which wrath was mingled with comic despair, "Have you ever done anything to deserve this?"

"Joe," Roosevelt answered solemnly, "I never have."

"Then I can't understand," Joe remarked, "why we're runnin' in such luck."

Roosevelt grinned at him and chuckled, and Joe Ferris grinned and chuckled; and after that the savage attentions of an unkind fate did not seem so bad.

They found the horses sooner than they expected and led them back to camp. Utterly weary, they wrapped themselves in their blankets once more and went to sleep. But rest was not for them that night. At three in the morning a thin rain began to fall, and they awoke to find themselves lying in four inches of water. Joe Ferris expected lamentations. What he heard was, "By Godfrey, but this is fun!"

They cowered and shivered under their blankets until dawn. Then, soaked to the skin, they made breakfast of Lang's adamantine biscuits, mounted their horses, and were off, glad to bid good-bye to the inhospitable pool.

A fine, drizzling mist, punctuated at intervals

by heavy downpours of rain, shrouded the desolate region and gathered them into a chilly desolation of its own.. They traveled by compass. It was only after hours that the mist lifted, revealing the world about them, and, in the center of it, several black objects slowly crossing a piece of rolling country ahead. They were buffalo.

They picketed the horses, and crept forward on their hands and knees through the soft, muddy prairie soil. A shower of cold rain blew up-wind straight in their faces and made the teeth chatter behind their blue lips. The rain was blowing in Roosevelt's eyes as he pulled the trigger. He missed clean, and the whole band plunged into a hollow and were off.

What Joe Ferris said upon that occasion remains untold. It was " one of those misses," Roosevelt himself remarked afterwards, " which a man to his dying day always looks back upon with wonder and regret." In wet, sullen misery he returned with Joe to the horses.

The rain continued all day, and they spent another wretched night. They had lived for two days on nothing but biscuits and rainwater, and privation had thoroughly lost whatever charm it might have had for an adventurous young man in search of experience. The next morning brought sunlight and revived spirits, but it brought no change in their luck.

" Bad luck followed us," Joe Ferris remarked long after, " like a yellow dog follows a drunkard."

Joe's horse nearly stepped on a rattlesnake, and narrowly escaped being bitten; a steep bluff broke away under their ponies' hoofs, and sent them sliding and rolling to the bottom of a long slope, a pile of intermingled horses and men. Shortly after, Roosevelt's horse stepped into a hole and turned a complete somersault, pitching his rider a good ten feet; and he had scarcely recovered his composure and his seat in the saddle, when the earth gave way under his horse as though he had stepped on a trap-door, and let him down to his withers in soft, sticky mud. They hauled the frightened animal out by the lariat, with infinite labor. Altogether it was not a restful Sunday.

More than once Joe Ferris looked at Roosevelt quizzically, wondering when the pleasant "four-eyed tenderfoot" would begin to worry about catching cold and admit at last that the game was too much for him. But the "tenderfoot," it happened, had a dogged streak. He made no suggestion of "quitting."

"He could stand an awful lot of hard knocks," Joe explained later, "and he was always cheerful. You just couldn't knock him out of sorts. He was entertaining, too, and I liked to listen to him, though, on the whole, he wasn't much on the talk. He said that he wanted to get away from politics, so I didn't mention political matters; and he had books with him and would read at odd times."

Joe began to look upon his "tenderfoot" with a kind of awe, which was not diminished when

Roosevelt, blowing up a rubber pillow which he carried with him, casually remarked one night that his doctors back East had told him that he did not have much longer to live, and that violent exercise would be immediately fatal.

They returned to Lang's, Roosevelt remarking to himself that it was " dogged that does it," and ready to hunt three weeks if necessary to get his buffalo.

If Lang had any notion that the privations of the hunt had dampened Roosevelt's enthusiasm for the frontier, Roosevelt himself speedily dispelled it.

Roosevelt had, for a year or more, felt the itch to be a monarch of acres. He had bought land at Oyster Bay, including an elevation known to the neighbors as Sagamore Hill, where he was building a house; but a view and a few acres of woodland could not satisfy his craving. He wanted expanses to play with, large works to plan and execute, subordinates to inspire and to direct. He had driven his uncles, who were as intensely practical and thrifty as Dutch uncles should be, and his sisters, who were, at least, very much more practical in money matters than he was, nearly frantic the preceding summer by declaring his intention to purchase a large farm adjoining the estate of his brother-in-law, Douglas Robinson, in the Mohawk Valley; for his kin knew, what he himself failed to recognize, that he was not made to be a farmer and that he who loved to be in the center of the seething world would explode, or burn himself out, in a countryside a night's run from anywhere. They knew also that farming was not a spiritual adventure, but a business, and that Theodore, with his generous habit of giving away a few thousands here and a few thousands there, was not exactly a business man. He had yielded to their abjurations; but his hankering for acres had remained.

Here in Dakota were all the acres that any man could want, and they were his for the asking.

To this vague craving to be monarch of all he surveyed (or nearly all), another emotion which Roosevelt might have identified with business acumen had during the past year been added. Together with a Harvard classmate, Richard Trimble, he had become interested in a ranching project known as the Teschmaker and Debillier Cattle Company, which "ran" some thousands of head of cattle fifty or sixty miles north of Cheyenne; and he had invested ten thousand dollars in it. Commander Gorringe, seeking to finance the enterprise in which he was involved, in the course of his hunting accounts doubtlessly spoke glowingly to Roosevelt of the huge profits that awaited Eastern dollars in the Bad Lands. Roosevelt, it appears, asked his uncle, James Roosevelt, his father's elder brother and head of the banking firm of Roosevelt and Son, whether he would advise him to invest a further sum of five thousand dollars in cattle in Dakota.

Uncle James, to whom, as investments, cattle ranches were in a class with gold mines, emphatically informed Theodore that he would not at all advise him to do anything of the kind. How deeply Roosevelt was impressed by this information subsequent events clearly indicate.

Roosevelt and Lang sat at the table long after Lincoln had cleared it that night. Joe and the Highlander were asleep, but Lincoln heard the two men talking and, years after, remembered the conversation of that momentous September night.

" Mr. Lang," said Roosevelt abruptly, " I have definitely decided to go into the cattle business. I want somebody to run cattle for me on shares or to take the management of my cattle under some arrangement to be worked out. Will you take charge of my cattle? "

The Scotchman, who was naturally deliberate, was not prepared to meet such precipitancy. He told Roosevelt that he appreciated his offer. " Unfortunately," he added reluctantly, " I am tied up with the other people."

Roosevelt's regret was evident. He asked Lang whether there was any one he would recommend. Without hesitation, Lang suggested Sylvane Ferris and Bill Merrifield. Early the next morning Lincoln Lang was dispatched to the Maltese Cross.

Meanwhile Roosevelt and Joe continued the pursuit of the elusive buffalo. But again luck was far from them. For two days they hunted in vain. When they returned to Lang's the second dusk, Sylvane and Merrifield were there waiting for them.

That evening, after supper, Roosevelt sat on a

log outside Lang's cabin with the two ranchmen and asked them how much in their opinion it would cost adequately to stock a cattle-ranch.

" Depends what you want to do," answered Sylvane. " But my guess is, if you want to do it right, that it'll spoil the looks of forty thousand dollars."

" How much would you need right off? " Roosevelt went on.

" Oh, a third would make a start."

" Could you boys handle the cattle for me? "

" Why, yes," said Sylvane in his pleasant, quiet drawl, " I guess we could take care of 'em 'bout as well as the next man."

" Why, I guess *so!* " ejaculated Merrifield.

" Well, will you do it? "

" Now, that's another story," said Sylvane. " Merrifield here and me is under contract with Wadsworth and Halley. We've got a bunch of cattle with them on shares. I guess we'd like to do business with you right enough, Mr. Roosevelt, but there's nothing we can do until Wadsworth and Halley releases us."

" I'll buy those cattle."

" All right," remarked Sylvane. " Then the best thing for us to do is to go to Minnesota an' see those men an' get released from our contract. When that's fixed up, we can make any arrangements you've a mind to."

" That will suit me."

Roosevelt drew a checkbook from his pocket,

and there, sitting on the log (oh, vision of Uncle James!) wrote a check, not for the contemplated five thousand dollars, but for fourteen, and handed it to Sylvane. Merrifield and Sylvane, he directed, were to purchase a few hundred head of cattle that fall in addition to the hundred and fifty head which they held on shares for Wadsworth.

" Don't you want a receipt? " asked Merrifield at last.

" Oh, that's all right," said Roosevelt. " If I didn't trust you men, I wouldn't go into business with you."

They shook hands all around; whereupon they dropped the subject from conversation and talked about game.

" We were sitting on a log," said Merrifield, many years later, " up at what we called Cannonball Creek. He handed us a check for fourteen thousand dollars, handed it right over to us on a verbal contract. He didn't have a scratch of a pen for it."

" All the security he had for his money," added Sylvane, " was our honesty."

The man from the East, with more than ordinary ability to read the faces of men, evidently thought that that was quite enough.

The next dawn Roosevelt did not go hunting as usual. All morning he sat over the table in the cabin with Lang and the two Canadians laboring over the contract which three of them were to sign in case his prospective partners were released from the obligation which for the time bound them. It

was determined that Ferris and Merrifield should go
at once to Minnesota to confer with Wadsworth
and Halley. Roosevelt, meanwhile, would continue
his buffalo hunt, remaining in the Bad Lands until
he received word that the boys from the Maltese
Cross were in a position to " complete the deal."
The wheels of the new venture having thus, in defiance of Uncle James, been set in motion, Roosevelt
parted from his new friends, and resumed the interrupted chase.

The red gods must have looked with favor on
Roosevelt's adventurous spirit, for luck turned
suddenly in his favor. Next morning he was
skirting a ridge of broken buttes with Joe Ferris,
near the upper waters of the Little Cannonball west
of Lang's camp over the Montana line, when suddenly both ponies threw up their heads and snuffed
the air, turning their muzzles toward a coulee that
sloped gently toward the creek-bottom they were
traversing. Roosevelt slipped off his pony and ran
quickly but cautiously up the side of the ravine. In
the soft soil at the bottom he saw the round prints
of a bison's hoof.

He came upon the buffalo an instant later, grazing
slowly up the valley. Both wind and shelter were
good, and he ran close. The bull threw back his
head and cocked his tail in the air.

Joe Ferris, who had followed close at Roosevelt's
heels, pointed out a yellow spot on the buffalo, just
back of the shoulder. " If you hit him there," he
whispered, " you'll get him right through the heart."

It seemed to Joe that the Easterner was extraordinarily cool, as he aimed deliberately and fired. With amazing agility the buffalo bounded up the opposite side of the ravine, seemingly heedless of two more bullets aimed at his flank.

Joe was ready to throw up his hands in despair. But suddenly they saw blood pouring from the bison's mouth and nostrils. The great bull rushed to the ridge at a lumbering gallop, and disappeared.

They found him lying in the next gully, dead, as Joe Ferris remarked, " as Methusalem's cat."

Roosevelt, with all his intellectual maturity, was a good deal of a boy, and the Indian war-dance he executed around the prostrate buffalo left nothing in the way of delight unexpressed. Joe watched the performance open-mouthed.

" I never saw any one so enthused in my life," he said in after days, " and, by golly, I was enthused myself for more reasons than one. I was plumb tired out, and, besides, he was so eager to shoot his first buffalo that it somehow got into my blood; and I wanted to see him kill his first one as badly as he wanted to kill it."

Roosevelt, out of the gladness of his heart, then and there presented him with a hundred dollars; so there was another reason for Joe to be happy.

They returned to Lang's, chanting pæans of victory. Early next day Roosevelt returned with Joe to the place where they had left the buffalo and with endless labor skinned the huge beast and brought the head and slippery hide to camp.

The next morning Roosevelt took his departure.

Gregor Lang watched the mounted figure ride off beside the rattling buckboard. " He is the most extraordinary man I have ever met," he said to Lincoln. " I shall be surprised if the world does not hear from him one of these days."

III

Some came for lungs, and some for jobs,
And some for booze at Big-mouth Bob's,
Some to punch cattle, some to shoot,
Some for a vision, some for loot;
Some for views and some for vice,
Some for faro, some for dice;
Some for the joy of a galloping hoof,
Some for the prairie's spacious roof,
Some to forget a face, a fan,
Some to plumb the heart of man;
Some to preach and some to blow,
Some to grab and some to grow,
Some in anger, some in pride,
Some to taste, before they died,
Life served hot and *a la cartee* —
And some to dodge a necktie-party.

From *Medora Nights*

ROOSEVELT remained in Little Missouri to wait for news from Merrifield and Sylvane, who had departed for Minnesota a day or two previous. Possibly it occurred to him that a few days in what was said to be the worst " town " on the Northern Pacific might have their charm.

Roosevelt was enough of a boy rather to relish things that were blood-curdling. Years after, a friend of Roosevelt's, who had himself committed almost every crime in the register, remarked, in commenting in a tone of injured morality on Roosevelt's frank regard for a certain desperate character, that " Roosevelt had a weakness for murderers." The reproach has a delightful suggestiveness. Whether it was merited or not is a large question on which Roosevelt himself might have discoursed with emphasis and humor. If he actually did possess such a weakness, Little Missouri and the boom town were fully able to satisfy it.

" Little Missouri was a terrible place," remarked, years after, a man who had had occasion to study it. It was, in fact, " wild and woolly " to an almost grotesque degree, and the boom town was if anything a little cruder than its twin across the river. The men who had drifted into Medora after the news was noised abroad that " a crazy Frenchman " was making ready to scatter millions there, were, many of them, outcasts of society, reckless, greedy, and conscienceless; fugitives from justice with criminal records, and gunmen who lived by crooked gambling and thievery of every sort. The best of those who had come that summer to seek adventure and fortune on the banks of the Little Missouri were men who cared little for their personal safety, courting danger wherever it beckoned, careless of life and limb, reticent of speech and swift of action, light-hearted and altogether human. They were the adventurous and unfettered spirits of hundreds of communities whom the restrictions of respectable society had galled. Here they were, elbowing each other in a little corner of sagebrush country where there was little to do and much whiskey to drink; and the hand of the law was light and far away.

Somewhere, hundreds of miles to the south, there was a United States marshal; somewhere a hundred and fifty miles to the east there was a sheriff. Neither Medora nor Little Missouri had any representative of the law whatsoever, no government or even a shadow of government. The feuds that arose were settled by the parties involved in the ancient manner of Cain.

Of the heterogeneous aggregation of desperate men that made up the population of the frontier settlement, Jake Maunders, the man who had lent Roosevelt a hammer and a buffalo-gun, was, by all odds, the most prominent and the least trustworthy.

He had been one of the first to settle at Little Missouri, and for a while had lived in the open as a hunter. But the influx of tourists and " floaters " had indicated to him a less arduous form of labor. He guided "tenderfeet," charging exorbitant rates; he gambled (cautiously); whenever a hunter left the Bad Lands, abandoning his shack, Maunders claimed it with the surrounding country, and, when a settler took up land near by, demanded five hundred dollars for his rights. A man whom he owed three thousand dollars had been opportunely kicked into oblivion by a horse in a manner that was mysterious to men who knew the ways of horses. He had shot MacNab, the Scotchman, in cold blood, as he came across the sagebrush flat from Bill Williams's saloon, kneeling at the corner of his shack with his rifle on his knee. Another murder was laid directly at his door. But the forces of law were remote from Little Missouri, and Jake Maunders not only lived, but flourished.

His enemies said he was " the sneakiest man in town, always figuring on somebody else doing the dirty work for him, and him reap the benefits"; but his friends said that "once Jake was your friend, he was your friend, and that was all there was to it." The truth remains that the friends Jake chose were all characters only a little less shady than himself.

Most prominent of these were the precious pair who "operated" Bill Williams's saloon. Bill Williams was a Welshman who had drifted into Little Missouri while the railroad was being built, and, recognizing that the men who made money in frontier settlements were the men who sold whiskey, had opened a saloon to serve liquid refreshment in various vicious forms to the grading crews and soldiers.

"He always reminded me of a red fox," said Lincoln Lang long after, "for, besides having a marked carroty complexion, there was a cunning leer in his face which seemed, as it were, to show indistinctly through the transparency of the manufactured grin with which he sought to cover it. When he got mad over something or other and swept the grin aside, I do not think that an uglier countenance ever existed on earth or in hell. He was rather short of stature, bullet-headed and bull-necked, with a sloping forehead and a somewhat underslung chin. His nose was red and bulbous, his eyes narrow-set beneath bushy red eyebrows. He had a heavy red moustache not altogether concealing an abnormally long mouth, and through it at times, when he smiled, his teeth showed like fangs."

He was a man of natural shrewdness, a money-maker, a gambler, and like Maunders (it was rumored) a brander of cattle that were not his. But he was not without a certain attractive quality, and when he was slightly drunk he was brilliant. He was deathly afraid of being alone, and had a habit on those infrequent occasions when his bar was for the moment deserted, of setting the chairs in orderly rows as in a chapel, and then preaching to them solemnly on the relative merits of King Solomon and Hiram, King of Tyre.

His partner, Jess Hogue, was the brains of the nefarious trio, a dark, raw-boned brute with an ugly, square-jawed, domineering face, a bellow like a bull's, and all the crookedness of Bill Williams without his redeeming wit. His record of achievement covered a broader field than that of either of his associates, for it began with a sub-contract on the New York water system, involved him with the United States Government in connection with a certain "phantom mail route" between Bismarck and Miles City, and started him on the road to affluence with the acquisition of twenty-eight army mules which, with the aid of Bill Williams and the skillful use of the peculiar type of intelligence with which they both seemed to be endowed, he had secured at less than cost from Fort Abraham Lincoln at Mandan.

Associated with Williams, Hogue, and Maunders, in their various ventures, was a man of thirty-eight or forty named Paddock, with florid cheeks, and a long, dark moustache and goatee that made him look something like Buffalo Bill and something like Simon Legree. He conducted the local livery-stable with much profit, for his rates were what was known to the trade as "fancy," and shared with Maunders whatever glory there was in being one of the most feared men in Little Missouri. Like Maunders, he had his defenders; and he had a pleasant-faced wife who gave mute tribute to a side of Jerry Paddock which he did not reveal to the world.

The banks of the Little Missouri in those days of September, 1883, were no place for soft hands or faint hearts; and a place for women only who had the tough fiber of the men. There were scarcely a half-dozen of them in all the Bad Lands up and down the river. In Little Missouri there were four — Mrs. Roderick, who was the cook at the Pyramid Park Hotel; Mrs. Paddock, wife of the livery-stable keeper; Mrs. Pete McGeeney who kept a boarding-house next to Johnny Nelson's store; and her neighbor and eternal enemy, Mrs. Fitzgerald. Pete McGeeney was a section-boss on the railroad, but what else he was, except the husband of Mrs. McGeeney, is obscure. He was mildly famous in Little Missouri because he had delirium tremens, and now and then when he went on a rampage had to be lassoed. Mrs. McGeeney's feud with Mrs. Fitzgerald was famous throughout the countryside. They lived within fifty feet of each other, which may have been the cause of the extreme bitterness between them, for they were both Irish and their tongues were sharp.

Little Missouri had, until now, known only one child, but that one had fully lived up to the best traditions of the community. It was Archie Maunders, his father's image and proudest achievement. At the age of twelve he held up Fitzgerald, the roadmaster, at the point of a pistol, and more than once delayed the departure of the Overland Express by shooting around the feet of the conductors.

Whether he was still the waiter at the Pyramid Park Hotel when Roosevelt arrived there is dark, for it was sometime that autumn that a merciful God took Archie Maunders to him before he could grow into the fullness of his powers. He was only thirteen or fourteen years old when he died, but even the guidebook of the Northern Pacific had taken notice of him, recounting the retort courteous he had delivered on one occasion when he was serving the guests at the hotel.

" Tea or coffee? " he asked one of the " dudes " who had come in on the Overland.

" I'll take tea, if you please," responded the tenderfoot.

" You blinkety blank son of a blank! " remarked Archie, " you'll take coffee or I'll scald you! "

The " dude " took coffee.

His " lip " was, indeed, phenomenal, and one day when he aimed it at Darius Vine (who was not a difficult mark), that individual bestirred his two hundred and fifty pounds and set about to thrash him. Archie promptly drew his " six-shooter," and as Darius, who was not conspicuous for courage, fled toward the Cantonment, Archie followed, shooting about his ears and his heels. Darius reached his brother's store, nigh dead, just in time to slam the door in Archie's face. Archie shot through the panel and brought Darius down with a bullet in his leg.

Archie's " gayety " with his " six-shooter " seemed to stir no emotion in his father except pride. But when Archie finally began to shoot at his own brother, Jake Maunders mildly protested. " Golly, golly," he exclaimed, " don't shoot at your brother. If you want to shoot at anybody, shoot at somebody outside the family."

Whether or not the boy saw the reasonableness of this paternal injunction is lost in the dust of the years. But the aphorism that the good die young has no significance so far as Archie Maunders is concerned.

The lawless element was altogether in the majority in the Bad Lands and thieving was common up and down the river and in the heart of the settlement itself. Maunders himself was too much of a coward to steal, too politic not to realize the disadvantage in being caught red-handed. Bill Williams was not above picking a purse when a reasonably safe occasion offered, but as a rule, like Maunders, he and his partner Hogue contrived to make some of the floaters and fly-by-nights, fugitives from other communities, do the actual stealing.

Maunders ruled by the law of the bully, and most men took him at the valuation of his " bluff."

But his attempt to intimidate Mrs. McGeeney was a rank failure. One of his hogs wandered south across the railroad track and invaded Mrs. Mc-Geeney's vegetable garden; whereupon, to discourage repetition, she promptly scalded it. Maunders, discovering the injury to his property, charged over to Mrs. McGeeney's house with blood in his eyes. She was waiting for him with a butcher-knife in her hand.

"Come on, ye damn bully!" she exclaimed. "Come on! I'm ready for ye!"

Maunders did not accept the invitation, and thereafter gave Mrs. McGeeney a wide berth.

There had been talk early in 1883 of organizing Billings County in which Little Missouri was situated. The stimulus toward this project had come from Jake Maunders, Bill Williams, and Hogue, backed by the unholy aggregation of saloon rats and floaters who customarily gathered around them. Merrifield and the Ferrises, who had taken the first steps in the community toward the reign of law when they had refused to buy stolen horses, were heartily anxious to secure some form of organized government, for they had no sympathy with the lawlessness that made the settlement a perilous place for honest men. But they were wise enough to see that the aim of Jake Maunders and his crew in organizing the county was not the establishment of law and order, but the creation of machinery for taxation on which they could wax fat. The Maltese Cross group therefore objected strenuously to any attempt on the part of the other group to force the organization of the county. Merrifield, Sylvane and Joe, and two or three ranchmen and cowboys who gathered around them, among them Gregor Lang and Bill Dantz (an attractive youngster of eighteen who had a ranch half a dozen miles south of the Maltese Cross), were in the minority, but they were respected and feared, and in the face of their opposition even such high-handed scoundrels as Maunders, Hogue, and Williams developed a vein of caution.

Meanwhile public safety was preserved in ways that were not altogether lawful, but were well known to all who lived in frontier communities.

"Many is the man that's cleared that bend west of Little Missouri with bullets following his heels," said Merrifield, years after. " That's the way we had of getting rid of people we didn't like. There was no court procedure, just a notice to get out of town and a lot of bullets, and, you bet, they got out."

Little Missouri's leading citizens were a wild crew, but with all their violence and their villainy, they were picturesque beings, and were by no means devoid of redeeming traits. Frank Vine, who evidently thought nothing of robbing his employers and was drunk more than half the time, had an equable temper which nothing apparently could ruffle, and a good heart to which no one in trouble ever seemed to appeal in vain. Mrs. McGeeney was a very " Lady of the Lamp " when any one was sick. Even Maunders had his graces. Roosevelt could not have lived among them a week without experiencing a new understanding of the inconsistencies that battle with each other in the making of men's lives.

IV

No, he was not like other men.
　　He fought at Acre (what's the date?),
Died, and somehow got born again
　　Seven hundred years too late.

It wasn't that he hitched his wagon
　　To stars too wild to heed his will —
He was just old Sir Smite-the-dragon
　　Pretending he was J. J. Hill.

And always when the talk was cattle
　　And rates and prices, selling, buying,
I reckon he was dreaming battle,
　　And, somewhere, grandly dying.

From *Medora Nights*

THE inhabitants of " Little Misery " who regarded law as a potential ball-and-chain were doing a thriving business by one crooked means or another and looked with uneasiness upon the coming of the cattlemen. There were wails and threats that autumn in Bill Williams's saloon over " stuck-up tenderfeet, shassayin' 'round, drivin' in cattle and chasin' out game."

" Maunders disliked Roosevelt from the first," said Bill Dantz. " He had no personal grudge against him, but he disliked him for what he represented. Maunders had prospered under the loose and lawless customs of the Northwest, and he shied at any man who he thought might try to interfere with them."

The coming of the Marquis de Mores six months previous had served greatly to heighten Maunders's personal prestige and to strengthen the lawless elements. For the Marquis was attracted by Jake's evident power, and, while he drew the crafty schemer into his inner counsels, was himself drawn into a subtle net that was yet to entangle both men in forces stronger than either.

When one day in March, 1883, a striking young Frenchman, who said he was a nobleman, came to Little Missouri with a plan ready-made to build a community there to rival Omaha, and a business that would startle America's foremost financiers, the citizens of the wicked little frontier settlement, who thought that they knew all the possibilities of " tenderfeet " and " pilgrims " and " how-do-you-do-boys," admitted in some bewilderment that they had been mistaken. The Frenchman's name was Antoine de Vallombrosa, Marquis de Mores. He was a member of the Orleans family, son of a duke, a " white lily of France," remotely in line for the throne; an unusually handsome man, tall and straight, black of hair and moustache, twenty-five or twenty-six years old, athletic, vigorous, and commanding. He had been a French officer, a graduate of the French military school of Saint Cyr, and had come to America following his marriage abroad with Medora von Hoffman, the daughter of a wealthy New York banker of German blood. His cousin, Count Fitz James, a descendant of the Jacobin exiles, had hunted in the Bad Lands the year previous, returning to France with stories of the new cattle country that stirred the Marquis's imagination. He was an adventurous spirit. " He had no judgment," said Merrifield, " but he was a fighter from hell." The stories of life on the frontier lured him as they had lured others, but the dreams that came to him were more complex and expensive dreams than those which came to the other young men who turned toward Dakota in those early eighties.

The Marquis arrived in Little Missouri with his father-in-law's millions at his back and a letter of introduction to Howard Eaton in his pocket. The letter, from a prominent business man in the East, ended, it seemed to Eaton, rather vaguely: " I don't know what experience he has had in business or anything of that kind, but he has some large views."

The Marquis enthusiastically unfolded these views. "I am going to build an abattoir. I am going to buy all the beef, sheep, and hogs that come over the Northern Pacific, and I am going to slaughter them here and then ship them to Chicago and the East."

" I don't think you have any idea how much stock comes over the Northern Pacific," Eaton remarked.

" It doesn't matter! " cried the Marquis. " My father-in-law has ten million dollars and can borrow ten million dollars more. I've got old Armour and the rest of them matched dollar for dollar."

Eaton said to himself that unquestionably the Marquis's views were " large."

"Do you think I am impractical?" the Marquis went on. "I am not impractical. My plan is altogether feasible. I do not merely think this. I know. My intuition tells me so. I pride myself on having a natural intuition. It takes me only a few seconds to understand a situation that other men have to puzzle over for hours. I seem to see every side of a question at once. I assure you, I am gifted in this way. I have wonderful insight."

But Eaton said to himself, "I wonder if the Marquis isn't raising his sights too high?"

The Marquis formed the Northern Pacific Refrigerator Car Company with two brothers named Haupt as his partners and guides; and plunged into his dream as a boy into a woodland pool. But it did not take him long to discover that the water was cold. Frank Vine offered to sell out the Little Missouri Land and Cattle Company to him for twenty-five thousand dollars, and when the Marquis, discovering that Frank had nothing to sell except a hazy title to a group of ramshackle buildings, refused to buy, Frank's employers intimated to the Marquis that there was no room for the de Mores enterprises in Little Missouri. The Marquis responded by buying what was known as Valentine scrip, or soldiers' rights, to the flat on the other side of the river and six square miles around it, with the determination of literally wiping Little Missouri off the map. On April Fool's Day, 1883 — auspicious date! — he pitched his tent in the sagebrush and founded the town of Medora.

The population of Little Missouri did not exhibit any noticeable warmth toward him or his dream. The hunters did not like " dudes " of any sort, but foreign " dudes " were particularly objectionable to them. His plans, moreover, struck at the heart of their free and untrammeled existence. As long as they could live by what their guns brought down, they were independent of the machinery of civilization. The coming of cattle and sheep meant the flight of antelope and deer. Hunters, to live, would have to buy and sell like common folk. That meant stores and banks, and these in time meant laws and police-officers; and police-officers meant the collapse of Paradise. It was all wrong.

The Marquis recognized that he had stepped in where, previously, angels had feared to tread. It occurred to him that it would be the part of wisdom to conciliate Little Missouri's hostile population. He began with the only man who, in that unstable community, looked solid, and appealed to Gregor Lang, suggesting a union of forces. Lang, who did not like the grandiose Frenchman, bluntly refused to entertain the idea.

" I am sorry," said the Marquis with a sincerity which was attractive and disarming. " I desire to be friends with every man."

The Marquis's efforts to win supporters were not altogether without success, for the liveryman, Jerry Paddock, became his foreman, and Jake Maunders, evidently seeing in the noble Frenchman one of those gifts from the patron saint of crooked men which come to a knave only once in a lifetime, attached himself to him and became his closest adviser. Maunders, as one who had known him well remarked long afterwards, "was too crooked to sleep in a roundhouse." Whether he set about deliberately to secure a hold on the Marquis, which the Marquis could never shake off, is a secret locked away with Maunders underground. If he did, he was more successful than wiser men have been in their endeavors. Insidiously he drew the Marquis into a quarrel, in which he himself was involved, with a hunter named Frank O'Donald and his two friends, John Reuter, known as "Dutch Wannigan," and Riley Luffsey. He was a crafty Iago, and the Marquis, born in a rose-garden and brought up in a hot-house, was guileless and trusting. Incidentally, the Marquis was "land hungry" and not altogether tactful in regarding the rights of others. Maunders carried bloodcurdling tales from the Marquis to O'Donald and back again, until, as Howard Eaton remarked, "every one got nervous."

"What shall I do?" the Marquis asked Maunders, unhappily, when Maunders reported that O'Donald was preparing for hostilities.

"Look out," answered Maunders, "and have the first shot."

The Marquis went to Mandan to ask the local magistrate for advice. "There is the situation," he said. "What shall I do?"

"Why, shoot," was the judicial reply.

He started to return to the center of hostilities.

A friend protested. "You'll get shot if you go down there," he declared.

The Frenchman shrugged his shoulders. "But I have got to go."

"Now, why do you have to go?"

"Why," replied the Marquis, "William is there. He is my valet. His father was my father's valet, and his grandfather was my grandfather's valet. I cannot leave William in the lurch."

Whereupon, smiling his engaging smile, he boarded the westbound express.

What followed is dead ashes, that need not be raked over. Just west of the town where the trail ran along the railroad track, the Marquis and his men fired at the hunters from cover. O'Donald and "Wannigan" were wounded, Riley was killed. Maunders, claiming that the hunters had started the shooting, charged them with manslaughter, and had them arrested.

The excitement in the little settlement was intense. Gregor Lang was outspoken in his indignation against the Marquis, and the few law-abiding citizens rallied around him. The Marquis was arrested and acquitted, but O'Donald and "Dutch Wannigan" were kept under lock and key. The better element in Little Missouri snorted in indignation and disgust, but for the moment there was nothing to be done about it. The excitement subsided. Riley Luffsey slept undisturbed on Graveyard Butte; the Marquis took up again the amazing activities which the episode of the quarrel had interrupted;

and Maunders, his mentor, flourished like the green bay tree. It was said that " after the murder, Maunders could get anything he wanted out of the Marquis "; so, from his point of view, the whole affair had been eminently successful.

All this was in the summer of 1883.

For all their violence and lawlessness there was no denying, meanwhile, that the settlements on both sides of the river, roughly known as Little Missouri, were beginning to flourish, and to catch the attention of a curious world.

The Mandan *Pioneer* spoke of surprising improvements; and even the Dickinson *Press*, which was published forty miles to the east and which as a rule regarded Little Missouri as an outrageous but interesting blot on the map of Dakota, was betrayed into momentary enthusiasm.

This town, situated in Pyramid Park on the banks of the Little Missouri River and surrounded by the Bad Lands with their fine scenery, is, at the present time, one of the most prosperous and rapidly growing towns along the line of the Northern Pacific. New buildings of every description are going up as fast as a large force of carpenters can do the work and an air of business and enterprise is apparent that would do honor to many an older town.

The " personals " that follow give a glimpse into the Little Missouri of which Roosevelt was a part during that third week of September, 1883.

NOTES

Business booms.

J. H. Butler is right on sight.

[McGeeney] and Walker are doing a good business.

Geo. Fitzpatrick is doing a rushing business.

J. B. Walker takes a good share of trade.

Anderson's restaurant refreshes the inner man.

Frank [Vine] rents the soldiers' quarters to tourists.

[P. McGeeney] will have a fine hotel when it is completed.

We found the Marquis de Mores a pleasant gentleman.

Little Missouri will double her population before spring.

The new depot will be soon completed and will be a good one.

It is worth remarking that Butler, McGeeney, Walker, Fitzpatrick, Anderson, and Frank Vine all conducted bars of one description or another. The " business " which is " booming " in the first line, therefore, seems to have been exclusively the business of selling and consuming liquor.

There is one further item in those " Notes ":

L. D. Rumsey, of Buffalo, N.Y., recently returned from a hunting expedition with Frank O'Donald. Frank is a good hunter and thoroughly posted about the country.

For the bloodthirsty desperado, by whose unconscious aid Maunders had contrived to get the Marquis into his power, was back in the Bad Lands, earning his living by hunting as he had earned it before the fatal June 26th when the Mar-

quis lost his head. There had been a " reconciliation." When O'Donald had returned to Little
Missouri from his sojourn in the Mandan jail, he
had been without money, and, as the Mandan
Pioneer explained, " the Marquis helped him out
by buying the hay on his ranch ' in stubble.' " He
bought the hay, it was rumored, for the sum of one
thousand dollars, which was high for hay which
would not begin growing for another eight months.
But the " reconciliation " was complete.

If Roosevelt met the Marquis during the week
he spent in Little Missouri, that September, there
is no record of that meeting. The Marquis was
here, there, and everywhere, for the stately house he
was building, on a grassy hill southward and across
the river from his new " town," was not yet completed, and he was, moreover, never inclined to stay
long on one spot, rushing to Miles City or St. Paul,
to Helena or to Chicago, at a moment's notice, in
pursuit of one or the other of his expensive dreams.

The Haupt brothers, it was said, were finding
their senior partner somewhat of a care. He bought
steers, and found, when he came to sell them as
beef, that he had bought them at too high a price;
he bought cows and found that the market would
not take cow-meat at all. Thereupon (lest the cold
facts which he had acquired concerning cattle should
rob him of the luxury of spacious expectations) he
bought five thousand dollars worth of broncos. He
would raise horses, he declared, on an unprecedented
scale.

The horses had barely arrived when the Marquis announced that he intended to raise sheep also. The Haupt brothers protested, but the Marquis was not to be diverted.

The hunters and cattlemen looked on in anger and disgust as sheep and ever more sheep began to pour into the Bad Lands. They knew, what the Marquis did not know, that sheep nibble the grass so closely that they kill the roots, and ruin the pasture for cattle and game. He tempered their indignation somewhat by offering a number of them a form of partnership in his enterprise. "His plan," says the guidebook of the Northern Pacific, published that summer of 1883, "is to engage experienced herders to the number of twenty-four, supply them with as many sheep as they may desire, and provide all necessary buildings and funds to carry on operations for a period of seven years. At the end of this time a division of the increase of the flocks is to be made, from which alone the Marquis is to derive his profits."

There was no one in the Bad Lands, that summer of 1883, who, if asked whether he knew anything about business or live stock or the laws of sidereal space, would not have claimed that he knew all that it was necessary for any man to know. The Marquis had no difficulty in finding the desired twenty-four. Each signed a solemn contract with him and let the sheep wander where they listed, eating mutton with relish and complaining to the Marquis of the depredations of the coyotes.

One who was more honest than the rest went to Herman Haupt at the end of August and drew his attention to the fact that many of the wethers and ewes were so old that they had no teeth to nibble with and were bound to die of starvation. Haupt rode from ranch to ranch examining the herds and came to the conclusion that six thousand out of twelve were too old to survive under the best conditions, and telegraphed the Marquis to that effect, advising that they be slaughtered at once.

The answer of the Marquis was prompt. " Don't kill any sheep," it ran. Haupt shrugged his shoulders. By the time Roosevelt left Little Missouri the end of September, the sheep were already beginning, one by one, to perish. But by this time the Marquis was absorbed in a new undertaking and was making arrangements to ship untold quantities of buffalo-meat and other game on his refrigerator cars to Eastern markets, unaware that a certain young man with spectacles had just shot one of the last buffalo that the inhabitants of Little Missouri were ever destined to see.

Roosevelt, learning a great deal about the ways of men who are civilized too little and men who are civilized too much, spent a week waiting in Little Missouri and roundabout for word from Merrifield and Sylvane. It came at last in a telegram saying that Wadsworth and Halley had given them a release and that they were prepared to enter into a new partnership. Roosevelt started promptly for St. Paul, and on September 27th signed a contract[1]

[1] See Appendix.

with the two Canadians. Sylvane and Merrifield thereupon went East to Iowa, to purchase three hundred head of cattle in addition to the hundred and fifty which they had taken over from Wadsworth and Halley; while Roosevelt, who a little less than three weeks previous had dropped off the train at Little Missouri for a hunt and nothing more, took up again the sober threads of life.

He returned East to his lovely young wife and a campaign for a third term in the New York Legislature, stronger in body than he had ever felt before. If he expected that his family would think as highly of his cattle venture as he did himself, he was doomed to disappointment. Those members of it whom he could count on most for sincere solicitude for his welfare were most emphatic in their disapproval. They considered his investment foolhardy, and said so. Uncle James and the other business men of the family simply threw up their hands in despair. His sisters, who admired him enormously and had confidence in his judgment, were frankly worried. Pessimists assured him that his cattle would die like flies during the winter.

He lost no sleep for apprehensions.

Little Missouri, meanwhile, was cultivating the air of one who is conscious of imminent greatness. The Marquis was extending his business in a way to stir the imagination of any community. In Miles City he built a slaughter-house, in Billings he built another. He established offices in St. Paul, in Brainerd, in Duluth. He built refrigerator plants and storehouses in Mandan and Bismarck and Vedalles and Portland.

His plan, on the surface, was practical. It was to slaughter on the range the beef that was consumed along the Northern Pacific Railway, west of St. Paul. The Marquis argued that to send a steer on the hoof from Medora to Chicago and then to send it back in the form of beef to Helena or Portland was sheer waste of the consumer's money in freight rates. A steer, traveling for days in a crowded cattle-car, moreover, had a way of shrinking ten per cent in weight. It was more expensive, furthermore, to ship a live steer than a dead one. Altogether, the scheme appeared to the Marquis as a heaven-sent inspiration; and cooler-headed business men than he accepted it as practical. The cities along the Northern Pacific acclaimed it enthusiastically, hoping that it meant cheaper beef; and presented the company that was exploiting it with all the land it wanted.

The Marquis might have been forgiven if, in the midst of the cheering, he had strutted a bit. But he did not strut. The newspapers spoke of his "modest bearing" as he appeared in hotel corridors in Washington and St. Paul and New York, with a lady whose hair was "Titan-red," as the *Pioneer Press* of St. Paul had it, and who, it was rumored, was a better shot than the Marquis. He had great charm, and there was something engaging in the perfection with which he played the *grand seigneur*.

"How did you happen to go into this sort of business?" he was asked.

"I wanted something to do," he answered.

In view of the fact that before his first abattoir was in operation he had spent upwards of three hundred thousand dollars, an impartial observer might have remarked that his desire for activity was expensive.

Unquestionably the Marquis had made an impression on the Northwest country. The hints he threw out concerning friends in Paris who were eager to invest five million dollars in Billings County were sufficient to cause palpitation in more than one Dakota bosom. The Marquis promised telephone lines up and down the river and other civic improvements that were dazzling to the imagination and stimulating to the price of building lots; and implanted firmly in the minds of the inhabitants of Medora the idea that in ten years their city would rival Omaha. Meanwhile, Little Missouri and the "boomtown" were leading an existence which seemed to ricochet back and forth between Acadian simplicity and the livid sophistication of a mining-camp.

"Sheriff Cuskelly made a business trip to Little Missouri," is the gist of countless "Notes" in the Dickinson *Press*, "and reports everything as lively at the town on the Little Muddy."

Lively it was; but its liveliness was not all thievery and violence. "On November 5th," the Dickinson *Press* announces, "the citizens of Little Missouri opened a school." Whom they opened it for is dark as the ancestry of Melchizedek. But from somewhere some one procured a teacher, and in the saloons the cowboys and the hunters, the horse-thieves and gamblers and fly-by-nights and painted ladies " chipped in " to pay his " board and keep." The charm of this outpouring of dollars in the cause of education is not dimmed by the fact that the school-teacher, in the middle of the first term, discovered a more profitable form of activity and deserted his charges to open a saloon.

Late in November a man of a different sort blew into town. His name was A. T. Packard. He was joyously young, like almost every one else in Little Missouri, except Maunders and Paddock and Captain Vine, having graduated from the University of Michigan only a year before. He drifted westward, and, having a taste for things literary, became managing editor of the Bismarck *Tribune*. Bismarck was lurid in those days, and editing a newspaper there meant not only writing practically everything in it, including the advertisements, but also persuading the leading citizens by main force that the editor had a right to say what he pleased. Packard had been an athlete in college, and his eyes gave out before his rule had been seriously disputed. After throwing sundry protesting malefactors downstairs, he resigned and undertook work a trifle less exacting across the Missouri River, on the Mandan *Pioneer*.

Packard became fascinated with the tales he heard of Little Missouri and Medora and, being foot loose, drifted thither late in November. It happened .that Frank Vine, who had by that time been deposed as agent of the Gorringe syndicate, was running the Pyramid Park Hotel. He had met Packard in Mandan and greeted him like a long-lost brother. As the newcomer was sitting in a corner of the barroom after supper, writing home, Frank came up and bent over him.

"You told me down in Mandan that you'd never seen an honest-to-goodness cowboy," he whispered. "See that fellow at the farther end of the bar? Well, that's a real cowboy."

Packard looked up. The man was standing with his back toward the wall, and it struck the tenderfoot that there was something in his attitude and in the look in his eye that suggested that he was on the watch and kept his back to the wall with a purpose. He wore the paraphernalia of the cowboy with ease and grace.

Packard started to describe him to his " folks " in distant Indiana. He described his hat, his face, his clothes, his shaps, his loosely hanging belt with the protruding gun. He looked up and studied the man; he looked down and wrote. The man finally became conscious that he was the subject of study. Packard observed Frank Vine whisper a word of explanation.

He finished his letter and decided to take it to the " depot " and ask the telegraph operator to mail it on the eastbound train that passed through Little Missouri at three. He opened the door. The night was black, and a blast of icy wind greeted him. He changed his mind.

The next afternoon he was riding up the river to the Maltese Cross when he heard hoofs behind him. A minute later the object of his artistic efforts of the night before joined him and for an hour loped along at his side. He was not slow in discovering that the man was pumping him. It occurred to him that turn-about was fair play, and he told him all the man wanted to know.

" So you're a newspaper feller," remarked the man at length. " That's damn funny. But I guess it's so if you say so. You see," he added, " Frank Vine he said you was a deputy-sheriff on the lookout for a horse-thief."

Packard felt his hair rise under his hat.

" Where was you going last night when you started to go out? "

" To the telegraph-office."

" I made up my mind you was going to telegraph."

" I was just going to mail a letter."

" Well, if you'd gone I'd have killed you."

Packard gasped a little. Frank Vine was a joker with a vengeance. They rode on, talking of lighter matters.[1]

Packard had come to the Bad Lands with the idea of spending the winter in the open, hunting, but he was a newspaper man from top to toe and in the back of his mind there was a notion that it would be a good deal of a lark, and possibly a not

---

[1] A year later, Packard, as Chief of Police, officiated at what was euphemistically known as a " necktie party " at which his companion of that ride was the guest of honor.

unprofitable venture, to start a weekly newspaper
in the Marquis de Mores's budding metropolis. He
had, at the tender age of thirteen, been managing
editor of a country newspaper, owned by his father,
and ever since had been drawn again and again
back into the " game " by that lure which few
men who yield to it are ever after able to resist.

He broached the matter to the Marquis. That
gentleman was patronizing, but agreed that a
special organ might prove of value to his Company.
He offered to finance the undertaking.

Packard remarked that evidently the Marquis
did not understand. If he started a paper it would
be an organ for nobody. He intended to finance it
himself and run it to please himself. All he wanted
was a building.

The Marquis, a little miffed, agreed to rent him
a building north of his general store in return for a
weekly advertisement for the Company. Packard
ordered his type and his presses and betook himself
to the solitude of the wintry buttes to think of a
name for his paper. His battle was half won when
he came back with the name of *The Bad Lands
Cowboy*.

His first issue came out early in February, 1884.
It was greeted with interest even by so mighty a
contemporary as the New York *Herald*.

We hail with pleasure the birth of a new Dakota
paper, the *Bad Lands Cowboy* [runs the note of welcome].
The *Cowboy* is really a neat little journal, with lots to
read in it, and the American press has every reason to be

proud of its new baby. We are quite sure it will live to be a credit to the family. The *Cowboy* evidently means business. It says in the introductory notice to its first number that it intends to be the leading cattle paper of the Northwest, and adds that it is not published for fun, but for $2 a year.

All the autumn and winter Medora and her rival across the river had been feverishly competing for supremacy. But Little Missouri, though she built ever so busily, in such a contest had not a chance in the world. For the Little Missouri Land and Stock Company, which was its only hope, was moribund, and the Marquis was playing, in a sense, with loaded dice. He spoke persuasively to the officials of the Northern Pacific and before the winter was well advanced the stop for express trains was on the eastern side of the river, and Little Missouri, protest as she would, belonged to the past. When the *Cowboy* appeared for the first time, Medora was in the full blaze of national fame, having " broken into the front page " of the New York *Sun*. For the Marquis was bubbling over with pride and confidence, and the tales he told a credulous interviewer filled a column. A few were based on fact, a few were builded on the nebulous foundation of hope, and a few were sheer romance. The most conspicuous case of romance was a story of the stage-line from Medora to the prosperous and wild little mining town of Deadwood, two hundred miles or more to the south.

" The Marquis had observed," narrates the interviewer, " that the divide on the top of the ridge between the Little Missouri and the Missouri Rivers was almost a natural roadway that led directly toward Deadwood. He gave this roadway needed artificial improvements, and started the Deadwood and Medora stage-line. This is now diverting the Deadwood trade to Medora, to the great advantage of both places."

Who, reading that sober piece of information, would have dreamed that the stage-line in question was at the time nothing but a pious hope?

The Dickinson *Press* was blunt in its comment. " Stages are not running from Medora to Deadwood," it remarked editorially, " nor has the roadway ever been improved. The Marquis should put a curb on his too vivid imagination and confine himself a little more strictly to facts."

But facts were not the things on which a nature like de Mores's fed.

His sheep meanwhile, were dying by hundreds every week. Of the twelve thousand he had turned loose on the range during the preceding summer, half were dead by the middle of January. There were rumors that rivals of the Marquis had used poison.

The loss [declared a dispatch to the *Minneapolis Journal*] can be accounted for on no other ground. It is supposed that malicious motives prompted the deed, as the Marquis is known to have had enemies since the killing of Luffsey.

If the Marquis took any stock in these suspicions, his partners, the Haupt brothers, did not. They knew that it was a physical impossibility to poison six thousand sheep scattered over ten thousand square miles of snowbound landscape.

The Haupts were by this time thoroughly out of patience with de Mores. There was a stormy meeting of the directors of the Northern Pacific Refrigerator Car Company in St. Paul, in the course of which the Haupt brothers told their distinguished senior partner exactly what they thought of his business ability; and suggested that the Company go into liquidation.

The Marquis jumped to his feet in a rage. " I won't let it go into liquidation," he cried. " My honor is at stake. I have told my friends in France that I would do so and so and so, that I would make money, a great deal of money. I must do it. Or where am I? "

The Haupts did not exactly know. They compromised with the Marquis by taking the bonds of the Company in exchange for their stock, and retired with inner jubilation at having been able to withdraw from a perilous situation with skins more or less intact.

The Marquis, as usual, secreted himself from the stern eyes of Experience, in the radiant emanations of a new dream. The Dickinson *Press* announced it promptly:

The Marquis de Mores has a novel enterprise under way, which he is confident will prove a success, it being a plan to raise 50,000 cabbages on his ranch at the Little

Missouri, and have them ready for the market April 1.
They will be raised under glass in some peculiar French
manner, and when they have attained a certain size,
will be transplanted into individual pots and forced
rapidly by rich fertilizers, made from the offal of the
slaughter-houses and for which preparation he owns
the patent. Should the cabbages come out on time, he
will try his hand on other kinds of vegetables, and
should he succeed the citizens along the line will have
an opportunity to get as early vegetables as those who
live in the sunny South.

The cabbages were a dream which seems never
to have materialized even to the point of being a
source of expense, and history speaks no more of it.

The boys at the Chimney Butte, meanwhile,
were hibernating, hunting as the spirit moved
them and keeping a general eye on the stock. Of
Roosevelt's three friends, Joe was the only one
who was really busy. Joe, it happened, was no
longer working for Frank Vine. He was now a
storekeeper. It was all due to the fateful hundred
dollars which he had loaned the unstable Johnny
Nelson.

For Johnny Nelson, so far as Little Missouri was
concerned, was no more. He had bought all his
goods on credit from some commission house in St.
Paul; but his payments, due mainly to the fact
that his receipts all drifted sooner or later into the
guileful hands of Jess Hogue, were infrequent and
finally stopped altogether. Johnny received word
that his creditor in St. Paul was coming to investigate him. He became frantic and confided the

awful news to every one he met. Hogue, Bill Williams, Jake Maunders, and a group of their satellites, hearing the doleful recital in Bill Williams's saloon, told Johnny that the sheriff would unquestionably close up his store and take everything away from him.

" You give me the keys," said Jake Maunders, " and I'll see that the sheriff don't get your stuff."

Johnny in his innocence gave up the keys. That night Jake Maunders and his " gang " entered the store and completely cleaned it out. They did not leave a button or a shoestring. It was said afterwards that Jake Maunders did not have to buy a new suit of clothes for seven years, and even Williams's two tame bears wore ready-made coats from St. Paul.

Johnny Nelson went wailing to Katie, his betrothed.

" I've lost everything!" he cried. " I've lost all my goods and I can't get more. I've lost my reputation. I can't marry you. I've lost my reputation."

Katie was philosophic about it. " That's all right, Johnny," she said comfortingly, " I lost mine long ago."

At that, Johnny "skipped the country." And so it was that Joe Ferris, to save his hundred dollars attached Johnny's building and became storekeeper.

For Roosevelt, two thousand miles to the east, the winter was proving exciting. He had won his reëlection to the Assembly with ease and had plunged into his work with a new vigor and a more solid self-reliance. He became the acknowledged leader of the progressive elements in the Legislature, the " cyclone member " at whom the reactionaries who were known as the " Black Horse Cavalry " sneered, but of whom, nevertheless, they were heartily afraid.

He " figured in the news," day in, day out, for the public, it seemed, was interested in this vigorous and emphatic young man from the " Silkstocking District " of New York. Roosevelt took his publicity with zest, for he was human and enjoyed the sensation of being counted with those who made the wheels go around. Meanwhile he worked all day and conversed half the night on a thousand topics which his ardor made thrilling. In society he was already somewhat of a lion; and he was only twenty-five years old.

Life was running, on the whole, very smoothly for Theodore Roosevelt when in January, 1884, he entered upon his third term in the Legislature. He was happily married, he had wealth, he had a notable book on the War of 1812 to his credit; he had, it seemed, a smooth course ahead of him, down pleasant roads to fame.

On February 12th, at ten o'clock in the morning, his wife gave birth to a daughter. At five o'clock the following morning his mother died. Six hours later his wife died.

He was stunned and dazed, but within a week after the infinitely pathetic double funeral he was back at his desk in the Assembly, ready to fling himself with every fiber of energy at his command into the fight for clean government. He supported civil service reform; he was chairman of a committee which investigated certain phases of New York City official life, and carried through the Legislature a bill taking from the Board of Aldermen the power to reject the Mayor's appointments. He was chairman and practically the only active member of another committee to investigate living conditions in the tenements of New York, and as spokesman of the worn and sad-looking foreigners who constituted the Cigar-Makers' Union, argued before Governor Cleveland for the passage of a bill to prohibit the manufacture of cigars in tenement-houses. His energy was boundless, it seemed, but the heart had gone out of him. He was restless, and thought longingly of the valley of the Little Missouri.

The news that came from the boys at Chimney Butte was favorable. The three hundred head of young cattle which Sylvane and Merrifield had bought in Iowa, were doing well in spite of a hard winter. Roosevelt, struck by Sylvane's enthusiastic report, backed by a painstaking account-sheet, wrote Sylvane telling him to buy a thousand or twelve hundred head more.

Sylvane's reply was characteristic and would have gratified Uncle James. "Don't put in any more money until you're sure we've scattered the other dollars right," he said in effect. "Better come out first and look around."

That struck Roosevelt as good advice, and he accepted it.

While Roosevelt was winning clear, meanwhile, of the tangles and snares in Albany, he was unconsciously being enmeshed in the web that was spinning at Medora.

It came about this way. The Marquis, who had many likable qualities, did not possess among them any strict regard for the rights of others. He had a curious obsession, in fact, that in the Bad Lands there were no rights but his; and with that point of view had directed his superintendent, a man named Matthews, to drive fifteen hundred head of cattle over on an unusually fine piece of bottom-land northwestward across the river from the Maltese Cross, which, by all the laws of the range, belonged to the " Roosevelt outfit." Matthews declared that the Marquis intended to hold the bottom permanently for fattening beef-cattle, and to build a cabin there.

" You'll have to move those cattle by daylight," said Merrifield, "or we'll move them for you. You can take your choice."

" I've got my orders from the Marquis to keep the cattle here," answered Matthews. " That's all there is to it. They'll stay here."

It was late at night, but Sylvane and Merrifield rode to Medora taking a neighboring cowboy named Pete Marlow along as witness, " for the Marquis is a hard man to deal with," remarked Merrifield. To Pete it was all the gayest sort of adventure.

He confided the object of the nocturnal expedition to the first man he came upon.

The Marquis was not at his home. The boys were told that he might still be at his office, though the time was nearing midnight.

Meanwhile Pete's news had spread. From the base of Graveyard Butte, Jake Hainsley, the superintendent of the coal mine, who dearly loved a fight, came running with a rifle in his hand. " I've got forty men myself," he cried, " and I've Winchesters for every mother's son of 'em, and if you need help you just let me know and we'll back you all right, we will."

The Marquis was in his office in Medora next to the new Company store, working with Van Driesche, his valet and secretary. He asked what the three men wanted of him at that hour in the night. Merrifield explained the situation.

They told him: " We want you to write an order to move those cattle at daylight."

" If I refuse? "

Sylvane and Merrifield had thoroughly discussed the question what they would do in case the Marquis refused. They would take tin pans and stampede the herd. They were under no illusions concerning the probabilities in case they took that means of ridding themselves of the unwelcome herd. There would be shooting, of course.

" Why, Marquis," said Merrifield, " if Matthews don't move those cattle, I guess there's nothing to it but what we'll have to move them ourselves."

The Marquis had not lived a year in the Bad Lands without learning something. In a more conciliatory mood he endeavored to find ground for a compromise. But " the boys " were not inclined to compromise with a man who was patently in the wrong. Finally, the Marquis offered them fifteen hundred dollars on the condition that they would allow him to use the piece of bottom-land for three weeks.

It was on its face a munificent offer; but Merrifield and Sylvane knew that the Marquis's " three weeks " might not terminate after twenty-one days. They knew something else. " After we had made our statement," Merrifield explained later, " no matter how much he had offered us we would not have accepted it. We knew there'd be no living with a man like the Marquis if you made statements and then backed down for any price."

Never draw your gun, ran a saying of the frontier, *unless you mean to shoot.*

" Marquis," said Merrifield, " we've made our statement once for all. If you don't see fit to write that order there won't be any more talk. We will move the cattle ourselves."

The Marquis was courteous and even friendly. " I am sorry you cannot do this for me," he said; but he issued the order. Merrifield and Sylvane themselves carried it to the offending superintendent. Matthews was furious; but he moved the cattle at dawn. The whole affair did not serve to improve the relations between the groups which the killing of Riley Luffsey had originally crystallized.

Roosevelt probably remained unaware of the interesting complications that were being woven for him in the hot-hearted frontier community of which he was now a part; for Merrifield and Sylvane, as correspondents, were laconic, not being given to spreading themselves out on paper. His work in the Assembly and the pre-convention campaign for presidential candidates completely absorbed his energies. He was eager that a reform candidate should be named by the Republicans, vigorously opposing both Blaine and Arthur, himself preferring Senator Edmunds of Vermont. He fought hard and up to a certain point successfully, for at the State Republican Convention held in Utica in April he thoroughly trounced the Old Guard, who were seeking to send a delegation to Chicago favorable to Arthur, and was himself elected head of the delegates at large, popularly known as the " Big Four."

He had, meanwhile, made up his mind that, however the dice might fall at the convention, he would henceforth make his home, for a part of the year at least, in the Bad Lands. He had two friends in Maine, backwoodsmen mighty with the axe, and born to the privations of the frontier, whom he decided to take with him if he could. One was " Bill " Sewall, a stalwart viking at the end of his thirties, who had been his guide on frequent occasions when as a boy in college he had sought health and good hunting on the waters of Lake Mattawamkeag; the other was Sewall's nephew,

Wilmot Dow. He flung out the suggestion to them, and they rose to it like hungry trout; for they had adventurous spirits.

The Republican National Convention met in Chicago in the first days of June. Roosevelt, supported by his friend Henry Cabot Lodge and a group of civil service reformers that included George William Curtis and Carl Schurz, led the fight for Edmunds. But the convention wanted Blaine, the " Plumed Knight "; and the convention got Blaine.

Roosevelt raged, but refused to follow Curtis and Schurz, who hinted darkly at " bolting the ticket." He took the first train to Dakota, sick at heart, to think things over.

V

He wears a big hat and big spurs and all that,
　　And leggins of fancy fringed leather;
He takes pride in his boots and the pistol he shoots
　　And he's happy in all kinds of weather;
He's fond of his horse, it's a broncho, of course,
　　For oh, he can ride like the devil;
He is old for his years and he always appears
　　Like a fellow who's lived on the level;
He can sing, he can cook, yet his eyes have the look
　　Of a man that to fear is a stranger;
Yes, his cool, quiet nerve will always subserve
　　For his wild life of duty and danger.
He gets little to eat, and he guys tenderfeet,
　　And for fashion, oh well! he's not in it;
But he'll rope a gay steer when he gets on its ear
　　At the rate of two-forty a minute.

Cowboy song

BLAINE was nominated on June 7th. On the 8th
Roosevelt was already in St. Paul, on his way to
the Bad Lands. A reporter of the *Pioneer Press*
interviewed him and has left this description of him
as he appeared fresh from the battle at Chicago:

He is short and slight and with rather an ordinary
appearance, although his frame is wiry and his flashing
eyes and rapid, nervous gestures betoken a hidden
strength. He is not at all an ideal Harvard alumnus,
for he lacks that ingrained conceit and grace of manner
that a residence at Cambridge insures. Although of
the old Knickerbocker stock, his manner and carriage
is awkward and not at all impressive.

He arrived in Medora on the evening of the 9th.
The Ferrises and Merrifield were at the "depot"
to meet him. They all adjourned to Packard's

printing office, since that was the only place in town of a semi-public character which was not at that hour in possession of a noisy aggregation of Medora's thirstiest citizens.

The office of the *Bad Lands Cowboy*, which stood under a gnarled cottonwood-tree north of the Marquis's store, was a one-room frame building which served as the editor's parlor, bedroom, and bath, as well as his printing-office and his editorial sanctum. It was built of perpendicular boards which let in the wintry blasts in spite of the two-inch strips which covered the joints on the outside. It had, in fact, originally served as the Marquis's blacksmith shop, and the addition of a wooden floor had not altogether converted it into a habitable dwelling, proof against Dakota weather. On this particular June night the thermometer was in the thirties and a cannon stove glowed red from a steady application of lignite.

A half-dozen voices greeted Roosevelt with pleas for the latest news of the "great Republican round-up." Roosevelt was not loath to unburden his soul. For an hour he told of the battles and the manipulations of the convention, of the stubborn fight against an impending nomination which he had known would be a fatal mistake, but which the majority seemed to be bound to make.

Packard told about it years afterward. "He gave us such a swinging description of the stirring scenes of the convention that the eyes of the boys were fairly popping out of their heads. But it was when he told how Roscoe Conkling attempted to dominate the situation and override the wishes of a large portion of the New York delegation that the fire really began to flash in his eyes. I can see him now as plainly as I did then, as he straightened up, his doubled fist in the air, his teeth glittering, and his eyes squinting in something that was far from a smile as he jerked out the words, 'By Godfrey! I will not be dictated to!'"

Roosevelt rode to the Maltese Cross next morning. The old stockade shack, with the dirt floor and dirt roof, had, as he had suggested, been converted into a stable, and a simple but substantial one-and-a-half story log cabin had been built with a shingle roof and a cellar, both luxuries in the Bad Lands. An alcove off the one large room on the main floor was set aside for Roosevelt's use as combined bedroom and study; the other men were quartered in the loft above. East of the ranch-house beside a patch of kitchen-garden, stood the strongly made circular horse-corral, with a snubbing-post in the middle, and at some distance from it the larger cow-corral for the branding of the cattle. Between them stood the cowsheds and the hayricks.

The ranch-buildings belonged to Sylvane Ferris and Merrifield. In buying out the Maltese Cross, Roosevelt had bought only cattle and horses; not buildings or land. The ranges on which his cattle grazed were owned by the Northern Pacific Railroad, and by the Government. It was the custom for ranchmen to claim for grazing purposes a certain stretch of land north, east, south, and west of the bottom on which the home ranch stood.

" You claim so much land each way," Sylvane explained to a tenderfoot a long time after, " according to how many cattle you have. For instance, if you have one hundred head of cattle, you don't require very much range; if you have a thousand head, you need so much more. There wouldn't be any sense of one man trying to crowd his cattle onto your range and starve out both outfits. So each man claims as much land as he needs. Of course, that doesn't mean that the other fellow doesn't get over on your range — that's the reason we brand our cattle; it simply means that a certain given number of cattle will have a certain given amount of grazing land. Our cattle may be on the other fellow's range and some of his may be on our range, but he'll claim so much land each way and we'll claim so much land each way, and then it doesn't make any difference if they do get on each other's territory, so long as there is enough grazing for the two outfits."

The range claimed by the " Maltese Cross outfit " extended northward to the river-crossing above Eaton's " Custer Trail Ranch," and southward to the crossing just below what was known as " Sloping Bottom," covering a territory that had a frontage of four miles on both sides of the river and extended back on each side for thirty miles to the heads of the creeks which emptied into the Little Missouri.

The cattle, Roosevelt found, were looking sleek

and well-fed. He had lost about twenty-five head
during the winter, partly from the cold, partly from
the attacks of wolves. There were, he discovered,
a hundred and fifty fine calves.

A new cowpuncher had been added to the Maltese
Cross outfit, he found, since the preceding autumn.
It was George Myers, whom he had met on the ride
down the river from Lang's. Roosevelt had purchased five hundred dollars' worth of barbed wire
and George was digging post-holes. He was a
boyish and attractive individual whom the *wanderlust* had driven westward from his home in Wis-
consin. His honesty fairly leaped at you out of
his direct, clear eyes.

Roosevelt spent two days contemplating his new
possessions. At the end of the second he had reached
a decision, and he announced it promptly. He told
Sylvane and Merrifield to get ready to ride to Lang's
with him the next day for the purpose of drawing
up a new contract. He had determined to make
cattle-raising his " regular business " and intended,
at once (in riotous defiance of Uncle James!), to
put a thousand head more on the range.

The Langs were situated seven miles nearer
civilization than they had been on Roosevelt's
previous visit, and were living in a dugout built
against a square elevation that looked like a low
fortress or the " barrow " of some dead Viking
chief. They were building a ranch-house in anticipation of the coming of Mrs. Lang and two children,
a girl of eighteen or nineteen and a son a half-dozen

years younger than Lincoln. The dugout was already overcrowded with three or four carpenters who were at work on the house, and Gregor Lang suggested that they ride five miles up the river to a cabin of his on what was known as "Sagebrush Bottom," where he and Lincoln had spent the winter. They had moved out of the shack on the Little Cannonball for two reasons. One was that a large cattle outfit from New Mexico, named the Berry-Boyce Cattle Company, had started a ranch, known as the "Three Seven," not half a mile down the river; the other was that Gregor Lang was by disposition not one who was able to learn from the experience of others. For it happened that, a few weeks after Roosevelt's departure in September, a skunk had invaded the cabin and made itself comfortable under one of the bunks. Lincoln and the Highlander were in favor of diplomacy in dealing with the invader. But Gregor Lang reached for a pitchfork. They pleaded with him, without effect. The skunk retaliated in his own fashion; and shortly after, they moved forever out of the cabin on the Little Cannonball.

Roosevelt, who recognized Gregor Lang's limitations, recognized also that the Scotchman was a good business man. He set him to work next morning drawing up a new contract. It called for further investment on his part of twenty-six thousand dollars to cover the purchase of a thousand head or more of cattle. Merrifield and Sylvane signed it and returned promptly to the Maltese Cross.

Roosevelt remained behind. " Lincoln," he said,
" there are two things I want to do. I want to
get an antelope, and I want to get a buckskin
suit."

Lincoln thought that he could help him to both.
Some twenty miles to the east lived a woman
named Mrs. Maddox who had acquired some fame
in the region by the vigorous way in which she
had handled the old reprobate who was her husband;
and by her skill in making buckskin shirts. She
was a dead shot, and it was said of her that even
" Calamity Jane," Deadwood's " first lady," was
forced " to yield the palm to Mrs. Maddox when
it came to the use of a vocabulary which adequately
searched every nook and cranny of a man's life
from birth to ultimate damnation."

They found her in her desolate, little mud-roofed
hut on Sand Creek, a mile south of the old Keogh
trail. She was living alone, having recently dismissed her husband in summary fashion. It seems
that he was a worthless devil, who, under the
stimulus of some whiskey he had obtained from
an outfit of Missouri "bull-whackers" who were
driving freight to Deadwood, had picked a quarrel
with his wife and attempted to beat her. She
knocked him down with a stove-lid lifter and the
" bull-whackers " bore him off, leaving the lady in
full possession of the ranch. She now had a man
named Crow Joe working for her, a slab-sided,
shifty-eyed ne'er-do-well, who was suspected of
stealing horses on occasion.

She measured Roosevelt for his suit[1] and gave him and Lincoln a dinner that they remembered. A vigorous personality spoke out of her every action. Roosevelt regarded her with mingled amusement and awe.

They found their antelope on the way home. They found two antelopes, in fact, but Roosevelt, who had been as cool as an Indian an instant before, was so elated when he saw the first drop to his rifle that he was totally incapacitated from aiming at the second when that animal, evidently bewildered, began to run in circles scarcely twenty-five yards away. He had dropped his gun with a whoop, waving his arms over his head and crying, " I got him! I got him! "

" Shoot the other one! " Lincoln called.

Roosevelt burst into a laugh. " I can't," he called back. " Not to save my life."

They met at the side of the antelope. " This would not have seemed nearly so good if somebody had not been here to see it," Roosevelt exclaimed. " Do you know what I am going to do? I am going to make you a present of my shot-gun."

Lincoln, being only sixteen, did not know exactly what to make of the generosity of this jubilant young man. It struck him that Roosevelt, in the excitement of the moment, was giving away a thing of great value and might regret it on sober

[1] The buckskin suit which was still doing service thirty years later, was made under the supervision of Mrs. Maddox by her niece, now Mrs. Olmstead, of Medora.

second thought. Lincoln replied that he could not accept the gift. It struck him that Roosevelt looked hurt for an instant.

They dressed the antelope together, Roosevelt taking the position of humble pupil. The next day he returned alone to the Maltese Cross.

He now entered with vigor into the life of a Dakota ranchman. The country was at its best in the clear June weather. The landscape in which the ranch-house was set had none of the forbidding desolateness of sharp bluff and scarred ravine that characterized the region surrounding Little Missouri. The door of the cabin looked out on a wide, semi-circular clearing covered with sagebrush, bordered on the east by a ring of buttes and grassy slopes, restful in their gray and green for eyes to gaze upon. Westward, not a quarter of a mile from the house, behind a hedge of cottonwoods, the river swung in a long circle at the foot of steep buttes crested with scoria. At the ends of the valley were glades of cottonwoods with grassy floors where deer hid among the buckbrush by day, or at dusk fed silently or, at the sound of a step, bounded, erect and beautiful, off into deeper shelter. In an almost impenetrable tangle of bullberry bushes, whose hither edge was barely one hundred yards from the ranch-house, two fawns spent their days. They were extraordinarily tame, and in the evenings Roosevelt could frequently see them from the door as they came out to feed. Walking on the flat after sunset, or riding home when night had fallen, he

would run across them when it was too dark to
make out anything but their flaunting white tails
as they cantered out of the way.

Roosevelt, who never did things by halves, took
up his new activities as though they constituted
the goal of a lifetime spent in a search for the ultimate good. Ranch-life was altogether novel to
him; at no point had his work or his play touched
any phase of it. He had ridden to hounds and was
a fair but by no means a " fancy " rider. His
experience in the Meadowbrook Hunt, however,
had scarcely prepared him adequately for combat
with the four-legged children of Satan that " mewed
their mighty youth " on the wild ranges of the
Bad Lands.

" I have a perfect dread of bucking," he confided
to an unseen public in a book which he began that
summer, " and if I can help it I never get on a
confirmed bucker." He could not always help it.
Sylvane, who could ride anything in the Bad Lands,
was wedded to the idea that any animal which by
main force had been saddled and ridden was a
" broke horse," and when Roosevelt would protest
mildly concerning this or that particularly vicious
animal, Sylvane would look at him in a grieved
and altogether captivating way, saying, " Why, I
call that a plumb gentle horse."

" When Sylvane says that a horse is ' plumb
gentle,' " remarked Roosevelt, on one occasion,
" then you want to look out."

Sylvane and Merrifield were to start for the East

to purchase the additional cattle on the 18th of June, and Roosevelt had determined to set forth on the same day for a solitary camping-trip on the prairie. Into the three or four intervening days he crowded all the experiences they would hold.

He managed to persuade Sylvane, somewhat against that individual's personal judgment (for Sylvane was suspicious of " dudes "), that he actually intended " to carry his own pack." Sylvane found, to his surprise, that the " dude " learnt quickly. He showed Roosevelt once how to saddle his horse, and thereafter Roosevelt saddled his horses himself. Sylvane was relieved in spirit, and began to look with new eyes on the " four-eyed tenderfoot " who was entrusting a fortune to his care.

There was no general round-up in the valley of the Little Missouri that spring of 1884, for the cattle had not had the opportunity to wander to any great distance, having been on the range, most of them, only a few months. The different " outfits," however, held their own round-ups, at each of which a few hundred cattle might be gathered from the immediate vicinity, the calves " cut out " and roped and branded, and turned loose again to wander undisturbed until the " beef round-up " in the fall.

At each of these round-ups, which might take place on any of a dozen bottoms up or down the river, the Maltese Cross " outfit " had to be represented, and Sylvane and Merrifield and George

Myers were kept busy picking up their "strays." Roosevelt rode with them, as "boss" and at the same time as apprentice. It gave him an opportunity to get acquainted with his own men and with the cowpunchers of half a dozen other "outfits." He found the work stirring and the men singularly human and attractive. They were free and reckless spirits, who did not much care, it seemed, whether they lived or died; profane youngsters, who treated him with respect in spite of his appearance because they respected the men with whom he had associated himself. They came from all parts of the Union and spoke a language all their own.

"We'll throw over an' camp to-night at the mouth o' Knutson Creek," might run the round-up captain's orders. "Nighthawk'll be corralin' the cavvy in the mornin' 'fore the white crow squeals, so we kin be cuttin' the day-herd on the bed-groun'. We'll make a side-cut o' the mavericks an' auction 'em off pronto soon's we git through."

All that was ordinary conversation. When an occasion arose which seemed to demand a special effort, the talk around the "chuck-wagon" was so riddled with slang from all corners of the earth, so full of startling imagery, that a stranger might stare, bewildered, unable to extract a particle of meaning. And through it blazed such a continual shower of oaths, that were themselves sparks of satanic poetry, that, in the phrase of one contemplative cowpuncher, "absodarnnlutely had to be parted in the middle to hold an extra one."

It was to ears attuned to this rich and racy music that Roosevelt came with the soft accents of his Harvard English. The cowboys bore up, showing the tenderfoot the frigid courtesy they kept for " dudes " who happened to be in company, which made it impolite or inexpedient to attempt " to make the sucker dance."

It happened, however, that Roosevelt broke the camel's back. Some cows which had been rounded up with their calves made a sudden bolt out of the herd. Roosevelt attempted to head them back, but the wily cattle eluded him.

" Hasten forward quickly there! " Roosevelt shouted to one of his men.

The bounds of formal courtesy could not withstand that. There was a roar of delight from the cowpunchers, and, instantly, the phrase became a part of the vocabulary of the Bad Lands. That day, and on many days thereafter when "Get a git on yuh!" grew stale and "Head off them cattle!" seemed done to death, he heard a cowpuncher shout, in a piping voice, " Hasten forward quickly there! "

Roosevelt, in fact, was in those first days considered somewhat of a joke. Beside Gregor Lang, forty miles to the south, he was the only man in the Bad Lands who wore glasses. Lang's glasses, moreover, were small and oval; Roosevelt's were large and round, making him, in the opinion of the cowpunchers, look very much like a curiously nervous and emphatic owl. They called him " Four Eyes,"

and spoke without too much respect, of " Roosen-
felder."

Merrifield rode to town with him one day and
stopped at the Marquis's company store to see a
man named Fisher, who had succeeded Edgar
Haupt as local superintendent of the Northern
Pacific Refrigerator Car Company, asking Fisher
as he was departing whether he did not want to
meet Roosevelt. Fisher had heard of the " four-
eyed dude from New York " and heard something
of his political reforming. He went outdoors with
Merrifield, distinctly curious.

Roosevelt was on horseback chatting with a
group of cowboys, and the impression he made on
Fisher was not such as to remove the natural
prejudice of youth against " reformers " of any
sort. What Fisher saw was " a slim, anæmic-look-
ing young fellow dressed in the exaggerated style
which new-comers on the frontier affected, and
which was considered indisputable evidence of
the rank tenderfoot." If any further proof of
Roosevelt's status was needed, the great round
glasses supplied it. Fisher made up his mind that
he knew all he needed to know about the new
owner of the Maltese Cross.

No doubt he expressed his opinions to Merrifield.
The taciturn hunter did not dispute his conclusions,
but a day or two after he dropped in on Fisher again
and said, " Get your horse and we'll take the young
fellow over the old Sully Trail and try out his nerve.
We'll let on that we're going for a little hunt."

Fisher agreed with glee in his heart. He knew the Sully Trail. It ran mainly along the sides of precipitous buttes, southeast of Medora, and, being old and little used, had almost lost the little semblance it might originally have had of a path where four-footed creatures might pick their way with reasonable security. A recent rain had made the clay as slippery as asphalt in a drizzle.

It occurred to Fisher that it was as truly wicked a trail as he had ever seen. Merrifield led the way; Fisher maneuvered for last place and secured it. In the most perilous places there was always something about his saddle which needed adjustment, and he took care not to remount until the danger was behind them. Roosevelt did not dismount for any reason. He followed where Merrifield led, without comment.

They came at last to a grassy slope that dipped at an angle of forty-five degrees to a dry creek-bed. "There goes a deer!" shouted Merrifield suddenly and started down the slope as fast as his horse could go. Roosevelt followed at the same speed. He and Merrifield arrived at the bottom at the identical moment; but with a difference. Roosevelt was still on his horse, but Merrifield and his pony had parted company about a hundred yards above the creek-bed and rolled the rest of the way. Fisher, who was conservative by nature, arrived in due course.

Roosevelt pretended to be greatly annoyed. "Now see what you've done, Merrifield," he exclaimed as that individual, none the worse for his tumble, drew himself to his feet. " That deer is in Montana by this time." Then he burst into laughter.

A suspicion took root in Fisher's mind that Merrifield had intended the hazardous performance as much for Fisher's education as for Roosevelt's. He was quite ready to admit that his first impression had been imperfect. Meanwhile, he wondered whether the joke was on himself or on Merrifield. Certainly it was not on the tenderfoot.

Roosevelt enjoyed it all with the relish of a gourmand at a feast cooked by the gods.

Theodore Roosevelt, the young New York reformer [remarked the *Bad Lands Cowboy*], made us a very pleasant call Monday in full cowboy regalia. New York will certainly lose him for a time at least, as he is perfectly charmed with our free Western life and is now figuring on a trip into the Big Horn country.

In a letter to his sister Anna, written from Medora, the middle of June, we have Roosevelt's own record of his reactions to his first experiences as an actual ranchman. "Bamie" or "Bye," as he affectionately called her, was living in New York. She had taken his motherless little Alice under her protecting wing, and, since the disasters of February, had been half a mother to him also.

Well, I have been having a glorious time here [he writes], and am well hardened now (I have just come in from spending thirteen hours in the saddle). For every day I have been here I have had my hands full. First and foremost, the cattle have done well, and I regard the outlook for making the business a success as being *very* hopeful. I shall buy a thousand more cattle and shall make it my regular business. In the autumn I shall bring out Sewall and Dow and put them on a ranch with very few cattle to start with, and in the course of a couple of years give them quite a little herd also.

I have never been in better health than on this trip. I am in the saddle all day long either taking part in the round-up of the cattle, or else hunting antelope (I got one the other day; another good head for our famous hall). I am really attached to my two " factors," Ferris and Merrifield, they are very fine men.

The country is growing on me, more and more; it has a curious, fantastic beauty of its own; and as I own six or eight horses I have a fresh one every day and ride on a lope all day long. How sound I do sleep at night now! There is not much game, however; the cattle-men have crowded it out and only a few antelope and deer remain. I have shot a few jackrabbits and curlews, with the rifle; and I also killed eight rattlesnakes.

To-morrow my two men go East for the cattle; and I will start out alone to try my hand at finding my way over the prairie by myself. I intend to take a two months' trip in the fall, for hunting; and may, as politics look now, stay away over Election day; so I shall return now very soon, probably leaving here in a week.

On the following day Ferris and Merrifield started for the East, and Roosevelt set out on his solitary hunting trip, half to test out his own qualities as a frontiersman and half to replenish the larder.

For the last week I have been fulfilling a boyish ambition of mine [he wrote to " Bamie " after his return to the Maltese Cross]; that is, I have been playing at frontier hunter in good earnest, having been off entirely alone, with my horse and rifle, on the prairie. I wanted to see if I could not do perfectly well without a guide, and I succeeded beyond my expectations. I shot a couple of antelope and a deer — and missed a great many more. I felt as absolutely free as a man could feel; as you know, I do not mind loneliness; and I enjoyed the trip to the utmost. The only disagreeable incident was one day when it rained. Otherwise the weather was lovely, and every night I would lie wrapped up in my blanket looking at the stars till I fell asleep, in the cool air. The country has widely different aspects in different places; one day I could canter hour after hour over the level green grass, or through miles of wild-rose thickets, all in bloom; on the next I would be amidst the savage desolation of the Bad Lands, with their dreary plateaus, fantastically shaped buttes, and deep, winding canyons. I enjoyed the trip greatly, and have never been in better health.

George Myers was holding the fort at the Maltese Cross, building his four-mile fence, keeping an eye on the horses and cattle and acting as general factotum and cook. He was successful in everything except his cooking. Even that was excellent, except for an occasional and unaccountable lapse; but those lapses were dire.

It happened that, on the day of his return to the semi-civilization of the Maltese Cross, Roosevelt intimated to George Myers that baking-powder biscuits would be altogether welcome. George was rather proud of his biscuits and set to work with energy, adding an extra bit of baking powder from the can on the shelf beside the stove to be sure that they would be light. The biscuits went into the oven looking as perfect as any biscuits which George had ever created. They came out a rich, emerald green.

Roosevelt and George Myers stared at them, wondering what imp in the oven had worked a diabolical transformation. But investigation proved that there was no imp involved. It was merely that Sylvane or Merrifield, before departing, had casually dumped soda into the baking-powder can.

Evidently Roosevelt thereupon decided that if accidents of that sort were liable to happen to George, he had better take charge of the culinary department himself. George was off on the range the following morning, and Roosevelt, who had stayed home to write letters, filled a kettle with dry rice, poured on what looked like a reasonable amount of water, and set it on the oven to cook. Somewhat to his surprise, the rice began to swell, brimming over on the stove. He dipped out what seemed to him a sufficient quantity, and returned to his work. The smell of burning rice informed him that there was trouble in the wind. The kettle, he found, was brimming over again. He dipped out more rice. All morning long he was dipping out rice. By the time George returned, every bowl in the cabin, including the wash-basin, was filled with half-cooked rice.

Roosevelt handed the control of the kitchen back to George Myers.

VI

Once long ago an ocean lapped this hill,
And where those vultures sail, ships sailed at will;
   Queer fishes cruised about without a harbor —
I will maintain there's queer fish round here still.
                                The Bad Lands Rubáiyát

THROUGH the long days of that soft, green June,
Roosevelt was making himself at home in his new
and strange surroundings. A carpenter, whose name
was the same as his trade, built him a bookcase
out of scraps of lumber, and on the shelves of it he
assembled old friends — Parkman and Irving and
Hawthorne and Cooper and Lowell, " Ike Marvel's
breezy pages and the quaint, pathetic character-
sketches of the Southern writers — Cable, Crad-
dock, Macon, Joel Chandler Harris, and sweet
Sherwood Bonner." Wherever he went he carried
some book or other about him, solid books as a rule,
though he was not averse on occasion to what
one cowpuncher, who later became superintendent
of education in Medora, and is therefore to be regarded as an authority, reproachfully described
as " trash." He consumed the " trash," it seems,
after a session of composition, which was laborious
to him, and which set him to stalking to and fro
over the floor of the cabin and up and down through
the sagebrush behind it.

He read and wrote in odd minutes, as his body
required now and then a respite from the outdoor

activities that filled his days; but in that first deep quaffing of the new life, the intervals out of the saddle were brief and given mainly to meals and sleep. As he plunged into books to extract from them whatever facts or philosophy they might hold which he needed to enrich his personality and his usefulness, so he plunged into the life of the Bad Lands seeking to comprehend the emotions and the mental processes, the personalities and the social conditions that made it what it was. With a warm humanity on which the shackles of social prejudice already hung loose, he moved with open eyes and an open heart among the men and women whom the winds of chance had blown together in the valley of the Little Missouri.

They were an interesting and a diverse lot. Closest to the Maltese Cross, in point of situation, were the Eatons, who had established themselves two years previously at an old stage station, five miles south of Little Missouri, on what had been the first mail route between Fort Abraham Lincoln and Fort Keogh. Custer had passed that way on his last, ill-fated expedition, and the ranch bore the name of the Custer Trail in memory of the little army that had camped beside it one night on the way to the Little Big Horn. The two-room shack of cottonwood logs and a dirt roof, which had been the station, was inhabited by calves and chickens who were kept in bounds by the stockade which only a little while before had served to keep the Indians at a distance.

The four Eaton brothers were men of education

and family, who had suffered financial reverses and migrated from Pittsburgh, where they lived, to " make their fortunes," as the phrase went, in the Northwest. A wealthy Pennsylvanian named Huidekoper, a lover of good horses, backed Howard at the Custer Trail and another Easterner named Van Brunt started a second ranch with him, known as the " V-Eye," forty miles down the river at the mouth of Beaver Creek; a third, named " Chris " McGee, who was a somewhat smoky light in the murk of Pennsylvania politics, went into partnership with Charles, at another ranch six miles up Beaver. The Custer Trail was headquarters for them all, and at the same time for an endless procession of Eastern friends who came for the hunting. The Eatons kept open house. Travelers wrote about the hospitality that even strangers were certain to find there, and carried away with them the picture of Howard Eaton, " who sat his horse as though he were a centaur and looked a picturesque and noble figure with his clean-shaven cheeks, heavy drooping moustache, sombrero, blue shirt, and neckerchief with flaming ends." About the time Roosevelt arrived, friends who had availed themselves of the Eaton hospitality until they were in danger of losing their self-respect, had prevailed on the reluctant brothers to make " dude-ranching" a business. " Eaton's dudes " became a notable factor in the Bad Lands. You could raise a laugh about them at Bill Williams's saloon when nothing else could wake a smile.

One of the few women up or down the river was living that June at the Custer Trail. She was Margaret Roberts, the wife of the Eatons' foreman, a, jovial, garrulous woman, still under thirty, with hair that curled attractively and had a shimmer of gold in it. She was utterly fearless, and was bringing up numerous children, all girls, with a cool disregard of wild animals and wilder men, which, it was rumored shocked her relatives " back East." She had been brought up in Iowa, but ten horses could not have dragged her back.

Four or five miles above the Maltese Cross lived a woman of a different sort who was greatly agitating the countryside, especially Mrs. Roberts. She had come to the Bad Lands with her husband and daughter since Roosevelt's previous visit, and established a ranch on what was known as " Tepee Bottom." Her husband, whose name, for the purposes of this narrative, shall be Cummins, had been sent to Dakota as ranch manager for a syndicate of Pittsburgh men, why, no one exactly knew, since he was a designer of stoves, and, so far as any one could find out, had never had the remotest experience with cattle. He was an excellent but ineffective little man, religiously inclined, and consequently dubbed " the Deacon." Nobody paid very much attention to him, least of all his wife. That lady had drawn the fire of Mrs. Roberts before she had been in the Bad Lands a week. She was a good woman, but captious, critical, complaining, pretentious. She had in her youth had social aspirations which her husband and a little town in Pennsylvania had been unable to gratify. She brought into her life in Dakota these vague, unsatisfied longings, and immediately set to work to remould the manners, customs, and characters of the community a little nearer to her heart's desire. To such an attitude there was, of course, only one reaction possible; and she got it promptly.

Mrs. Roberts, energetic, simple-hearted, vigorous, plain-spoken, was the only woman within a dozen miles, and it was not long before Mrs. Roberts hated Mrs. Cummins as Jeremiah hated Babylon. For Mrs. Cummins was bent on spreading "culture," and Mrs. Roberts was determined that by no seeming acquiescence should it be spread over her.

"Roosevelt was a great visitor," said Howard Eaton in after time. "When he first came out there, he was a quiet sort of a fellow, with not much to say to anybody, but the best kind of a mixer I ever saw."

The Bad Lands no doubt required the ability to mix with all manner of men, for it was all manner of men that congregated there. Roosevelt evaded the saloons but established friendly relations with the men who did not. When he rode to town for his mail or to make purchases at Joe Ferris's new store, he contracted the habit of stopping at the office of the *Bad Lands Cowboy*, where those who loved conversation more than whiskey had a way of foregathering.

It was there that he came to know Hell-Roaring Bill Jones.

Bill Jones was a personage in the Bad Lands. He was, in fact, more than that. He was (like Roosevelt himself) one of those rare beings who attain mythical proportions even in their lifetime and draw about themselves the legendry of their generation. Bill Jones was the type and symbol of the care-free negation of moral standards in the wild little towns of the frontier, and men talked of him with an awe which they scarcely exhibited toward any symbol of virtue and sobriety. He said things and he did things which even a tolerant observer, hardened to the aspect of life's seamy side, might have felt impelled to call depraved, and yet Bill Jones himself was not depraved. He was, like the community in which he lived, " free an' easy." Morality meant no more to him than grammar. He outraged the one as he outraged the other, without malice and without any sense of fundamental difference between himself and those who preferred to do neither.

The air was full of tales of his extraordinary doings, for he was a fighter with pistols and with fists and had an ability as a " butter " which was all his own and which he used with deadly effect. What his history had been was a secret which he illuminated only fitfully. It was rumored that he had been born in Ireland of rather good stock, and in the course of an argument with an uncle of his with whom he lived had knocked the uncle down. Whether he had killed him the rumors failed to tell, but the fact that Bill Jones had found it necessary " to dust " to America, under an assumed name, suggested several things. Being inclined to violence, he naturally drifted to that part of the country where violence seemed to be least likely to have serious consequences. By a comic paradox, he joined the police force of Bismarck. He casually mentioned the fact one day to Roosevelt, remarking that he had left the force because he " beat the Mayor over the head with his gun one day."

" The Mayor, he didn't mind it," he added, " but the Superintendent of Police guessed I'd better resign."

He was a striking-looking creature, a man who could turn dreams into nightmares, merely by his presence in them. He was rather short of stature, but stocky and powerfully built, with a tremendous chest and long, apelike arms, hung on a giant's shoulders. The neck was a brute's, and the square protruding jaw was in keeping with it. His lips were thin, his nose was hooked like a pirate's, and his keen black eyes gleamed from under the bushy black eyebrows like a grizzly's from a cave. He was not a thing of beauty, but, at the back of his unflinching gaze, humor in some spritely and satanic shape was always disporting itself, and there was, as Lincoln Lang described it, "a certain built-in look of drollery in his face," which made one forget its hardness.

He was feared and, strange to say, he was loved

by the very men who feared him. For he was genial, and he could build a yarn that had the architectural completeness of a turreted castle, created out of smoke by some imaginative minstrel of hell. His language on all occasions was so fresh and startling that men had a way of following him about just to gather up the poppies and the night-shade of his exuberant conversation.

As Will Dow later remarked about him, he was " an awfully good man to have on your side if there was any sassing to be done."

Roosevelt was not one of those who fed on the malodorous stories which had gained for their author the further sobriquet of "Foul-mouthed Bill"; but he rather liked Bill Jones.[1] It happened one day, in the *Cowboy* office that June, that the genial repro-bate was holding forth in his best vein to an admir-ing group of cowpunchers.

Roosevelt, who was inclined to be reserved in the company of his new associates, endured the flow of indescribable English as long as he could. Then, suddenly, in a pause, when the approving laughter had subsided, he began slowly to " skin his teeth."

[1] "As I recall Bill, his stories were never half as bad as Frank [Vine's], for instance. Where he shone particularly was in excoriating those whom he did not like. In this connection he could — and did — use the worst expressions I have ever heard. He was a born cynic, who said his say in 'plain talk,' not 'langwidge.' For all that, he was filled to the neck with humor, and was a past-master in the art of re-partee, always in plain talk, remember. Explain it if you can. Bill was roundly hated by many because he had a way of talking straight truth. He had an uncanny knack of seeing behind the human scenery of the Bad Lands, and always told right out what he saw. That is why they were all afraid of him." — *Lincoln Lang*.

"Bill Jones," he said, looking straight into the saturnine face, and speaking in a low, quiet voice, "I can't tell why in the world I like you, for you're the nastiest-talking man I ever heard."

Bill Jones's hand fell on his "six-shooter." The cowpunchers, knowing their man, expected shooting. But Bill Jones did not shoot. For an instant the silence in the room was absolute. Gradually a sheepish look crept around the enormous and altogether hideous mouth of Bill Jones. "I don't belong to your outfit, Mr. Roosevelt," he said, "and I'm not beholden to you for anything. All the same, I don't mind saying that mebbe I've been a little too free with my mouth."

They became friends from that day.

If Roosevelt had tried to avoid the Marquis de Mores on his trips to the Marquis's budding metropolis in those June days, he would scarcely have succeeded. The Marquis was the most vivid feature of the landscape in and about Medora. His personal appearance would have attracted attention in any crowd. The black, curly hair, the upturned moustaches, waxed to needle-points, the heavy eyelids, the cool, arrogant eyes, made an impression which, against that primitive background, was not easily forgotten. His costume, moreover, was extraordinary to the point of the fantastic. It was the Marquis who always seemed to wear the widest sombrero, the loudest neckerchief. He went armed like a battleship. A correspondent of the Mandan *Pioneer* met him one afternoon returning from the pursuit of a band of cattle which had stampeded. "He was armed to the teeth," ran his report. "A formidable-looking belt encircled his waist, in which was stuck a murderous-looking knife, a large navy revolver, and two rows of cartridges, and in his hand he carried a repeating rifle."

A man who appeared thus dressed and accoutered would either be a master or a joke in a community like Medora. There were several reasons why he was never a joke. His money had something to do with it, but the real reason was, in the words of a contemporary, that "when it came to a showdown, the Marquis was always there." He completely dominated the life of Medora. His hand was on everything, and everything, it seemed, belonged to him. It was quite like "Puss in Boots." His town was really booming and was crowding its rival on the west bank completely out of the picture. The clatter of hammers on new buildings sounded, in the words of the editor of the *Cowboy*, "like a riveting machine." The slaughter-house had already been expanded. From Chicago came a score or more of butchers, from the range came herds of cattle to be slaughtered. The side-track was filled with empty cars of the Northern Pacific Refrigerator Car Company, which, as they were loaded with dressed beef, were coupled on fast east-bound trains. The Marquis, talking to newspaper correspondents, was glowing in his accounts of the blooming of his desert rose. He announced that it already had six hundred inhabitants. Another, calmer witness estimated fifty. The truth was probably a hundred, including the fly-by-nights. Unquestionably, they made noise enough for six hundred.

The Marquis, pending the completion of his house, was living sumptuously in his private car, somewhat, it was rumored, to the annoyance of his father-in-law, who was said to see no connection between the rough life of a ranchman, in which the Marquis appeared to exult, and the palace on wheels in which he made his abode. But he was never snobbish. He had a friendly word for whoever drifted into his office, next to the company store, and generally " something for the snake-bite," as he called it, that was enough to bring benedictions to the lips of a cowpuncher whose dependence for stimulants was on Bill Williams's " Forty-Mile Red-Eye." To the men who worked for him he was extraordinarily generous, and he was without vindictiveness toward those who, since the killing of Luffsey, had openly or tacitly opposed him. He had a grudge against Gregor Lang,[1] whose aversion to titles and all that went with them had not remained unexpressed during the year that had intervened since that fatal June 26th, but if he held any rancor toward Merrifield or the Ferrises, he did not reveal it. He was learning a great deal incidentally.

---

[1] "He held the grudge all right, and it may have been largely because father sided against him in regard to the killing. But I think the main reason was because father refused to take any hand in bringing about a consolidation of interests. Pender was a tremendously rich man and had the ear of some of the richest men in England, such as the Duke of Sutherland and the Marquis of Tweeddale."—*Lincoln Lang.*

Shortly before Roosevelt's arrival from the Chicago convention, the Marquis had stopped at the Maltese Cross one day for a chat with Sylvane. He was dilating on his projects, " spreading himself " on his dreams, but in his glowing vision of the future, he turned, for once, a momentary glance of calm analysis on the past.

" If I had known a year ago what I know now," he said rather sadly, " Riley Luffsey would never have been killed."

It was constantly being said of the Marquis that he was self-willed and incapable of taking advice. The charge was untrue. The difficulty was rather that he sought advice in the wrong quarters and lacked the judgment to weigh the counsel he received against the characters and aims of the men who gave it. He was constantly pouring out the tale of his grandiose plans to Tom and Dick and Abraham, asking for guidance in affairs of business and finance from men whose knowledge of business was limited to frontier barter and whose acquaintance with finance was of an altogether dubious and uneconomic nature. He was possessed, moreover, by the dangerous notion that those who spoke bluntly were, therefore, of necessity opposed to him and not worth regarding, while those who flattered him were his friends whose counsel he could trust.

It was this attitude of mind which encumbered his project for a stage-line to the Black Hills with difficulties from the very start. The project itself was feasible. Deadwood could be reached only by stage from Pierre, a matter of three hundred miles. The distance to Medora was a hundred miles shorter. Millions of pounds of freight were accumulating for lack of proper transportation facilities to Deadwood. That hot little mining town, moreover, needed contact with the great transcontinental system, especially in view of the migratory movement, which had begun early in the year, of the miners from Deadwood and Lead to the new gold-fields in the Cœur d'Alênes in Idaho.

Bill Williams and Jess Hogue, with the aid of the twenty-eight army mules which they had acquired in ways that invited research, had started a freight-line from Medora to Deadwood, but its service turned out to be spasmodic, depending somewhat on the state of Medora's thirst, on the number of " suckers " in town who had to be fleeced, and on the difficulty under which both Williams and Hogue seemed to suffer of keeping sober when they were released from their obvious duties in the saloon. There appeared to be every reason, therefore, why a stage-line connecting Deadwood with the Northern Pacific, carrying passengers, mail, and freight, and organized with sufficient capital, should succeed.

Dickinson, forty miles east, was wildly agitating for such a line to run from that prosperous little community to the Black Hills. The Dickinson *Press* and the *Bad Lands Cowboy* competed in deriding each other's claims touching " the only feasible route." The *Cowboy* said that the Medora line would be more direct. The *Press* agreed, but replied that the country through which it would have to go was impassable even for an Indian on a pony. The *Cowboy* declared that " the Dickinson road strikes gumbo from the start "; and the *Press* with fine scorn answered, " This causes a smile to percolate our features. From our experience in the Bad Lands we know that after a slight rain a man can carry a whole quarter-section off on his boots, and we don't wear number twelves either." The *Cowboy* insisted that the Dickinson route " is at best a poor one and at certain seasons impassable." The *Press* scorned to reply to this charge, remarking merely from the heights of its own eight months' seniority, " The *Cowboy* is young, and like a boy, going through a graveyard at night, is whistling to keep up courage."

There the debate for the moment rested. But Dickinson, which unquestionably had the better route, lacked a Marquis. While the *Press* was printing the statements of army experts in support of its claims, de Mores was sending surveyors south to lay out his route. From Sully Creek they led it across the headwaters of the Heart River and the countless affluents of the Grand and the Cannonball, past Slim Buttes and the Cave Hills, across the valleys of the Bellefourche and the Moreau, two hundred and twenty-five miles into the Black Hills and Deadwood. Deadwood gave the Marquis a public reception, hailing him as a benefactor of the race, and the Marquis, flushed and seeing visions, took a flying trip to New York and presented a petition to the directors of the Northern Pacific for a railroad from Medora to the Black Hills.

The dream was perfect, and everybody (except the Dickinson *Press*) was happy. Nothing remained but to organize the stage company, buy the coaches, the horses and the freight outfits, improve the highway, establish sixteen relay stations, and get started. And there, the real difficulties commenced.

The Marquis, possibly feeling that it was the part of statesmanship to conciliate a rival, forgot apparently all other considerations and asked Bill Williams, the saloon-keeper, to undertake the organization of the stage-line. Williams assiduously disposed of the money which the Marquis put in his hands, but attained no perceptible results. The Marquis turned next to Bill Williams's partner in freighting and faro and asked Jess Hogue to take charge. Hogue, who was versatile and was as willing to cheat a man in one way as in another, consented and for a time neglected the card-tables of Williams's " liquor-parlor " to enter into negotiations for the construction of the line. He was a clever man and had had business experience of a sort, but his interest in the Deadwood stage-line did not reach beyond the immediate opportunity it offered of acquiring a substantial amount of the Marquis's money. He made a trip or two to Bismarck and Deadwood; he looked busy; he promised great things; but nothing happened. The Marquis, considerably poorer in pocket, deposed his second manager as he had deposed the first, and looked about for an honest man.

One day Packard, setting up the *Cowboy*, was amazed to see the Marquis come dashing into his office.

" I want you to put on the stage-line for me," he ejaculated.

Packard looked at him. "But Marquis," he answered, " I never saw a stage or a stage-line. I don't know anything about it."

" It makes no difference," cried the Frenchman. " You will not rob me."

Packard admitted the probability of the last statement. They talked matters over. To Packard, who was not quite twenty-four, the prospect of running a stage-line began to look rather romantic. He set about to find out what stage-lines were made of, and went to Bismarck to study the legal document the Marquis's lawyers had drawn up. It specified, in brief, that A. T. Packard was to be sole owner of the Medora and Black Hills Stage and Forwarding Company when it should have paid for itself from its net earnings, which left nothing to be desired, especially as the total receipts from sales of building lots in Medora and elsewhere were to be considered part of the earnings. It was understood that the Marquis was to secure a mail contract from the Post-Office Department effective with the running of the first stage sometime in June. Packard attached his name to the document, and waited for the money which the Marquis had agreed to underwrite to set the organization in motion.

Day after day he waited in vain. Weeks passed. In June began an exodus from the Black Hills to the Cœur d'Alênes that soon became a stampede. With an exasperation that he found it difficult to control, Packard heard of the thousands that were taking the roundabout journey by way of Pierre or Miles City. He might, he knew, be running every north-bound coach full from front to hind boot and from thorough-brace to roof-rail; and for once the Marquis might make some money. He pleaded for funds in person and by wire. But the Marquis, for the moment, did not have any funds to give him.

Roosevelt and the Marquis were inevitably thrown together, for they were men whose tastes in many respects were similar. They were both fond of hunting, and fond also of books, and the Marquis, who was rather solitary in his grandeur and possibly a bit lonely, jumped at the opportunity Roosevelt's presence in Medora offered for companionship with his own kind. Roosevelt did not like him. He recognized, no doubt, that if any cleavage should come in the community to which they both belonged, they would, in all probability, not be found on the same side.

VII

An oath had come between us — I was paid by Law and Order;
He was outlaw, rustler, killer — so the border whisper ran;
Left his word in Caliente that he'd cross the Rio border —
Call me coward? But I hailed him — "Riding close to daylight, Dan!"

Just a hair and he'd have got me, but my voice, and not the warning,
Caught his hand and held him steady; then he nodded, spoke my name,
Reined his pony round and fanned it in the bright and silent morning,
Back across the sunlit Rio up the trail on which he came.
                                        HENRY HERBERT KNIBBS

IT was already plain that there were in fact two distinct groups along the valley of the Little Missouri. There are always two groups in any community (short of heaven); and the fact that in the Bad Lands there was a law-abiding element, and another element whose main interest in law was in the contemplation of its fragments, would not be worth remarking if it had not happened that the Marquis had allowed himself to be maneuvered into a position in which he appeared, and in which in fact he was, the protector of the disciples of violence. This was due partly to Maunders's astute manipulations, but largely also to the obsession by which apparently he was seized that he was the lord of the manor in the style of the *ancien régime*, not to be bothered in his beneficent despotism with the restrictions that kept the common man in his place. As a foreigner he naturally cared little for the political development of the region: as long as his own possessions, therefore, were not tampered with, he was not greatly disturbed by any depredations which his neighbors might suffer. He employed hands without number; he seemed to believe any " fool lie " a man felt inclined to tell him; he distributed blankets, saddles and spurs. Naturally, Maunders clung to him like a leech with his train of lawbreakers about him.

The immunity which Maunders enjoyed and radiated over his followers was only one factor of many in perpetuating the lawlessness for which the Bad Lands had for years been famous. Geography favored the criminal along the Little Missouri. Montana was a step or two to the west, Wyoming was a haven of refuge to the southwest, Canada was within easy reach to the north. A needle in a haystack, moreover, was less difficult to lay one's finger upon than a " two-gun man " tucked away in one of a thousand ravines, scarred with washouts and filled with buckbrush, in the broken country west of Bullion Butte.

Western Dakota was sanctuary, and from every direction of the compass knaves of varying degrees of iniquity and misguided ability came to enjoy it. There was no law in the Bad Lands but " six-shooter law." The days were reasonably orderly, for there were " jobs " for every one; but the nights were wild. There was not much diversion of an uplifting sort in Medora that June of 1884. There was not even an " op'ry house." Butchers and cowboys, carpenters and laborers, adventurous young college graduates and younger sons of English noblemen, drank and gambled and shouted and " shot up the town together " with " horse-rustlers " and faro-dealers and " bad men " with notches on their guns. " Two-gun men " appeared from God-knows-whence, generally well supplied with money, and disappeared, the Lord knew whither, appearing elsewhere, possibly, with a band of horses whose brands had melted away under the appli- cation of a red-hot frying-pan, or suffered a sea- change at the touch of a " running iron." Again they came to Medora, and again they disappeared. The horse-market was brisk at Medora, though only the elect knew where it was or who bought and sold or from what frantic owner, two hundred miles to the north or south, the horses had been spirited away.

It was a gay life, as Packard remarked.

The " gayety " was obvious even to the most casual traveler whose train stopped for three noisy minutes at the Medora " depot." " Dutch Wanni- gan," when he remarked that " seeing the trains come in was all the scenery we had," plumbed the depths of Medora's hunger " for something to happen." A train (even a freight) came to stand for excitement, not because of any diversion it brought of itself out of a world of " dudes " and police-officers, but because of the deviltry it never failed to inspire in certain leading citizens of Medora.

For Medora had a regular reception committee, whose membership varied, but included always the most intoxicated cowpunchers who happened to be in town. Its leading spirits were Bill Williams, the saloon-keeper, Van Zander, the wayward but attractive son of a Dutch patrician, and his bosom friend, Hell-Roaring Bill Jones; and if they were fertile in invention, they were no less energetic in carrying their inventions into execution. To shoot over the roofs of the cars was a regular pastime, to shoot through the windows was not unusual, but it was a genius who thought of the notion of crawling under the dining-car and shooting through the floor. He scattered the scrambled eggs which the negro waiter was carrying, but did no other damage. These general salvos of greeting, Bill Jones, Bill Williams, and the millionaire's son from Rotterdam were accustomed to vary by specific attention to passengers walking up and down the platform.

It happened one day that an old man in a derby hat stepped off the train for a bit of an airing while the engine was taking water. Bill Jones, spying the hat, gave an indignant exclamation and promptly shot it off the man's head. The terrified owner hurried into the train, leaving the brim behind.

" Come back, come back! " shouted Bill Jones, " we don't want the blinkety-blank thing in Medora."

The old man, terrified, looked into Bill Jones's sinister face. He found no relenting there. Deeply humiliated, he walked over to where the battered brim lay, picked it up, and reëntered the train.

Medora, meanwhile, was acquiring a reputation

for iniquity with overland tourists which the cowboys felt in duty bound to live up to. For a time
the trains stopped both at Medora and Little
Missouri. On one occasion, as the engine was taking
water at the wicked little hamlet on the west bank,
the passengers in the sleeping-car, which was
standing opposite the Pyramid Park Hotel, heard
shots, evidently fired in the hotel. They were
horrified a minute later to see a man, apparently
dead, being carried out of the front door and
around the side of the hotel to the rear. A minute
later another volley was heard, and another " dead "
man was seen being carried out. It was a holocaust
before the train finally drew out of the station,
bearing away a car-full of gasping " dudes."

They did not know that it was the same man who
was being carried round and round, and only the
wise ones surmised that the shooting was a volley
fired over the " corpse " every time the " procession " passed the bar.

All this was very diverting and did harm to
nobody. Roosevelt himself, no doubt, took huge
satisfaction in it. But there were aspects of
Medora's disregard for the conventions which were
rather more serious. If you possessed anything of
value, you carried it about with you if you expected
to find it when you wanted it. You studied the
ways of itinerant butchers with much attention,
and if you had any cattle of your own, you kept an
eye on the comings and goings of everybody who
sold beef or veal. The annoying element in all this

vigilance, however, was that, even if you could point your finger at the man who had robbed you, it did not profit you much unless you were ready to shoot him. A traveling salesman, whose baggage had been looted in Medora, swore out a warrant in Morton County, a hundred and fifty miles to the east. The Morton County sheriff came to serve the warrant, but the warrant remained in his pocket. He was "close-herded" in the sagebrush across the track from the "depot" by the greater part of the male population, on the general principle that an officer of the law was out of place in Medora whatever his mission might be; and put on board the next train going east.

In all the turmoil, the Marquis was in his element. He was never a participant in the hilarity and he was never known to "take a drink" except the wine he drank with his meals. He kept his distance and his dignity. But he regarded the lawlessness merely as part of frontier life, and took no steps to stop it. Roosevelt was too young and untested a member of the community to exert any open influence during those first weeks of his active life in the Bad Lands. It remained for the ex-baseball player, the putative owner of a stage-line that refused to materialize, to give the tempestuous little community its first faint notion of the benefits of order.

Packard, as editor of the *Bad Lands Cowboy*, had, in a manner entirely out of proportion to his personal force, or the personal force that any other man except the most notable might have brought to bear, been a civilizing influence from the beginning. The train that brought his presses from the East brought civilization with it, a somewhat shy and wraithlike civilization, but yet a thing made in the image and containing in itself the germ of that spirit which is the antithesis of barbarism, based on force, being itself the visible expression of the potency of ideas. The *Bad Lands Cowboy* brought the first tenuous foreshadowing of democratic government to the banks of the Little Missouri, inasmuch as it was an organ which could mould public opinion and through which public opinion might find articulation. It was thus that a youngster, not a year out of college, became, in a sense, the first representative of the American idea in the Marquis de Mores's feudal appanage.

Packard was extraordinarily well fitted not only to be a frontier editor, but to be a frontier editor in Medora. His college education gave him a point of contact with the Marquis which most of the other citizens of the Bad Lands lacked; his independence of spirit, on the other hand, kept him from becoming the Frenchman's tool. He was altogether fearless, he was a crack shot and a good rider, and he was not without effectiveness with his fists. But he was also tactful and tolerant; and he shared, and the cowboys knew he shared, their love of the open country and the untrammeled ways of the frontier. Besides, he had a sense of humor, which, in Medora in the spring of 1884, was better than great riches.

The *Cowboy* was Packard and Packard was the *Cowboy*. He printed what he pleased, dictating his editorials, as it were, " to the machine," he himself being the machine translating ideas into type as they came. His personal responsibility was absolute. There was no one behind whom he could hide. If any one objected to any statement in Medora's weekly newspaper, he knew whom to reproach. " Every printed word," said Packard, a long time after, " bore my brand. There were no mavericks in the *Bad Lands Cowboy* articles. There was no libel law; no law of any kind except six-shooter rights. And I was the only man who never carried a six-shooter."

To a courageous man, editing a frontier paper was an adventure which had thrills which editors in civilized communities never knew. Packard spoke his mind freely. Medora gasped a little. Packard expressed his belief that a drunken man who kills, or commits any other crime, should be punished for the crime and also for getting drunk, and then there was trouble; for the theory of the frontier was that a man who was drunk was not responsible for what he did, and accidents which happened while he was in that condition, though unfortunate, were to be classed, not with crimes, but with tornadoes and hailstorms and thunder bolts, rather as " acts of God." The general expression of the editor's opposition to this amiable theory brought only rumblings, but the specific applications brought indignant citizens with six-

shooters. Packard had occasion to note the merits
as a lethal weapon of the iron " side-stick " with
which he locked his type forms. It revealed itself
as more potent than a six-shooter, and a carving-
knife was not in a class with it; as he proved to the
satisfaction of all concerned when a drunken
butcher, who attempted to cut a Chinaman into
fragments, came to the *Cowboy* office, "to forestall
adverse comment in the next issue."

Packard was amused to note how much his
ability to defend himself simplified the problem
of moulding public opinion in Medora.

The law-abiding ranchmen along the Little
Missouri, who found a spokesman in the editor of
the *Cowboy*, recognized that what the Bad Lands
needed was government, government with a club
if possible, but in any event something from which
a club could be developed. But the elements of
disorder, which had been repulsed when they had
suggested the organization of Billings County a
year previous, now vigorously resisted organization
when the impetus came from the men who had
blocked their efforts. But the *Cowboy* fought val-
iantly, and the Dickinson *Press* in its own way did
what it could to help.

Medora is clamoring for a county organization in
Billings County [the editor reported.] We hope they
will get it. If there is any place along the line that needs
a criminal court and a jail it is Medora. Four-fifths of
the business before our justice of the peace comes from
Billings County.

A week later, the *Press* reported that the county was about to be organized and that John C. Fisher and A. T. Packard were to be two out of the three county commissioners. Then something happened. What it was is shrouded in mystery. Possibly the Marquis, who had never been acquitted by a jury of the killing of Riley Luffsey, decided at the last minute that, in case the indictment, which was hovering over him like an evil bird, should suddenly plunge and strike, he would stand a better chance away from Medora than in it. A word from him to Maunders and from Maunders to his " gang " would unquestionably have served to bring about the organization of the county; a word spoken against the move would also have served effectually to block it. There was, however, a certain opposition to the movement for organization on the part of the most sober elements of the population. Some of the older ranchmen suggested to Packard and to Fisher that they count noses. They did so, and the result was not encouraging. Doubtless they might organize the county, but the control of it would pass into the hands of the crooked. Whatever causes lay behind the sudden evaporation of the project, the fact stands that for the time being the Bad Lands remained under the easy-going despotism of the Marquis de Mores and his prime minister, Jake Maunders, unhampered and unillumined by the impertinences of democracy.

The Dickinson *Press* had truth on its side when it uttered its wail that Medora needed housing facilities for the unruly. Medora had never had a jail. Little Missouri had had an eight by ten shack which one man, who knew some history, christened " the Bastile," and which was used as a sort of convalescent hospital for men who were too drunk to distinguish between their friends and other citizens when they started shooting. But a sudden disaster had overtaken the Bastile one day when a man called Black Jack had come into Little Missouri on a wrecking train. He had a reputation that extended from Mandan to Miles City for his ability to carry untold quantities of whiskey without showing signs of intoxication; but Little Missouri proved his undoing. The " jag " he developed was something phenomenal, and he was finally locked up in the Bastile by common consent. The train crew, looking for Black Jack at three in the morning, located him after much searching. But the Bastile had been built by the soldiers and resisted their efforts to break in. Thereupon they threw a line about the shack and with the engine hauled it to the side of a flatcar attached to the train. Then with a derrick they hoisted Little Missouri's only depository for the helpless inebriate on the flatcar and departed westward. At their leisure they chopped Black Jack out of his confinement. They dumped the Bastile over the embankment somewhere a mile west of town.

The collapse of the efforts of the champions of order to organize the county left the problem of dealing with the lawlessness that was rampant, as before, entirely to the impulse of outraged individuals. There was no court, no officer of the law. Each man was a law unto himself, and settled his own quarrels. The wonder, under such circumstances, is not that there was so much bloodshed, but that there was so little. There was, after all, virtue in the anarchy of the frontier. Personal responsibility was a powerful curb-bit.

In the Bad Lands, in June, 1884, there was a solid minority of law-abiding citizens who could be depended on in any crisis. There was a larger number who could be expected as a rule to stand with the angels, but who had friendly dealings with the outlaws and were open to suspicion. Then there was the indeterminate and increasing number of men whose sources of revenue were secret, who toiled not, but were known to make sudden journeys from which they returned with fat " rolls " in their pockets. It was to curb this sinister third group that Packard had attempted to organize the county. Failing in that project, he issued a call for a " mass meeting."

The meeting was duly held, and, if it resembled the conference of a committee more than a popular uprising, that was due mainly to the fact that a careful census taken by the editor of the *Cowboy* revealed that in the whole of Billings County, which included in its limits at that time a territory the size of Massachusetts, there lived exactly one hundred and twenty-two males and twenty-seven females. There was a certain hesitancy on the part even of the law-abiding to assert too loudly their opposition to the light-triggered elements which were "frisking" their horses and cattle. The "mass meeting" voted, in general, that order was preferable to disorder and adjourned, after unanimously electing Packard chief of police (with no police to be chief of) and the Marquis de Mores head of the fire department (which did not exist).

"I have always felt there was something I did not know back of that meeting," said Packard afterward. "I think Roosevelt started it, as he and I were agreed the smaller ranches were losing enough cattle and horses to make the difference between profit and loss. It was a constant topic of conversation among the recognized law-and-order men and all of us agreed the thieves must be checked. I don't even remember how the decision came about to hold the meeting. It was decided to hold it, however, and I gave the notice wide publicity in the *Bad Lands Cowboy*. I was never more surprised than when Merrifield nominated me for chief of police. Merrifield was a partner with Roosevelt and the Ferris boys in the Chimney Butte Ranch and I have always thought he and Roosevelt had agreed beforehand to nominate me."

Packard took up his duties, somewhat vague in his mind concerning what was expected of him. There was no organization behind him, no executive committee to give him instructions. With a large liberality, characteristic of the frontier, the "mass meeting" had left to his own discretion the demar-

cation of his "authority" and the manner of its
assertion. His "authority," in fact, was a gigantic
bluff, but he was not one to let so immaterial a
detail weaken his nerve.

The fire department died still-born; but the
police force promptly asserted itself. Packard had
decided to "work on the transients" first, for he
could persuade them, better than he could the
residents, that he had an organization behind him,
with masks and a rope. From the start he made it
a point not to mix openly in any "altercation,"
where he could avoid it, for the simple reason that
the actual fighting was in most cases done by
professional "bad men," and the death of either
party to the duel, or both, was considered a source
of jubilation rather than of regret. He devoted his
attention mainly to those "floaters" whom he
suspected of being in league with the outlaws, or
who, by their recklessness with firearms, made
themselves a public nuisance. He seldom, if ever,
made an arrest. He merely drew his man aside
and told him that "it had been decided" that he
should leave town at once and never again appear
in the round-up district of the Bad Lands. In no
case was his warning disobeyed. On the few occasions when it was necessary for him to interfere
publicly, there were always friends of order in the
neighborhood to help him seal the exile in a box
car and ship him east or west on the next freight.
A number of hilarious disciples of justice varied
this proceeding one evening by breaking open the

car in which one of Packard's prisoners lay confined and tying him to the cowcatcher of a train which had just arrived. Word came back from Glendive at midnight that the prisoner had reached his destination in safety, though somewhat breathless, owing to the fact that the cowcatcher " had picked up a Texas steer on the way."

Packard's activity as chief of police had value in keeping the " floaters " in something resembling order; but it scarcely touched the main problem with which the law-abiding ranchmen had to contend, which was the extinction of the horse and cattle thieves.

To an extraordinary extent these thieves possessed the Bad Lands. They were here, there, and everywhere, sinister, intangible shadows, weaving in and out of the bright-colored fabric of frontier life. They were in every saloon and in almost every ranch-house. They rode on the round-ups, they sat around the camp-fire with the cowpunchers. Some of the most capable ranchmen were in league with them, bankers east and west along the railroad were hand in glove with them. A man scarcely dared denounce the thieves to his best friend for fear his friend might be one of them.

There were countless small bands which operated in western Dakota, eastern Montana, and northwestern Wyoming, each loosely organized as a unit, yet all bound together in the tacit fellowship of outlawry. The most tangible bond among them was that they all bought each other's stolen horses, and were all directors of the same " underground railway." Together they constituted not à band, but a " system," that had its tentacles in every horse and cattle " outfit" in the Bad Lands.

As far as the system had a head at all, that head was a man named Axelby. Other men stole a horse here or there, but Axelby stole whole herds of fifty and a hundred at one daring sweep. He was in appearance a typical robber chieftain, a picturesque devil with piercing black eyes and a genius for organization and leadership. In addition to his immediate band, scores of men whom he never saw, and who were scattered over a territory greater than New England, served him with absolute fidelity. They were most of them saloon-keepers, gamblers, and men who by their prominence in the community would be unsuspected; and there were among them more than a few ranchmen who were not averse to buying horses under the market price. With the aid of these men, Axelby created his smooth-running " underground railway " from the Big Horn Mountains and the Black Hills north through Wyoming, Dakota, and Montana. His agents in the settlements performed the office of spies, keeping him in touch with opportunities to operate on a large scale; and the ranchmen kept open the " underground " route by means of which he was able to spirit his great herds of horses across the Canadian line.

By the spring of 1884, Axelby's fame had reached

the East, and even the New York *Sun* gave him a
column:

Mr. Axelby is said to be at the head of a trusty band
as fearless and as lawless as himself. The Little Missouri
and Powder River districts are the theater of his operations. An Indian is Mr. Axelby's detestation. He kills
him at sight if he can. He considers that Indians have
no right to own ponies and he takes their ponies whenever he can. Mr. Axelby has repeatedly announced his
determination not to be taken alive. The men of the
frontier say he bears a charmed life, and the hairbreadth
'scapes of which they have made him the hero are numerous and of the wildest stamp.

During the preceding February, Axelby and his
band had had a clash with the Federal authorities,
which had created an enormous sensation up and
down the Little Missouri, but had settled nothing
so far as the horse-thieves were concerned. In the
Bad Lands the thieves became daily more pestifer-
ous. Two brothers named Smith and two others
called " Big Jack " and " Little Jack " conducted
the major operations in Billings County. They had
their cabin in a coulee west of the Big Ox Bow,
forty miles south of Medora, in the wildest part of
the Bad Lands, and " worked the country " from
there north and south. They seldom stole from
white men, recognizing the advisability of not
irritating their neighbors too much, but drove off
Indian ponies in herds. Their custom was to steal
Sioux horses from one of the reservations, keep
them in the Scoria Hills a month or more until

all danger of pursuit was over, and then drive them north over the prairie between Belfield and Medora, through the Killdeer Mountains to the north-eastern part of the Territory. There they would steal other horses from the Grosventres Indians, and drive them to their cache in the Scoria Hills whence they could emerge with them at their good pleasure and sell them at Pierre. There had been other " underground railways," but this had a charm of its own, for it " carried freight " both ways. Occasionally the thieves succeeded in selling horses to the identical Indians they had originally robbed. The efficiency of it all was in its way magnificent.

Through the record of thievery up and down the river, that spring of 1884, the shadow of Jake Maunders slips in and out, making no noise and leaving no footprints. It was rumored that when a sheriff or a United States marshal from somewhere drifted into Medora, Maunders would ride south in the dead of night to the Big Ox Bow and give the thieves the warning; and ride north again and be back in his own shack before dawn. It was rumored, further, that when the thieves had horses to sell, Maunders had " first pick." His own nephew was said to be a confederate of Big Jack. One day that spring, the Jacks and Maunders's nephew, driving a herd of trail-weary horses, stopped for a night at Lang's Sage Bottom camp. They told Lincoln Lang that they had bought the horses in Wyoming. Maunders sold the herd himself, and the news that came from the south that the herd had been stolen made no perceptible ruffle. The ranchmen had enough difficulty preserving their own property and were not making any altruistic efforts to protect the horses of ranchmen two hundred miles away. Maunders continued to flourish. From Deadwood came rumors that Joe Morrill, the deputy marshal, was carrying on a business not dissimilar to that which was making Maunders rich in Medora.

When even the officers of the law were in league with the thieves or afraid of them, there was little that the individual could do except pocket his losses with as good grace as possible and keep his mouth shut. The " system " tolerated no interference with its mechanism.

Fisher, smarting under the theft of six of the " top " horses from the Marquis de Mores's " outfit " called one of the cowboys one day into his office. His name was Pierce Bolan, and Fisher knew him to be not only absolutely trustworthy, but unusually alert.

" You're out on the range all the time," said Fisher. " Can't you give me a line on the fellows who are getting away with our horses? "

The cowboy hesitated and shook his head. " If I knew," he answered, " I wouldn't dare tell you. My toes would be turned up the first time I showed up on the range."

" What in —— are we going to do? "

" Why, treat the thieves considerate," said Bolan. " Don't get 'em sore on you. When one of them comes up and wants the loan of a horse, why, let him have it."

Fisher turned to the foreman of one of the largest " outfits " for advice and received a similar answer. The reputable stockmen were very much in the minority, it seemed, and wise men treated the thieves with " consideration " and called it insurance.

There were ranchmen, however, who were too high-spirited to tolerate the payment of such tribute in their behalf, and too interested in the future of the region as a part of the American commonwealth to be willing to temporize with outlaws. Roosevelt was one of them, in the valley of the Little Missouri. Another, across the Montana border in the valley of the Yellowstone, was Granville Stuart.

Stuart was a " forty-niner," who had crossed the continent in a prairie-schooner as a boy and had drifted into Virginia City in the days of its hot youth. He was a man of iron nerve, and when the time came for a law-abiding minority to rise against a horde of thieves and desperadoes, he naturally became one of the leaders. He played an important part in the extermination of the famous Plummer band of outlaws in the early sixties, and was generally regarded as one of the most notable figures in Montana Territory.

At the meeting of the Montana Stockgrowers' Association, at Miles City in April, there had been much discussion of the depredations of the horse and cattle thieves, which were actually threatening to destroy the cattle industry. The officers of the law had been helpless, or worse, in dealing with the situation, and the majority of the cattlemen at the convention were in favor of raising a small army of cowboys and " raiding the country."

Stuart, who was president of the Association, fought the project almost single-handed. He pointed out that the " rustlers " were well organized and strongly fortified, each cabin, in fact, constituting a miniature fortress. There was not one of them who was not a dead shot and all were armed with the latest model firearms and had an abundance of ammunition. No " general clean-up " on a large scale could, Stuart contended, be successfully carried through. The first news of such a project would put the thieves on their guard, many lives would unnecessarily be sacrificed, and the law, in the last analysis, would be on the side of the " rustlers."

The older stockmen growled and the younger stockmen protested, intimating that Stuart was a coward; but his counsel prevailed. A number of them, who " stood in " with the thieves in the hope of thus buying immunity, carried the report of the meeting to the outlaws. The " rustlers " were jubilant and settled down to what promised to be a year of undisturbed " operations."

Stuart himself, however, had long been convinced that drastic action against the thieves must be taken; and had quietly formulated his plan. When the spring round-up was over, late in June, he called a half-dozen representative ranchmen from both sides of the Dakota-Montana border together at his ranch, and presented his project. It was promptly accepted, and Stuart himself was put in charge of its execution.

Less than ten men in the whole Northwest knew of the movement that was gradually taking form under the direction of the patriarchal fighting man from Fergus County; but the Marquis de Mores was one of those men. He told Roosevelt. Stuart's plan, it seems, was to organize the most solid and reputable ranchmen in western Montana into a company of vigilantes similar to the company which had wiped out the Plummer band twenty years previous. Groups of indignant citizens who called themselves vigilantes had from time to time attempted to conduct what were popularly known as " necktie parties," but they had failed in almost every case to catch their man, for the reason that the publicity attending the organization had given the outlaws ample warning of their peril. It was Stuart's plan to organize in absolute secrecy, and fall on the horse-thieves like a bolt from the blue.

The raid was planned for late in July. It was probably during the last days of June that Roosevelt heard of it. With him, when the Marquis unfolded the project to him, was a young Englishman named Jameson (brother of another Jameson who was many years later to stir the world with a raid of another sort). Roosevelt and young Jameson, who shared a hearty dislike of seeing lawbreakers triumphant, and were neither of them averse to a little danger in confounding the public enemy, announced with one accord that they intended to join Stuart's vigilantes. The Marquis had already made up his mind that in so lurid an adventure he would not be left out. The three of them took a west-bound train and met Granville Stuart at Glendive.

But Stuart refused pointblank to accept their services. They were untrained for frontier conditions, he contended; they were probably reckless and doubtlessly uncontrollable; and would get themselves killed for no reason; above all, they were all three of prominent families. If anything happened to them, or if merely the news were spread abroad that they were taking part in the raid, the attention of the whole country would be drawn to an expedition in which the element of surprise was the first essential for success.

The three young argonauts pleaded, but the old pioneer was obdurate. He did not want to have them along, and he said so with all the courtesy that was one of his graces and all the precision of phrase that a life in the wild country had given him. Roosevelt and the Englishman saw the justice of the veteran's contentions and accepted the situation, but the Marquis was aggrieved. Granville Stuart, meanwhile, having successfully sidetracked the three musketeers, proceeded silently to gather his clansmen.

VIII

All day long on the prairies I ride,
Not even a dog to trot by my side;
My fire I kindle with chips gathered round,
My coffee I boil without being ground.

I wash in a pool and wipe on a sack;
I carry my wardrobe all on my back;
For want of an oven I cook bread in a pot,
And sleep on the ground for want of a cot.

My ceiling is the sky, my floor is the grass,
My music is the lowing of the herds as they pass;
My books are the brooks, my sermons the stones,
My parson is a wolf on his pulpit of bones.

Cowboy song

ROOSEVELT'S first weeks at the Maltese Cross proved one thing to him beyond debate; that was, that the cabin seven miles south of Medora was not the best place in the world to do literary work. The trail south led directly through his dooryard, and loquacious cowpunchers stopped at all hours to pass the time of day. It was, no doubt, all " perfectly bully "; but you did not get much writing done, and even your correspondence suffered.

Roosevelt had made up his mind, soon after his arrival early in the month, to bring Sewall and Dow out from Maine, and on his return from his solitary trip over the prairie after antelope, he set out to locate a site for a ranch, where the two backwoodsmen might hold some cattle and where at the same time he might find the solitude he needed for his literary work. On one of his exploring expeditions down the river, he met Howard Eaton riding south to the railroad from his V-Eye Ranch at the mouth of the Big Beaver, to receive a train-load of cattle. He told Eaton the object of his journeying, and Eaton, who knew the country better possibly than any other man in the Bad Lands, advised him to look at a bottom not more than five miles up the river from his own ranch. Roosevelt rode there promptly. The trail led almost due north, again and again crossing the Little Missouri which wound in wide sigmoid curves, now between forbidding walls of crumbling lime-stone and baked clay, now through green acres of pasture-land, or silvery miles of level sagebrush.

The country was singularly beautiful. On his left, as he advanced, grassy meadows sloped to a wide plateau, following the curve of the river. The valley narrowed. He forded the stream. The trail rose sharply between steep walls of olive and lavender that shut off the sun; it wound through a narrow defile; then over a plateau, whence blue seas of wild country stretched northward into the haze; then sharply down again into a green bottom, walled on the west by buttes scarred like the face of an old man. He forded the stream once more, swung round a jutting hill, and found the end of the bottom-land in a grove of cottonwoods under the shadow of high buttes. At the edge of the river he came upon the interlocked antlers of two elk who had died in combat. He determined that it was there that his "home-ranch" should stand.

For three weeks Roosevelt was in the saddle every day from dawn till night, riding, often in no company but his own, up and down the river, restless and indefatigable. On one of his solitary rides he stopped at Mrs. Maddox's hut to call for the buckskin suit he had ordered of her. She was a woman of terrible vigor, and inspired in Roosevelt a kind of awe which none of the " bad men " of the region had been able to make him feel.

She invited him to dinner. While she was preparing the meal, he sat in a corner of the cabin. He had a habit of carrying a book with him wherever he went and he was reading, altogether absorbed, when suddenly Mrs. Maddox stumbled over one of his feet.

" Take that damn foot away! " she cried in tones that meant business.[1] Roosevelt took his foot away, " and all that was attached to it," as one of his cowboy friends explained subsequently, waiting outside until the call for dinner came. He ate the dinner quickly, wasting no words, not caring to run any risk of stirring again the fury of Mrs. Maddox.

It was on another solitary ride, this time in pursuit of stray horses,— the horses, he found, were

---

[1] " I am inclined to doubt the truth of this story. Mrs. Maddox was a terror only to those who took her wrong or tried to put it over her. Normally she was a very pleasant woman with a good, strong sense of humor. My impression is she took a liking to T. R. that time I took him there to be measured for his suit. If she ever spoke as above, she must have been on the war-path about something else at the time." — *Lincoln Lang.*

always straying,— that he had an adventure of a more serious and decidedly lurid sort. The horses had led him a pace through the Bad Lands westward out over the prairie, and night overtook him not far from Mingusville, a primitive settlement named thus with brilliant ingenuity by its first citizens, a lady by the name of Minnie and her husband by the name of Gus. The " town " — what there was of it — was pleasantly situated on rolling country on the west bank of Beaver Creek. Along the east side of the creek were high, steep, cream-colored buttes, gently rounded and capped with green, softer in color than the buttes of the Bad Lands and very attractive in spring in their frame of grass and cottonwoods and cedars. Mingusville consisted of the railroad station, the section-house, and a story-and-a-half " hotel " with a false front. The " hotel " was a saloon with a loft where you might sleep if you had courage.

Roosevelt stabled his horse in a shed behind the " hotel," and started to enter.

Two shots rang out from the barroom.

He hesitated. He had made it a point to avoid centers of disturbance such as this, but the night was chilly and there was no place else to go. He entered, with misgivings.

Inside the room were several men, beside the bartender, all, with one exception, " wearing the kind of smile," as Roosevelt said, in telling of the occasion, " worn by men who are making-believe to like what they don't like." The exception was a shabby-looking individual in a broad-brimmed hat who was walking up and down the floor talking and swearing. He had a cocked gun in each hand. A clock on the wall had two holes in its face, which accounted for the shots Roosevelt had heard.

It occurred to Roosevelt that the man was not a "bad man" of the really dangerous, man-killer type; but a would-be "bad man," a bully who for the moment was having things all his own way.

"Four-eyes!" he shouted as he spied the newcomer.

There was a nervous laugh from the other men who were evidently sheepherders. Roosevelt joined in the laugh.

"Four-eyes is going to treat!" shouted the man with the guns.

There was another laugh. Under cover of it Roosevelt walked quickly to a chair behind the stove and sat down, hoping to escape further notice.

But the bully was not inclined to lose what looked like an opportunity to make capital as a "bad man" at the expense of a harmless "dude" in a fringed buckskin suit. He followed Roosevelt across the room.

"Four-eyes is going to treat," he repeated.

Roosevelt passed the comment off as a joke. But the bully leaned over Roosevelt, swinging his guns, and ordered him, in language suited to the surroundings, " to set up the drinks for the crowd."

For a moment Roosevelt sat silent, letting the

filthy storm rage round him. It occurred to him in a flash that he was face to face with a crisis vastly more significant to his future than the mere question whether or not he should let a drunken bully have his way. If he backed down, he said to himself, he would, when the news of it spread abroad, have more explaining to do than he would care to undertake. It was altogether a case of " Make good now, or quit! "

The bully roared, " Set up the drinks! "

It struck Roosevelt that the man was foolish to stand so near, with his heels together. " Well, if I've got to, I've got to," he said and rose to his feet, looking past his tormentor.

As he rose he struck quick and hard with his right just to one side of the point of the jaw, hitting with his left as he straightened out, and then again with his right.

The bully fired both guns, but the bullets went wide as he fell like a tree, striking the corner of the bar with his head. It occurred to Roosevelt that it was not a case in which one could afford to take chances, and he watched, ready to drop with his knees on the man's ribs at the first indication of activity. But the bully was senseless. The sheep-herders, now loud in their denunciations, hustled the would-be desperado into a shed.

Roosevelt had his dinner in a corner of the dining-room away from the windows, and he went to bed without a light. But the man in the shed made no move to recover his shattered prestige. When he came to, he went to the station, departing on a freight, and was seen no more.

The news of Roosevelt's encounter in the " rum-hole " in Mingusville spread as only news can spread in a country of few happenings and much conversation. It was the kind of story that the Bad Lands liked to hear, and the spectacles and the fringed buckskin suit gave it an added attraction. " Four-eyes " became, overnight, " Old Four Eyes," which was another matter.

" Roosevelt was regarded by the cowboys as a good deal of a joke until after the saloon incident," said Frank Greene, a local official of the Northern Pacific, many years later. " After that it was different."

Roosevelt departed for the East on July 1st. On the 4th, the Mandan *Pioneer* published an editorial about him which expressed, in exuberant Dakota fashion, ideas which may well have been stirring in Roosevelt's own mind.

Our friends west of us, at Little Missouri, are now being made happy by the presence among them of that rare bird, a political reformer. By his enemies he is called a dude, an aristocrat, a theorist, an upstart, and the rest, but it would seem, after all, that Mr. Roosevelt has something in him, or he would never have succeeded in stirring up the politicians of the Empire State. Mr. Roosevelt finds, doubtless, the work of a reformer to be a somewhat onerous one, and it is necessary, for his mental and physical health, that he should once and again leave the scene of his political labors and refresh himself with a little ozone, such as is to be found pure and unadulterated in the Bad Lands. Mr. Roosevelt is

not one of the fossilized kind of politicians who believes
in staying around the musty halls of the Albany capitol
all the time. He thinks, perhaps, that the man who
lives in those halls, alternating between them and the
Delavan House, is likely to be troubled with physical
dyspepsia and mental carbuncles. Who knows but that
John Kelly might to-day be an honored member of
society — might be known outside of New York as a
noble Democratic leader — if he had been accustomed
to spend some of his time in the great and glorious West?
Tammany Hall, instead of being to-day the synonym for
all that is brutal and vulgar in politics, might be to-day
another name for all that is fresh, and true, ozonic and
inspiring in the political arena. If the New York politicians only knew it, they might find it a great advantage
to come once or twice a year to West Dakota, to blow
the cobwebs from their eyes, and get new ambitions,
new aspirations, and new ideas. Mr. Roosevelt, although
young, can teach wisdom to the sophisticated machine
politicians, who know not the value to an Easterner of
a blow among the fresh, fair hills of this fair territory.

One wonders whether the editor is not, in part,
quoting Roosevelt's own words. No doubt, Roosevelt was beginning already to realize what he was
gaining in the Bad Lands.

Roosevelt spent three weeks or more in the East;
at New York where the politicians were after him,
at Oyster Bay where he was building a new house,
and at Chestnut Hill near Boston, which was closely
connected with the memories of his brief married
life. Everywhere the reporters tried to extract
from him some expression on the political campaign,
but on that subject he was reticent. He issued

a statement in Boston, declaring his intention to vote the Republican ticket, but further than that he refused to commit himself. But he talked of the Bad Lands to any one who would listen.

I like the West and I like ranching life [he said to a reporter of the New York *Tribune* who interviewed him at his sister's house a day or two before his return to Dakota]. On my last trip I was just three weeks at the ranch and just twenty-one days, of sixteen hours each, in the saddle, either after cattle, taking part in the " round-up," or hunting. It would electrify some of my friends who have accused me of representing the kid-gloved element in politics if they could see me galloping over the plains, day in and day out, clad in a buckskin shirt and leather chaparajos, with a big sombrero on my head. For good, healthy exercise I would strongly recommend some of our gilded youth to go West and try a short course of riding bucking ponies, and assist at the branding of a lot of Texas steers.

There is something charmingly boyish in his enthusiasm over his own manly valor and his confidence in its " electrifying " effect.

Roosevelt wrote to Sewall immediately after his arrival in the East, telling him that he would take him West with him. Toward the end of July, Sewall appeared in New York with his stalwart nephew in tow. The contract they entered into with Roosevelt was merely verbal. There was to be a three-year partnership. If business were prosperous, they were to have a share in it. If it were not, they were to have wages, whatever happened.

"What do you think of that, Bill?" asked Roosevelt.

"Why," answered Bill in his slow, Maine way, "I think that's a one-sided trade. But if you can stand it, I guess we can."

That was all there was to the making of the contract. On the 28th the three of them started westward.

In the cattle country, meanwhile, things had been happening. Shortly after Roosevelt's departure for the East, Granville Stuart had gathered his clans, and, suddenly and without warning, his bolt from the blue had fallen upon the outlaws of Montana. At a cabin here, at a deserted lumber-camp there, where the thieves, singly or in groups, made their headquarters, the masked riders appeared and held their grim proceedings. There was no temporizing, and little mercy. Justice was to be done, and it was done with all the terrible relentlessness that always characterizes a free citizen when he takes back, for a moment, the powers he has delegated to a government which in a crisis has proved impotent or unwilling to exercise them. A drumhead court-martial might have seemed tedious and technical in comparison with the sharp brevity of the trials under the ominous cottonwoods.

Out of the open country, where "Stuart's vigilantes" were swooping on nest after nest of the thieves, riders came with stories that might well have sent shudders down the backs even of innocent men. The newspapers were filled with

accounts of lifeless bodies left hanging from countless cottonwoods in the wake of the raiders, tales of
battles in which the casualties were by no means
all on one side, and snatches of humor that was
terrible against the background of black tragedy.
Some of the stories were false, some were fantastic
exaggerations of actual fact sifted through excited
imaginations. Those that were bare truth were in
all conscience grim enough for the most morbid
mind. The yarns flew from mouth to mouth, from
ranch to ranch. Cowboys were hard to hold to
their work. Now that a determined man had shown
the way, everybody wanted to have a part in the
last great round-up of the unruly. The excitement
throughout the region was intense. Here and
there subsidiary bands were formed to " clean up
the stragglers." Thoughtful men began to have
apprehensions that it might prove more difficult to
get the imp of outraged justice back into the bottle
than it had been to let him out.

The raiders skirted the Bad Lands on the north,
pushing on east to the Missouri, and for a time
Medora's precious collection of desperadoes remained undisturbed. There were rumors that
Maunders was on the books of Stuart's men, but
under the wing of the Marquis he was well protected, and that time, at least, no raiders came
to interrupt his divers and always profitable activities.

Roosevelt reached Medora with Sewall and Dow
on July 31st. A reporter of the *Pioneer* interviewed

him while the train was changing engines at Mandan.

Theodore Roosevelt, the New York reformer, was on the west-bound train yesterday, *en route* to his ranch near Little Missouri [ran the item in the next day's issue]. He was feeling at his best, dressed in the careless style of the country gentleman of leisure, and spoke freely on his pleasant Dakota experience and politics in the East. He purposes spending several weeks on his ranch, after which he will return East. . . . Mr. Roosevelt believes that the young men of our country should assume a spirit of independence in politics. He would rather be forced to the shades of private life with a short and honorable career than be given a life tenure of political prominence as the slave of a party or its masters.

Roosevelt brought his two backwoodsmen straight to the Maltese Cross. The men from Maine were magnificent specimens of manhood. Sewall, nearing forty, with tremendous shoulders a little stooped as though he were accustomed to passing through doorways that were too low for him; Dow, twenty-eight or twenty-nine, erect and clear-eyed. They looked on the fantastic landscape with quiet wonderment.

"Well, Bill," remarked Roosevelt that night, "what do you think of the country?"

"Why," answered the backwoodsman, "I like the country well enough. But I don't believe that it's much of a cattle country."

"Bill," said Roosevelt vigorously, "you don't know anything about it. Everybody says that it is."

Sewall laughed softly. " It's a fact that I don't know anything about it," he said. " I realize that. But it's the way it looks to me, like not much of a cattle country."

During Roosevelt's absence in the East, Merrifield and Sylvane had returned from Iowa with a thousand head of yearlings and " two-year-olds." A hundred head of the original herd, which had become accustomed to the country, he had already set apart for the lower ranch, and the day after his arrival he sent the two backwoodsmen north with them, under the general and vociferous direction of a certain Captain Robins. The next day, in company with a pleasant Englishman who had accompanied him West, he rode up the river to Lang's.

The ranch of the talkative Scotchman had suffered a joyous change since Roosevelt's last visit. A week or two previous Gregor Lang's wife had arrived from Ireland with her daughter and younger son, and a visit at Yule, as Lang had called his ranch, was a different thing from what it had been when it had been under masculine control. The new ranch-house was completed, and though it was not large it was vastly more homelike than any other cabin on the river with the possible exception of the Eatons'. It stood in an open flat, facing north, with a long butte behind it; and before it, beyond a wide semi-circle of cottonwoods that marked the river's course, low hills, now gray and now green, stretching away to the horizon. It was a curiously Scotch landscape, especially at dusk or in misty weather, which was no doubt a reason why Gregor Lang had chosen it for his home.

Mrs. Lang proved to be a woman of evident character and ability. She was well along in the forties, but in her stately bearing and the magnificent abundance of her golden hair, that had no strand of gray in it, lay more than a hint of the beauty that was said to have been hers in her youth. There was wistfulness in the delicate but firm mouth and chin; there was vigor in the broad forehead and the well-proportioned nose; and humor in the shrewd, quiet eyes set far apart. She belonged to an old Border family, and had lived all her life amid the almost perfect adjustments of well-to-do British society of the middle class, where every cog was greased and every wheel was ball-bearing. But she accepted the grating existence of the frontier with something better than resignation, and set about promptly in a wild and alien country to make a new house into a new home.

While Roosevelt was getting acquainted with the new-comers at Yule, Sewall and Dow were also getting acquainted with many people and things that were strange to them. They took two days for the ride from the Maltese Cross to the site of the new ranch, for the river was high and they were forced to take a roundabout trail over the prairie; the cattle, moreover, could be driven only at a slow pace; but even twenty-odd miles a day was more than a Maine backwoodsman enjoyed as initiation in horsemanship. Dow was mounted on an excellent trained horse, and being young and supple was able to do his share in spite of his discomfort. But the mare that had been allotted to Sewall happened also to be a tenderfoot, and they did not play a conspicuous rôle in the progress of the cattle.

Captain Robins was not the sort to make allowances when there was work to be done. He was a small, dark man with a half-inch beard almost completely covering his face, a " seafaring man " who had got his experience with cattle in South America; "a man of many orders" as Sewall curtly described him in a letter home. He rode over to where Sewall was endeavoring in a helpless way to make the mare go in a general northerly direction.

Sewall saw him coming, and wondered why he thought it necessary to come at such extraordinary speed.

The Captain drew rein sharply at Sewall's side. " Why in hell don't you ride in and do something? " he roared.

Sewall knew exactly why he didn't. He had known it for some time, and he was nettled with himself, for he had not been accustomed " to take a back seat for any one " when feats that demanded physical strength and skill were to be done. Robins was very close to him, and Sewall's first impulse was to take him by the hair. But it occurred to him that the seafaring man was smaller than he, and that thought went out of his head.

" I know I'm not doing anything," he said at

last gruffly. "I don't know anything about what I'm trying to do and I think I've got a horse as green as I am. But don't you ever speak to me in such a manner as that again as long as you live."

There was a good deal that was impressive about Sewall, his shoulders, his teeth that were like tombstones, his vigorous, brown beard, his eyes that had a way of blazing. The Captain did not pursue the discussion.

"That Sewall is a kind of quick-tempered fellow," he remarked to Dow.

"I don't think he is," said the younger man quietly.

"He snapped me up."

"You must have said something to him, for he ain't in the habit of doing such things."

The Captain dropped the subject for the time being.

Roosevelt, after two days at Lang's, returned to the Maltese Cross and then rode northward to look after the men from Maine.

Captain Robins's report was altogether favorable. "You've got two good men here, Mr. Roosevelt," said he. "That Sewall don't calculate to bear anything. I spoke to him the other day, and he snapped me up so short I did not know what to make of it. But," he added, "I don't blame him. I did not speak to him as I ought."

This was what Bill himself would have called "handsome." Roosevelt carried the gruff apology to Sewall, and there was harmony after that between the lumberjack and the seafaring man, punching cattle together in the Bad Lands.

The cattle which Captain Robins and his two tenderfeet from Maine had driven down the river from the Maltese Cross were intended to be the nucleus of the Elkhorn herd. They were young grade short-horns of Eastern origin, less wild than the long-horn Texas steers, but liable, on new ground, to stray off through some of the innumerable coulees stretching back from the river, and be lost in the open prairie. The seafaring man determined, therefore, that they should be " close-herded " every night and " bedded down " on the level bottom where the cabin stood which was their temporary ranch-house. So each dusk, Roosevelt and his men drove the cattle down from the side valleys, and each night, in two-hour " tricks " all night long, one or the other of them rode slowly and quietly round and round the herd, heading off all that tried to stray. This was not altogether a simple business, for there was danger of stampede in making the slightest unusual noise. Now and then they would call to the cattle softly as they rode, or sing to them until the steers had all lain down close together.

It was while Roosevelt was working at Elkhorn that he received a call from Howard Eaton, who was his neighbor there as well as at the Maltese Cross, since his ranch at the mouth of Big Beaver Creek was only five miles down the Little Missouri from the place where Roosevelt had " staked his claim." Eaton brought Chris McGee, his partner, with him. Roosevelt had heard of McGee, not altogether favorably, for McGee was the Republican " boss " of Pittsburgh in days when " bosses " were in flower.

" Are you going to stay out here and make ranching a business? " asked Eaton.

" No," Roosevelt answered. " For the present I am out here because I cannot get up any enthusiasm for the Republican candidate, and it seems to me that punching cattle is the best way to avoid campaigning."

Eaton asked McGee on the way home how Roosevelt stood in the East. " Roosevelt is a nice fellow," remarked McGee, " but he's a damned fool in politics."

Roosevelt remained with Robins and the men from Maine for three days, varying his life in the saddle with a day on foot after grouse when the larder ran low. It was all joyous sport, which was lifted for a moment into the plane of adventure by a communication from the Marquis de Mores.

That gentleman wrote Roosevelt a letter informing him that he himself claimed the range on which Roosevelt had established himself.

Roosevelt's answer was brief and definite. He had found nothing but dead sheep on the range, he wrote, and he did not think that they would hold it.

There the matter rested.

" You'd better be on the lookout," Roosevelt

remarked to Sewall and Dow, as he was making ready to return to the Maltese Cross. "There's just a chance there may be trouble."

"I cal'late we can look out for ourselves," announced Bill with a gleam in his eye.

IX

Young Dutch Van Zander, drunkard to the skin,
Flung wide the door and let the world come in —
The world, with daybreak on a thousand buttes!
"Say, is this heaven, Bill — or is it gin?"

Bad Lands Rubáiyát

ROOSEVELT returned to the upper ranch on August 11th.

Everything so far has gone along beautifully [he wrote to his sister on the following day]. I had great fun in bringing my two backwoods babies out here. Their absolute astonishment and delight at everything they saw, and their really very shrewd, and yet wonderfully simple remarks were a perpetual delight to me.

I found the cattle all here and looking well; I have now got some sixteen hundred head on the river. I mounted Sewall and Dow on a couple of ponies (where they looked like the pictures of discomfort, Sewall remarking that his only previous experience in the equestrian line was when he " rode logs "), and started them at once off down the river with a hundred head of cattle, under the lead of one of my friends out here, a grumpy old sea captain, who has had a rather diversified life, trying his hand as sailor, buffalo hunter, butcher, apothecary (*mirabile dictu*), and cowboy. Sewall tried to spur his horse which began kicking and rolled over with him into a washout.

Sewall, meanwhile, was also writing letters " to the folks back East," and the opinions he expressed about the Bad Lands were plain and unvarnished.

It is a dirty country and very dirty people on an average [he wrote his brother Samuel in Island Falls], but I think it is healthy. The soil is sand or clay, all dust or all mud. The river is the meanest apology for a frog-pond that I ever saw. It is a queer country, you would like to see it, but you would not like to live here long. The hills are mostly of clay, the sides of some very steep and barren of all vegetation. You would think cattle would starve there, but all the cattle that have wintered here are fat now and they say here that cattle brought from any other part will improve in size and quality. Theodore thinks I will have more than $3000.00 in three years if nothing happens. He is going to put on a lot of cattle next year.

This is a good place for a man with plenty of money to make more, but if I had enough money to start here I never would come, think the country ought to have been left to the annimils that have laid their bones here.

Roosevelt had, ever since the Chicago convention, planned to go on an extensive hunting trip, partly to take his mind from the political campaign, from which, in his judgment, the course of events had eliminated him, and partly to put himself out of reach of importunate politicians in various parts of the country, who were endeavoring to make him commit himself in favor of the Republican candidate in a way that would make his preconvention utterances appear insincere and absurd. The tug of politics was strong. He loved " the game " and he hated to be out of a good fight. To safeguard himself, therefore, he determined to hide himself in the recesses of the Big Horn Mountains in Wyoming.

In a day or two I start out [he wrote on August 12th

to his friend Henry Cabot Lodge, who had suffered defeat at his side at the convention] with two hunters, six riding-ponies, and a canvas-topped " prairie schooner " for the Bighorn Mountains. You would be amused to see me, in my broad sombrero hat, fringed and beaded buckskin shirt, horsehide chaparajcs or riding-trousers, and cowhide boots, with braided bridle and silver spurs. I have always liked horse and rifle, and being, like yourself, " ein echter Amerikaner," prefer that description of sport which needs a buckskin shirt to that whose votaries adopt the red coat. A buffalo is nobler game than an anise-seed bag, the Anglomaniacs to the contrary notwithstanding.

He did not start on the day he had planned, for the reason that the six riding-ponies which he needed were not to be had for love or money in the whole length and breadth of the Bad Lands. He sent Sylvane with another man south to Spearfish in the Black Hills to buy a " string " of horses. The other man was Jack Reuter, otherwise known as " Dutch Wannigan." For " Wannigan," like his fellow " desperado," Frank O'Donald, had returned long since to the valley of the Little Missouri and taken up again the activities which the Marquis had rudely interrupted. But, being a simple-hearted creature, he had sold no crop of hay to the Marquis " in stubble " for a thousand dollars, like his craftier associate. He had merely " gone to work." The fact that it happened to be Roosevelt for whom he went to work had something to do, no doubt, with the subsequent relations between Roosevelt and the Marquis.

Various forces for which the Marquis himself could claim no responsibility had, meanwhile, been conspiring with him to " boom " his new town. The glowing and distinctly exaggerated accounts of farming conditions in the Northwest, sent broadcast by the railroad companies, had started a wave of immigration westward which the laments of the disappointed seemed to have no power to check. " City-boomers," with their tales of amazing fortunes made overnight, lured men to a score of different " towns " along the Northern Pacific that were nothing but two ruts and a section-house. From the south rolled a tide of another sort. The grazing-lands of Texas were becoming overstocked, and up the broad cattle-trail came swearing cowboys in broad sombreros, driving herds of long-horned cattle into the new grazing-country. Altogether, it was an active season for the saloon-keepers of Medora.

The Marquis was having endless trouble with the plans for his stage-line and was keeping Packard on tenterhooks. Packard twiddled his thumbs, and the Marquis, plagued by the citizens of the Black Hills whom he had promised the stage- and freight-line months previous, made threats one day and rosy promises the next. It was the middle of August before Packard received directions to go ahead.

Roosevelt did not see much of the genial editor of the *Cowboy* during those August days while he was waiting for Sylvane and " Dutch Wannigan " to return from Spearfish with the ponies, for Packard, knowing that every hour was precious, was rushing frantically to and fro, buying lumber and feed, pegging out the sites of his stage-stations, his eating-houses, his barns and his corrals, and superintending the constructing crews at the dozen or more stops along the route.

Roosevelt, meanwhile, was obviously restless and seemed to find peace of mind only in almost continuous action. After two or three days at the Maltese Cross, he was back at Elkhorn again, forty miles away, and the next day he was once more on his travels, riding south. Sewall went with him, for he wanted the backwoodsman to accompany him on the trip to the Big Horn Mountains. Dow remained with the seafaring man, looking crestfallen and unhappy.

During the days that he was waiting for Sylvane to return, Roosevelt touched Medora and its feverish life no more than absolute necessity demanded, greeting his acquaintances in friendly fashion, but tending strictly to business. It seems, however, that he had already made a deep impression on his neighbors up and down the river. The territory was shortly to be admitted to statehood and there were voices demanding that Theodore Roosevelt be Dakota's first representative in Congress.

In commenting upon the rumor that Theodore Roosevelt had come to Dakota for the purpose of going to Congress [said the Bismarck *Weekly Tribune* in an

editorial on August 8th], the Mandan *Pioneer* takes
occasion to remark that young Roosevelt's record as a
public man is above reproach and that he is "a vigorous
young Republican of the new school." Such favorable
comment from a Mandan paper tends to substantiate
the rumor that the young political Hercules has already
got the West Missouri section solid.

" If he concludes to run," remarked the *Pioneer*,
" he will give our politicians a complete turning
over."

What sirens were singing to Roosevelt of political
honors in the new Western country, and to what
extent he listened to them, are questions to which
neither his correspondence nor the newspapers
of the time provide an answer. It is not unreason-
able to believe that the possibility of becoming a
political power in the Northwest allured him.
His political position in the East was, at the
moment, hopeless. Before the convention, he had
antagonized the " regular " Republicans by his
leadership of the Independents in New York, which
had resulted in the complete defeat of the " organization " in the struggle over the " Big Four " at
Utica; after the convention, he had antagonized
the Independents by refusing to " bolt the ticket."
He consequently had no political standing, either
within the party, or without. The Independents
wept tears over him, denouncing him as a traitor;
and the " regulars," even while they were calling
for his assistance in the campaign, were whetting
their knives to dirk him in the back.

If the temptation ever came to him to cut what remained of his political ties in the East and start afresh in Dakota, no evidence of it has yet appeared. A convention of the Republicans of Billings County was held in the hall over Bill Williams's new saloon in Medora on August 16th. Roosevelt did not attend it. Sylvane and "Wannigan" had returned from Spearfish and Roosevelt was trying out one of the new ponies at a round-up in the Big Ox Bow thirty miles to the south.

We have been delayed nearly a week by being forced to get some extra ponies [he wrote his sister Anna on the 17th]. However, I was rather glad of it, as I wished to look thoroughly through the cattle before going. To-morrow morning early we start out. Merrifield and I go on horseback, each taking a spare pony; which will be led behind the wagon, a light " prairie schooner " drawn by two stout horses, and driven by an old French Canadian. I wear a sombrero, silk neckerchief, fringed buckskin shirt, sealskin chaparajos or riding-trousers; alligator-hide boots; and with my pearl-hilted revolver and beautifully finished Winchester rifle, I shall feel able to face anything.

There is no question that Roosevelt's costume fascinated him. It was, in fact, gorgeous beyond description.

How long I will be gone I cannot say; we will go in all nearly a thousand miles. If game is plenty and my success is good, I may return in six weeks; more probably I shall be out a couple of months, and if game is so scarce that we have to travel very far to get it, or if our horses give out or run away, or we get caught by the snow, we may be out very much longer — till toward Christmas; though I will try to be back to vote.

Yesterday I rode seventy-two miles between dawn and darkness; I have a superb roan pony, or rather horse; he looks well with his beautifully carved saddle, plaited bridle, and silver inlaid bit, and seems to be absolutely tireless.

I grow very fond of this place, and it certainly has a desolate, grim beauty of its own, that has a curious fascination for me. The grassy, scantily wooded bottoms through which the winding river flows are bounded by bare, jagged buttes; their fantastic shapes and sharp, steep edges throw the most curious shadows, under the cloudless, glaring sky; and at evening I love to sit out in front of the hut and see their hard, gray outlines gradually grow soft and purple as the flaming sunset by degrees softens and dies away; while my days I spend generally alone, riding through the lonely rolling prairie and broken lands.

If, on those solitary rides, Roosevelt gave much thought to politics, it was doubtless not on any immediate benefit for himself on which his mind dwelt. Sewall said, long afterward, that " Roosevelt was always thinkin' of makin' the world better, instead of worse," and Merrifield remembered that even in those early days the " Eastern tenderfoot " was dreaming of the Presidency. It was a wholesome region to dream in. Narrow notions could not live in the gusty air of the prairies, and the Bad Lands were not conducive to sentimentalism.

X

The pine spoke, but the word he said was "Silence";
    The aspen sang, but silence was her theme.
The wind was silence, restless; and the voices
Of the bright forest-creatures were as silence
    Made vocal in the topsy-turvy of dream.

Paradise Found

ROOSEVELT started for the Big Horn Mountains
on August 18th, but Sewall, after all, did not go
with him. Almost with tears, he begged off. " I'd
always dreamed of hunting through that Big Horn
country," he said long afterward. " I had picked
that out as a happy hunting ground for years and
years, and I never wanted to go anywhere so much
as I wanted to go along with Theodore on that
trip." But the memory of the lonely look in Will
Dow's face overcame the soft-hearted backwoodsman at the last minute. He pointed out to Roosevelt that one man could not well handle the logs
for the new ranch-house and suggested that he be
allowed to rejoin Will Dow.

Early on the morning of the 18th, Roosevelt
set his caravan in motion for the long journey.
For a hunting companion he had Merrifield and for
teamster and cook he had a French Canadian named
Norman Lebo, who, as Roosevelt subsequently
remarked, to Lebo's indignation (for he prided
himself on his scholarship), " possessed a most
extraordinary stock of miscellaneous mis-informa-
tion upon every conceivable subject." He was a

short, stocky, bearded man, a born wanderer, who had left his family once for a week's hunting trip and remained away three years, returning at last only to depart again, after a week, for further Odyssean wanderings. " If I had the money," he had a way of saying, " no two nights would ever see me in the same bed." It was rumored that before Mrs. Lebo had permitted her errant spouse to go out of her sight, she had secured pledges from Roosevelt guaranteeing her three years' subsistence, in case the *wanderlust* should once more seize upon her protector and provider.

Roosevelt rode ahead of the caravan, spending the first night with the Langs, who were always friendly and hospitable and full of good talk, and rejoining Merrifield and " the outfit " on the Keogh trail a few miles westward next morning. Slowly and laboriously the " prairie schooner " lumbered along the uneven route. The weather was sultry, and as they crossed the high divide which separated the Little Missouri basin from the valley of the Little Beaver they saw ahead of them the towering portents of storm. The northwest was already black, and in a space of time that seemed incredibly brief the masses of cloud boiled up and over the sky. The storm rolled toward them at furious speed, extending its wings, as it came, as though to gather in its victims.

Against the dark background of the mass [Roosevelt wrote, describing it later] could be seen pillars and clouds of gray mist, whirled hither and thither by the wind,

and sheets of level rain driven before it. The edges of
the wings tossed to and fro, and the wind shrieked and
moaned as it swept over the prairie. It was a storm of
unusual intensity; the prairie fowl rose in flocks from
before it, scudding with spread wings toward the thickest
cover, and the herds of antelope ran across the plain
like race-horses to gather in the hollows and behind
the low ridges.

We spurred hard to get out of the open, riding with
loose reins for the creek. The center of the storm swept
by behind us, fairly across our track, and we only got a
wipe from the tail of it. Yet this itself we could not
have faced in the open. The first gust caught us a few
hundred yards from the creek, almost taking us from
the saddle, and driving the rain and hail in stinging
level sheets against us. We galloped to the edge of a
deep wash-out, scrambled into it at the risk of our
necks, and huddled up with our horses underneath the
windward bank. Here we remained pretty well sheltered
until the storm was over. Although it was August, the
air became very cold. The wagon was fairly caught, and
would have been blown over if the top had been on;
the driver and horses escaped without injury, pressing
under the leeward side, the storm coming so level that
they did not need a roof to protect them from the hail.
Where the center of the whirlwind struck, it did great
damage, sheets of hailstones as large as pigeons' eggs
striking the earth with the velocity of bullets; next day
the hailstones could have been gathered up by the bushel
from the heaps that lay in the bottom of the gullies
and ravines.

They made camp that night at the edge of the
creek whose banks had given them what little
shelter there was on the plateau where the storm
had struck them. All night the rain continued in

a drizzle punctuated at intervals by sharp showers. Next morning the weather was no better, and after a morning's struggle with the wagon along the slippery trail of gumbo mud, they made what would under other circumstances have been a " dry camp." They caught the rain in their slickers and made their coffee of it, and spent another more or less uncomfortable night coiling themselves over and around a cracker-barrel which seemed to take up the whole interior of the wagon.

The weather cleared at last, and they pushed on southwestward, between Box Elder Creek and Powder River. It was dreary country through which Lebo and his prairie schooner made their slow and creaking way, and Roosevelt and Merrifield, to whom the pace was torture, varied the monotony with hunting expeditions on one-side or the other of the parallel ruts that were the Keogh trail. It was on one of these trips that Roosevelt learned a lesson which he remembered.

They had seen a flock of prairie chickens and Roosevelt had started off with his shot-gun to bring in a meal of them. Suddenly Merrifield called to him. Roosevelt took no heed.

" Don't you shoot! " cried Merrifield.

Roosevelt, with his eyes on the chickens, proceeded on his way undeterred. Suddenly, a little beyond where he had seen the prairie fowl go to covert, a mountain lion sprang out of the brush and bounded away. Roosevelt ran for his rifle, but he was too late. The lion was gone.

Merrifield's eyes were blazing and his remarks were not dissimilar. "Now, whenever I hold up my hand," he concluded, "you stop still where you are. Understand?"

Roosevelt, who would have knocked his ranch-partner down with earnestness and conviction if he had thought Merrifield was in the wrong, meekly bore the hunter's wrath, knowing that Merrifield was in the right; and thereafter on the expedition obeyed orders with a completeness that occasionally had its comic aspects. But Merrifield had no more complaints to make.

They plodded on, day after day, seeing no human being. When at last they did come upon a lonely rider, Roosevelt instantly pressed him into service as a mail carrier, and wrote two letters.

The first was to his sister Anna.

I am writing this on an upturned water-keg, by our canvas-covered wagon, while the men are making tea, and the solemn old ponies are grazing round about me. I am going to trust it to the tender mercies of a stray cowboy whom we have just met, and who may or may not post it when he gets to "Powderville," a delectable log hamlet some seventy miles north of us. We left the Little Missouri a week ago, and have been traveling steadily some twenty or thirty miles a day ever since, through a desolate, barren-looking and yet picturesque country, part of the time rolling prairie and part of the time broken, jagged Bad Lands. We have fared sumptuously, as I have shot a number of prairie chickens, sage hens and ducks, and a couple of fine bucks — besides missing several of the latter that I ought to have killed.

Every morning we get up at dawn, and start off by six o'clock or thereabouts, Merrifield and I riding off among the hills or ravines after game, while the battered " prairie schooner," with the two spare ponies led behind, is driven slowly along by old Lebo, who is a perfect character. He is a weazened, wiry old fellow, very garrulous, brought up on the frontier, and a man who is never put out or disconcerted by any possible combination of accidents. Of course we have had the usual incidents of prairie travel happen to us. One day we rode through a driving rainstorm, at one time developing into a regular hurricane of hail and wind, which nearly upset the wagon, drove the ponies almost frantic, and forced us to huddle into a gully for protection. The rain lasted all night and we all slept in the wagon, pretty wet and not very comfortable. Another time a sharp gale of wind or rain struck us in the middle of the night, as we were lying out in the open (we have no tent), and we shivered under our wet blankets till morning. We go into camp a little before sunset, tethering two or three of the horses, and letting the others range. One night we camped in a most beautiful natural park; it was a large, grassy hill, studded thickly with small, pine-crowned chalk buttes, with very steep sides, worn into the most outlandish and fantastic shapes. All that night the wolves kept up a weird concert around our camp — they are most harmless beasts.

The second letter was to his friend Lodge, who was in the midst of a stiff fight to hold his seat in Congress.

You must pardon the paper and general appearance of this letter, as I am writing out in camp, a hundred miles or so from any house; and indeed, whether this letter is, or is not, ever delivered depends partly on

Providence, and partly on the good-will of an equally inscrutable personage, either a cowboy or a horse-thief, whom we have just met, and who has volunteered to post it — my men are watching him with anything but friendly eyes, as they think he is going to try to steal our ponies. (To guard against this possibility he is to sleep between my foreman and myself — delectable bedfellow he'll prove, doubtless.)

I have no particular excuse for writing, beyond the fact that I would give a good deal to have a talk with you over political matters, just now. I heartily enjoy this life, with its perfect freedom, for I am very fond of hunting, and there are few sensations I prefer to that of galloping over these rolling, limitless prairies, rifle in hand, or winding my way among the barren, fantastic and grimly picturesque deserts of the so-called Bad Lands; and yet I cannot help wishing I could be battling along with you, and I cannot regret enough the unfortunate turn in political affairs that has practically debarred me from taking any part in the fray. I have received fifty different requests to speak in various places — among others, to open the campaign in Vermont and Minnesota. I am glad I am not at home; I get so angry with the "mugwumps," and get to have such scorn and contempt for them, that I know I would soon be betrayed into taking some step against them, much more decided than I really ought to take.

The hunting trips which Roosevelt and Merrifield made on this side or the other of the trail had their charm, and their perils also. There was one excursion, while the wagon was crawling up the Clear Fork of the Powder River, which for several reasons remained memorable.

The party was out of food, for the country they

had been traversing was not favorable for game, and Roosevelt and Merrifield started forth one afternoon, with hope goaded by necessity, to replenish the larder.

Where the hilly country joined the river bottom, it broke off into steep bluffs, presenting an ascent before which even a bronco, it seemed, had his hesitations. Roosevelt and his companion rode into a washout, and then, dismounting led their ponies along a clay ledge from which they turned off and went straight up an almost perpendicular sandy bluff. As Merrifield, who was in the lead, turned off the ledge, his horse, plunging in his attempt to clamber up the steep bluff, overbalanced himself, and for a second stood erect on his hind legs trying to recover his equilibrium. As Roosevelt, who was directly beneath him, made a frantic leap with his horse to one side, Merrifield's pony rolled over backwards, turned two complete somersaults and landed with a crash at the bottom of the washout, feet uppermost. They did not dare to hope that the horse would not be " done for," but he proved on investigation to be very much alive. Without aid he struggled to his feet, looking about in a rather shame-faced fashion, apparently none the worse for his fall. With vigorous pulling, they drew Roosevelt's pony to the top, and by the same method, augmented with coaxing and abuse, they brought his fellow to his side at last, and proceeded on their excursion.

Late in the afternoon they came on three blacktail deer. Roosevelt took a running shot at two hundred yards and missed, took another and missed again, though this time he managed to turn the animals in their flight. They disappeared round the shoulder of a bluff, and Roosevelt, suspecting that they would reappear when they had recovered from their terror, elevated his sights to four hundred yards and waited. It was not long before one of the three stepped out. Roosevelt raised his rifle. The shot, at that distance, was almost impossible, but there was zest in the trying. Suddenly another buck stepped out and walked slowly toward the first. Roosevelt waited until the heads were in line and fired. Over went both bucks. Roosevelt paced off the distance. It was just four hundred and thirty-one long paces.

It was while they were ascending the Clear Fork of the Powder that they discovered a band of Indians camped a short distance from the place where they themselves had halted for the night.

"I'm going over to see those Indians," remarked Merrifield after dinner that evening.

"What do you want to go over there for?" asked Roosevelt.

"Out in this country," responded the hunter dryly, "you always want to know who your neighbors are."

They rode over together. The Indians were Cheyennes. Experience had taught Merrifield that nothing was so conducive to peaceful relations with a red neighbor as to prove to him that you could

beat him at his own game. He consequently suggested a shooting-match. The Indians agreed. To
Roosevelt's astonishment they proved to be very
bad shots, and not only Merrifield, but Roosevelt
himself, completely outclassed them in the com-
petition. The Indians were noticeably impressed.
Merrifield and Roosevelt rode back to their camp
conscious that so far as those particular Indians
were concerned no anxiety need disturb their
slumbers.

"Indians," remarked Merrifield later, "are the
best judges of human nature in the world. When
an Indian finds out that you are a good shot, he
will leave you absolutely alone to go and come as
you like. Indians are just like white men. They
are not going to start something when they know
you can out-shoot them."

For three weeks they traveled through desolation
before they came at last to the goal of their journey.
At the foot of the first steep rise, on the banks of
Crazy Woman Creek, a few miles south of the army
post at Buffalo, they left the wagon, and following
an old Indian trail started into the mountains,
driving their pack-ponies before them.

It was pleasant, after three burning weeks of
treeless prairie, to climb into the shadowy greenness
of the mountains. All about them was the music of
running water, where clear brooks made their
way through deep gorges and under interlacing
boughs. Groves of great pines rose from grassy
meadows and fringed the glades that lay here and

there like quiet parks in the midst of the wilderness.

The hunters pitched their camp at last in a green valley beside a boisterous mountain brook. The weather was clear, with thin ice coursing the dark waters of the mountain tarns, and now and again slight snowfalls that made the forest gleam and glisten in the moonlight like fairyland. Through the frosty air they could hear the vibrant, musical notes of the bull elk far off, calling to the cows or challenging one another.

No country could have been better adapted to still hunting than the great, pine-clad mountains, studded with open glades. Roosevelt loved the thrill of the chase, but he loved no less the companionship of the majestic trees and the shy wild creatures which sprang across his path or ran with incredible swiftness along the overhanging boughs. Moving on noiseless moccasins he caught alluring glimpses of the inner life of the mountains.

The days passed very pleasantly in the crystal air and vibrant solitude of their mountain hunting grounds. The fare that old Lebo provided was excellent, and to the three men, who had for weeks been accustomed to make small fires from dried brush or from sagebrush roots laboriously dug out of the ground, it was a treat to sit at night before the roaring pine-logs.

" We've come to a land at last," remarked the quaint old teamster with satisfaction, " where the wood grows on trees."

They shot several elk promptly, but the grizzlies

they were after eluded them. At last, after a week,
Merrifield, riding into camp one dusk, with a shout
announced that he had come upon grizzly-bear
signs some ten miles away. They shifted camp
at once.

That afternoon, on a crag overlooking a wild
ravine, Roosevelt shot another great bull elk. To
Merrifield it seemed as though the elk might con-
stitute a day's satisfactory achievement. But
Roosevelt was indefatigable. " Now," he said with
gusto, contemplating the magnificent antlers, " we'll
go out to-night and get a bear."

But that night they found nothing. Returning
next day with Merrifield for the carcass of the elk,
however, they found that a grizzly had been feeding
on it. They crouched in hiding for the bear's
return. Night fell, owls began to hoot dismally
from the tops of the tall trees, and a lynx wailed
from the depths of the woods, but the bear did not
come.

Early next morning they were again at the elk
carcass. The bear had evidently eaten his fill
during the night. His tracks were clear, and they
followed them noiselessly over the yielding carpet of
moss and pine-needles, to an elk-trail leading into
a tangled thicket of young spruces.

Suddenly Merrifield sank on one knee, turning
half round, his face aflame with excitement.
Roosevelt strode silently past him, his gun " at
the ready."

There, not ten steps off, was the great bear,

slowly rising from his bed among the young spruces. He had heard the hunters and reared himself on his haunches. Seeing them, he dropped again on all-fours, and the shaggy hair on his neck and shoulders bristled as he turned toward them.

Roosevelt aimed fairly between the small, glittering eyes, and fired.

Doubtless my face was pretty white [Roosevelt wrote " Bamie " a week later,] but the blue barrel was as steady as a rock as I glanced along it until I could see the top of the bead fairly between his two sinister-looking eyes; as I pulled the trigger I jumped aside out of the smoke, to be ready if he charged, but it was needless, for the great brute was struggling in his death agony, and as you will see when I bring home his skin, the bullet hole was as exactly between his eyes as if I had measured the distance with a carpenter's rule.

At last, one cool morning, when the branches of the evergreens were laden with the feathery snow that had fallen overnight, the hunters struck camp, and in single file, with the pack-ponies laden with the trophies of the hunt, moved down through the woods and across the canyons to the edge of the great table-land, then slowly down the steep slope to its foot, where they found the canvas-topped wagon. Next day they set out on the three-hundred-mile journey home to the Maltese Cross.

For once I have made a very successful hunting trip [Roosevelt wrote " Bamie " from Fort McKinney.] I have just come out of the mountains and will start at once for the Little Missouri, which I expect to reach in a fortnight, and a week afterwards will be on my way home. Merrifield killed two bears and three elk; he has been an invaluable guide for game, and of course the real credit for the bag rests with him, for he found most of the animals. But I really shot well this time. Merrifield, who is a perfectly fearless and reckless man, has no more regard for a grizzly bear than he has for a jack-rabbit; the last one he killed, he wished to merely break his leg with the first shot " so as to see what he'd do." I had not at all this feeling, and fully realized that we were hunting dangerous game; still I never made steadier shooting than at the grizzlies. I had grand sport with the elk, too, and the woods fairly rang with my shouting when I brought down my first lordly bull, with great branching antlers; but after I had begun bear-killing, other sport seemed tame.

So I have had good sport; and enough excitement and fatigue to prevent overmuch thought; and, moreover, I have at last been able to sleep well at night. But unless I was bear-hunting all the time I am afraid I should soon get as restless with this life as with the life at home.

XI

The rattlesnake bites you, the scorpion stings,
The mosquito delights you with buzzing wings;
The sand-burrs prevail, and so do the ants,
And those who sit down need half-soles on their pants.

Cowboy song

THE day that Roosevelt started south on his journey to the mountains, Sewall returned north down the river to rejoin his nephew. Will Dow was watching the cattle on the plateau a few miles south of Elkhorn Bottom, near the mouth of the defile which the cowboys called Shipka Pass.

"You never looked so good to me," he said to Sewall that night, " as you did when I saw your head coming up the Shipka Pass."

They worked together among the cattle for another two or three weeks. They were on the best of terms with Captain Robins by this time, for there was much to like and much to respect in the gruff, dark little seafaring man, who had suffered shipwreck in more ways than one, and was out on the plains because of a marriage that had gone on the rocks. He was an excellent man with the horses, and good company about a camp-fire, for somewhere he had picked up an education and was well-informed. He gave the two tenderfeet a good training in the rudiments of " cattle-punching," sending first one and then the other off to distant round-ups to test their abilities among strangers.

Sewall proved unadaptable, for he was rather old to learn new tricks so far removed from the activities that were familiar to him; but Dow became a " cow-hand " overnight.

Experience was not greatly mollifying Sewall's opinion of the region in which his lot had been cast.

The sun when it shines clear [he wrote his brother Sam after he had been in the Bad Lands six weeks] strikes the bare sides of the Buttes and comes down on the treeless bottoms hot enough to make a Rattlesnake pant. If you can get in the shade there is most always a breeze. The grand trouble is you can't get in the shade. There's no shade to get into and the great sandy Desert is cool compared with some of the gulches, but as you ride it is not quite so bad. The Ponys when they are up to some trick are lively and smart, all other times they are tired, are very tame and look very meek and gentle. But just let one of them get the start of you in any way and you are left. Am glad to say mine has never really got the start yet. We have had a number of differences and controverseys, but my arguments have always prevailed so far.

About the middle of September, the two backwoodsmen moved down to Elkhorn Bottom, leaving Robins in charge of the cattle. Dow went away on a round-up and Sewall undertook to put in livable shape a dugout that stood on the river-bank some thirty or forty yards from the place which Roosevelt had, on a previous visit, selected as the site for the ranch-house which Sewall and Dow were to build. The shack had belonged to a hunter who had left the country, and was not sumptuous in its fittings.

Dow returned from the round-up with interesting news. The Marquis, it seemed, had by no means resigned his claim to the territory on which Roosevelt had established "squatter's rights." Dow overheard one of the Marquis's men confiding to another that "there'd be some dead men round that Elkhorn shack some day."

Sewall received the news with calm satisfaction. "Well," he drawled, "if there's going to be any dead men hereabouts, I cal'late we can fix it so it won't be us."

Sewall and Dow began cutting timber for the house in a thick grove of cottonwoods two or three hundred yards from the river, keeping a weather eye open for trouble. A day or two after Dow's return from the round-up, one of the Marquis's men rode up to them where they were working.

"There's a vigilance committee around, I hear," he remarked casually. "You haven't seen anything of 'em yet hereabouts, have you? I hear they're considerin' makin' a call on you folks."

The men from Maine said to each other that the thing began to look "smoky." They consulted Captain Robins, who agreed that "smoky" was the word, and they carried rifles after that when they went to cut timber.

For they knew very well that the hint which the Marquis's man had lightly thrown out was no idle attempt at intimidation based on nothing but the hope that the Easterners were timid. The activities of Granville Stuart's raiders had stimulated the formation of other vigilance committees, inspired in part by less lofty motives than those which impelled the president of the Montana Stockgrowers' Association and his friends. On the border between Dakota and Montana a company of rough characters who called themselves vigilantes began to make themselves the topic of excited conversation. They were said to be after horse-thieves, but it became noticeable that their activities seemed to be directed mainly against the small ranchers on the edge of the Bad Lands. It was rumored that certain large ranchmen were backing them in the hope of driving the " nesters " out of the country.

The cowmen here are opposed, not only to the Indians, but also to white settlers [wrote the Western correspondent of the New York *Sun*]. They want the land these white and red settlers are taking up. Vast tracts — uncultivated ranges, not settlements — are what they desire. The small holder — the man with a little bunch of cattle — is not wanted. They freeze him out. Somehow he loses cattle, or they are killed by parties unknown.

Sewall and Dow had a right to keep their guns near them while they were at work in the grove on Elkhorn Bottom.

Meanwhile, the endeavors of Granville Stuart's vigilantes were having their results. The precipitous methods of the " stranglers," as they were grimly called, began to give the most hardened " the creeps." Who the " stranglers " themselves were, nobody seemed to know. It was rumored, on the one hand, that they included the biggest ranch-owners in the Northwest; on the other hand, it was stated that they were bands of lawless Texans driven out of the Panhandle and hired by the ranch-men at thirty dollars a month " to clean up the country." Whoever they were, they moved swiftly and acted without hesitation. The newspapers said little about them, partly because they knew little, partly because there was a general tacit under-standing that the whole thing, though necessary, was a disagreeable business, and the less said of it the better.

The truth seems to be that behind the whole movement to rid eastern Montana and western Dakota of the horse-thieves was a loose organiza-tion of cattlemen of which Granville Stuart and his friends were the directing heads. What funds were needed they provided. They designated, moreover, certain responsible men in the different round-up districts, to whom subordinate bands of the " stranglers " reported from time to time for orders. Each subordinate band operated independently of the others, and the leader in one district knew nothing as a rule of the operations of the other bands. He told the " stranglers " what men to " get," and that was all; and a day or two later a man here and a man there would be found dangling from a cottonwood.

In certain cases, Packard, who successfully com-bined the functions of law officer and news-gatherer, knew beforehand what men were to be hanged. On one occasion he was informed that two notorious characters were to be done away with on the following Thursday. The operations of the stranglers were as a rule terrifyingly punctual, and as Thursday was the day on which the *Cowboy* went to press, he announced in it, with an awful punctuality of his own, the sudden demise of the thieves in question.

He carried the papers to the depot to put them on the afternoon train bound for the west, for the *Cowboy* was popular with the passengers and he disposed of an edition of seven or eight hundred weekly with them in excess of his regular edition. As he was about to step on the train, two men stepped down. They were the horse-thieves whose death he had too confidently announced.

He stared at them, shocked to the marrow, feeling as though he had seen ghosts. Would they stay in Medora, or would they go on to where frontier justice was awaiting them? Would they see the announcement in the *Cowboy?* He remembered that they could not read.

Fascinated, he watched them. The train started. The two men jumped aboard.

That night they were hanged.

Exactly what relation the vigilance committee which was seeking to drive the " nesters " out of western Montana bore to Granville Stuart's organization, is difficult to determine. They had probably originally been one of the subordinate bands, who were " feeling their oats," and, under the pretense of " cleaning up the country," were cleaning up personal scores. The captain of the band was a man called " Flopping Bill," a distinctly shady character, and the band itself was made up of irresponsible creatures who welcomed the opportunity to do, in the cause of righteousness, a number of things for which under ordinary circumstances they would have been promptly hanged. Their first act as a body was to engage a French Canadian named Louis La Pache as guide. La Pache was himself awaiting trial at Miles City for horse-stealing, but there is no indication in the records that he was chosen because he was ready to turn State's evidence. He was merely the type that Flopping Bill's guardians of law and order would naturally choose.

The raiders began their activities near the mouth of Beaver Creek, not ten miles from the spot where Sewall and Dow (with their rifles at hand) were hewing timber for the new house. Two cowpunchers had recently started a ranch there. They were generally considered honest, but the vigilantes had marked them for destruction, and descended upon the ranch ready to hang any one in sight. They found only a hired man, an Englishman, for the ranchmen had got wind of the raid and fled; and spent their enthusiasm for order in " allowing the Englishman to feel the sansation of a lariat round his neck," as the record runs, releasing him on his promise to leave the country forever. Thereupon they nailed a paper, signed with skull and crossbones, on the door of the cabin ordering the ranchmen " to vacate "; and proceeded to other pastures.

They stopped at a half dozen ranches, terrorizing and burning, but catching no horse-thieves. It is impossible through the obscurity that shrouds the grim events of that autumn to determine to what extent they were honestly in pursuit of law-breakers or were merely endeavoring, at the behest of some of the great cattle-owners, to drive the small stockmen out of the country. Their motives were possibly mixed. The small ranchers were notoriously not always what they seemed. Most of the horse-thieves posed as "nesters," hiding in underground stables by day the horses they stole by night. Each registered his own brand and sometimes more than one; but the brands were carefully contrived. If you intended, for instance, to prey on the great herds of the "Long X outfit," thus ✕, you called your brand "Four Diamonds," marking it thus ⬦⬦. A quick fire and a running iron did the trick. It was all very simple and very profitable and if you were caught there was always a Certain Person (to whom you were accustomed to give an accounting), and beyond him a vague but powerful Somebody Else to stand between you and the law. There would be no trial, or, if there were a trial, there would be no witnesses, or, if there were witnesses, there would be a lenient judge and a skeptical jury. The methods of Flopping Bill's party were no doubt reprehensible, but in attacking some of the little "nesters" the raiders came close to the heart of many troubles.

But indiscriminate terrorizing by any one in any

cause was not to the taste of the ranchmen up and down the Little Missouri who happened to be law-abiding. The raiders were starting prairie fires, moreover, with the purpose evidently of destroying the ,pasture of the small stockmen, and were in consequence vitally affecting the interests of every man who owned cattle anywhere in the valley. That these acts of vandalism were the work of a body from another Territory, invading the Bad Lands for purposes of reform, did not add greatly to their popularity. The ranchmen set about to organize a vigilance committee of their own to repel the invaders, if necessary, by force.

Whether the raiders got wind of this purpose is not known, but they evidently decided that they had overplayed their hand, for they suddenly veered in their course and troubled the Bad Lands no more. But before they went they dropped a bomb which did more than many conflagrations to carry out their ostensible mission as discouragers of evil-doing.

It happened that not far from Elkhorn Bottom the vigilantes came upon Pierce Bolan, who, it will be remembered, had some time previous discoursed to Fisher on the merits of the " considerate treatment " in relations with horse-thieves. He was himself as honest as daylight, but, as ill-luck would have it, the raiders found him afoot, and, assuming that he was about to steal a horse, called on him to confess. He declared that he had nothing to confess. The raiders thereupon threw a rope around his neck and drew him up in such a way that his feet just touched the ground. The victim continued to proclaim his innocence and the vigilantes finally released him, but not until he was unconscious. When he came to, the raiders were gone, but near-by he found a paper possibly dropped not altogether inadvertently. It bore the names of fifteen men along the Little Missouri whom Granville Stuart's committee had marked for punishment.

What Bolan did with the list, to whom he showed the list, in what way he reached the men whose names were on the list — all that is lost to history. All that we know is that there was a great scattering during the succeeding days, and certain men who were thought most reputable discovered suddenly that they had pressing business in California or New York.

" I never saw a full list of the names on that paper," said Fisher years afterward, " and knew nothing of what was going on until two of them came to me about the matter. They found that I was really ignorant and then asked what I would do if in their place. I advised hiding out for a while until matters had cooled off, which they did."

Who the men were whose names were on that list is a secret which those who held it never revealed and inquisitive minds along the Little Missouri could never definitely solve. Rumor suggested this man and that whose ways had been devious, but only one name was ever mentioned with certainty. That name was Maunders. No one seemed to question that if any one was going to be hanged, Maunders was the most likely candidate.

That gentleman, meanwhile, was fully aware that he had been marked for slaughter, but he kept his head, and, trusting no doubt to the protection of the Marquis, calmly remained in Medora, refusing by flight to present his enemies with evidence of an uneasy conscience. To his friends he declared that Fisher alone was responsible for having his name placed on the list, and breathed dire threats against the manager of the Marquis's Refrigerator Company.

Fisher was not greatly disturbed by the rumors that reached him of Maunders's determination to kill him at the first opportunity. He even went hunting alone with the outwardly affable " bad man."

Some of the " boys " thought he was taking unnecessary risks, and told him so. " You're taking a big chance in going out alone with Maunders. He's got it in for you."

Fisher smiled. " Perhaps you haven't noticed," he said, " that I always make certain that one or the other of you fellows sees us leave. Maunders would break his neck to see me get back safely."

Unquestionably, Maunders had an almost over-developed bump of caution. He left Fisher unharmed and turned his attention to the two backwoodsmen from Maine who were holding down the most desirable claim north of Medora for an Eastern tenderfoot.

One Sunday morning late in September Sewall

was alone in the dugout at the river-bank. Dow was off on a stroll and Sewall was writing his weekly letter home, when he suddenly heard hoof-beats punctuated with shots. He went to the door. Six rough-looking characters on horseback were outside with smoking rifles in their hands. He knew only one of them, but he was evidently the leader. It was Maunders. Sewall took in the situation and invited them all inside.

The men had been drinking, and, suspecting that they would be hungry, Sewall offered them food. Dow was an excellent cook and in the ashes of the hearth was a pot of baked beans, intended for their own midday meal. Sewall, keeping carefully within reach of one or the other of his weapons which hung on the wall, set the pot before the evil-faced gunmen.

Maunders, who was slightly drunk, ate ravenously and directly began to sing the praises of the beans. Sewall filled his plate, and filled it again.

" I thought I would do everything I could to make them comfortable," he remarked, telling about it later, " and then if they cooked up any racket we should have to see what the end would be. I knew that if they were well filled, it would have a tendency to make them good-natured, and besides that it puts a man in rather an awkward position, when he's got well treated, to start a rumpus."

Sewall watched the men unostentatiously, but with an eagle eye. He had made up his mind that if there were to be any dead men thereabouts Maunders was to be the first. " He being the leader I thought I would make sure of him whatever happened to me."

He noted, not without satisfaction, that the men were looking around the cabin, regarding the weapons with attention. He showed Maunders about. The gunman agreed without enthusiasm that they had " got things fixed up in very fine shape," and departed. He treated Sewall most affably thereafter, but the backwoodsmen were made aware in one way and another that the old mischief-maker had not yet given up the idea of driving Theodore Roosevelt and his " outfit " off the claim at Elkhorn Bottom.

XII

It was underneath the stars, the little peeking stars,
  That we lay and dreamed of Eden in the hills;
We were neither sad nor gay, but just wondering, while we lay,
  What a mighty lot of space creation fills.

Our fire was just a spark; dot of red against the dark,
  And around the fire an awful lot of night.
The purple, changing air was as quiet as a prayer,
  And the moon came up and froze the mountains white.
                                HENRY HERBERT KNIBBS

THE " boss " of Elkhorn Ranch, meanwhile, oblivi-
ous of the heat which he was generating in the
Marquis's Prime Minister, was taking his slow
course northeastward across Wyoming to the Bad
Lands. It was long and weary traveling across
the desolate reaches of burnt prairie. The horses
began to droop. At last, in some heavy sand-hills
east of the Little Beaver, one of the team pulling
the heavily laden wagon played out completely,
and they had to put the toughest of the saddle
ponies in his place. Night was coming on fast
as they crossed the final ridge and came in sight
of as singular a bit of country as any of them had
ever seen. Scattered over a space not more than
three quarters of a mile square were countless isolated buttes of sandstone, varying in height from
fifteen to fifty feet. Some of them rose as sharp
peaks or ridges or as connected chains, but the
greater number by far were topped with diminutive
table-lands, some thirty feet across, some seventy,

some two hundred. The sides were perpendicular, and were cut and channeled by the weather into most curious caves and columns and battlements and spires. Here and there ledges ran along the faces of the cliffs and eerie protrusions jutted out from the corners. Grave pine-trees rose loftily among the strange creations of water and wind set in a desert of snow-white sand. It was a beautiful and fantastic place and they made their camp there.

The moon was full and the night clear. In an angle of a cliff they built a roaring pine-log fire whose flames, leaping up the gray wall, made wild sport of the bold corners and strange-looking escarpments of the rock. Beyond the circle that the firelight brought luridly to life, the buttes in the moonlight had their own still magic. Against the shining silver of the cliffs the pines showed dark and somber, and when the branches stirred, the bright light danced on the ground making it appear like a sheet of molten metal.

It was like a country seen in a dream.

The next morning all was changed. A wild gale was blowing and rain beat about them in level sheets. A wet fog came and went and gave place at last to a steady rain, as the gale gave place to a hurricane. They spent a miserable day and night shifting from shelter to shelter with the shifting wind; another day and another night. Their provisions were almost gone, the fire refused to burn in the fierce downpour, the horses drifted far off before the storm. . . .

" Fortunately," remarked Roosevelt later, " we had all learned that, no matter how bad things were, grumbling and bad temper can always be depended upon to make them worse, and so bore our ill-fortune, if not with stoical indifference, at least in perfect quiet."

The third day dawned crisp and clear, and once more the wagon lumbered on. They made camp that night some forty miles southwest of Lang's. They were still three days from home, three days of crawling voyaging beside the fagged team. The country was monotonous, moreover, without much game.

" I think I'd like to ride in and wake the boys up for breakfast," remarked Merrifield.

" Good!" exclaimed Roosevelt. " I'll do it with you."

Merrifield argued the matter. Roosevelt had been in the saddle all day and it was eighty miles to the Maltese Cross.

" I'm going with you. I want to wind up this trip myself," said Roosevelt, and there the argument ended.

At nine o'clock they saddled their tough little ponies, and rode off out of the circle of firelight. The October air was cool in their faces as they loped steadily mile after mile over the moonlit prairie.

Roosevelt later described that memorable ride.

The hoof-beats of our horses rang out in steady rhythm through the silence of the night, otherwise unbroken save now and then by the wailing cry of a coyote. The rolling plains stretched out on all sides of us, shimmering in the clear moonlight; and occasionally a band of spectral-looking antelope swept silently away from before our path. Once we went by a drove of Texan cattle, who stared wildly at the intruders; as we passed they charged down by us, the ground rumbling beneath their tread, while their long horns knocked against each other with a sound like the clattering of a multitude of castanets. We could see clearly enough to keep our general course over the trackless plain, steering by the stars where the prairie was perfectly level and without landmarks; and our ride was timed well, for as we galloped down into the valley of the Little Missouri the sky above the line of the level bluffs in our front was crimson with the glow of the unrisen sun.

Roosevelt rode down to Elkhorn a day or two after his return to the Maltese Cross, and found Sewall and Dow busy cutting the timber for the new house, which was to stand in the shade of a row of cottonwood trees overlooking the broad, shallow bed of the Little Missouri. They were both mighty men with the axe. Roosevelt worked with them for a few days. He himself was no amateur, but he could not compete with the stalwart backwoodsmen.

One evening he overheard Captain Robins ask Dow what the day's cut had been. " Well, Bill cut down fifty-three," answered Dow. " I cut forty-nine, and the boss," he added dryly, not realizing that Roosevelt was within hearing — " the boss he beavered down seventeen."

Roosevelt remembered the tree-stumps he had seen gnawed down by beavers, and grinned.

Roosevelt found that the men from Maine were adapting themselves admirably to their strange surroundings. Dow was already an excellent cowhand. Sewall's abilities ran in other directions.

We are hewing away at the stuff for the house [Sewall wrote his brother on October 19th]. It is to be 60 ft. long and 30 wide, the walls 9 ft. high, so you can see it is quite a job to hew it out on three sides, but we have plenty of time. Theodore wants us to ride and explore one day out of each week and we have to go to town after our mail once a week, so we don't work more than. half the time. It is a good job and a big one, but we have lots of time between this and spring.

Meanwhile, he stubbornly insisted that the country was not adapted to cattle.

I think I already see a good many drawbacks to this country [he wrote]. The Stock business is a new business in the Bad Lands and I can't find as anybody has made anything at it, yet *they all expect to*. I think they have all lost as yet. Talked the other day with one of the biggest Stock men here. He is hired by the month to boss. He said nobody knew whether there was anything in it or not, yet. He had been here three years and sometimes thought there was not much in it, said it was very expensive and a great many outs to it and I believe he told the truth. Out about town they blow it up, want to get everybody at it they can. We shall see in time. Can tell better in the spring after we see how they come in with their cattle.

The truth was, Bill knew the ways of cattle, for he had run cattle in the open in Maine under climatic conditions not dissimilar to those of the Dakota country. His experience had taught him that when a cow is allowed to have one calf after another without special feeding, she is more than likely to die after the third calf. He knew also that when a cow calves in cold weather, she is likely to freeze her udder and be ruined, and lose the calf besides.

" Those cows will either have to be fed," he said to Roosevelt, " or they'll die."

Roosevelt took Sewall's pessimism with a grain of salt. " No one hereabouts seems to think there's any danger of that sort," he said. " I think, Bill, you're wrong."

" I hope I am," said Bill; and there the matter dropped.

It was while Roosevelt was working at Elkhorn that further rumors of trouble came from the party of the Marquis. Maunders insisted that he had a prior claim to the shack in which Sewall and Dow were living and all the land that lay around it, and demanded five hundred dollars for his rights. Roosevelt had from the first scouted the claim, for Maunders had a way of claiming any shack which a hunter deserted anywhere. Vague threats which Maunders was making filled the air, but did not greatly disturb Roosevelt. Sewall and Dow, however, had heard a rumor which sounded authentic and might require attention. Maunders had said that he was going to shoot Roosevelt at the next opportunity. They passed the news on to " the boss."

This was decidedly interesting. Maunders was

known as a good shot and was well protected by the Marquis.

Roosevelt promptly saddled his horse and rode back up the river. Maunders's shack stood on the west bank a few hundred yards from the Pyramid Park Hotel. Roosevelt knocked on the door. Maunders opened it.

" Maunders," said Roosevelt sharply, " I understand that you have threatened to kill me on sight. I have come over to see when you want to begin the killing and to let you know that, if you have anything to say against me, now is the time for you to say it."

Maunders looked unhappy. After a brief conversation it appeared that Maunders did not after all want to shoot him. He had been " misquoted," he said. They parted, understanding one another perfectly.

Roosevelt left Medora on October 7th, bound for New York. He had decided, after all, not to remain aloof from the political campaign. He deeply distrusted the Democratic Party, on the one hand, and he was enraged at the nominations of the Republican Party, on the other; but the " Mugwumps," those Republicans who, with a self-conscious high-mindedness which irritated him almost beyond words, were supporting the Democratic nominee, he absolutely despised. Besides, it was not in him to be neutral in any fight. He admitted that freely. During the final weeks of the campaign he made numerous speeches in New York and elsewhere which were not neutral in the least.

By leaving Medora on the 7th of October he missed a memorable occasion, for on the following day Packard at last opened his stage-line. The ex-baseball player had met and surmounted an array of obstacles that would have daunted anybody but a youngster on the Western frontier. He had completed his building operations by the end of September, and by the first of October he had distributed his hostlers, his eating-house keepers, his helpers and his " middle-route " drivers, among the sixteen relay-stations that lined the wheel-tracks which the Marquis was pleased to call the " highway " to the Black Hills. The horses which he had purchased in a dozen different places in the course of the summer were not such as to allay the trepidation of timid travelers. They had none of them been broken to harness before Packard's agents had found them and broken them in their own casual and none too gentle fashion. Packard would have preferred to have horses which had become accustomed to the restraining hand of man, but " harness-broke " horses were rare in that country. Besides, they were expensive, and, with the money coming from the Marquis only in little sums, long-delayed, Packard that summer was hunting bargains. As it was, Baron von Hoffman, who was a business man of vision and ability, was none too pleased with the mounting expenses of his son-in-law's new venture.

" How many horses have you bought? " he asked Packard one day rather sharply.

" A hundred and sixty-six."

" How many are you using on the stage-line? "

" A hundred and sixty."

" What are you doing with the other six? "

" They're out on the line."

" Humph! " grunted the Baron in despair. " Eating their heads off! "

What the Baron said to the Marquis is lost to history. The family in the new house across the river from Medora had plenty of dignity and pride. Whatever disagreements they had they kept securely within their own walls, and there was nothing but a growing querulousness in the voice of the man who held the purse-strings to reveal to the world that Baron von Hoffman was beginning to think he was laying away his money in a hole that had no bottom. Something of that feeling seems to have been in the Marquis's own mind, for in the interviews he gave to the newspapers the words " I won't be bled " recur.

On the first of October, Packard was ready for the " dress rehearsal " of his stage-line. That performance partook of more than the usual quantity of hazard connected with such occasions. At every station, for instance, some or all of the six horses had to be roped, thrown, and blindfolded before they would let themselves be harnessed. To adjust the harness was itself a ticklish undertaking and had to be done with minute regard for sensitive nerves, for if any part of it struck a horse except with the pressure of its own weight, the devil was loose again, and anything might happen. But even when the harness was finally on the refractory backs, the work was not half done. Still blind-folded, the horses had to be driven, pulled, pushed, and hauled by main force to their appointed places in front of the coach. Noiselessly, one at a time, the tugs were attached to the single-tree, and carefully, as though they were dynamite, the reins were handed to the driver. At the Moreau Station, two thirds of the way to Deadwood, all six horses, it happened were practically unbroken broncos. The driver was on his box with Packard at his side, as they prepared to start, and at the head of each horse stood one of the station-hands.

" Ready? " asked the man at the head of the near leader.

" All set," answered the other helpers.

" Let 'er go! " called the driver.

The helpers jerked the blinds from the horses' eyes. The broncos jumped into their collars as a unit. As a unit, however, they surged back, as they became suddenly conscious of the horror that they dreaded most — restraint. The off leader made a wild swerve to the right, backing toward the coach, and dragging the near leader and the near swing-horse from their feet. The off leader, unable to forge ahead, made a wild leap for the off swing horse, and fairly crushed him to earth with his feet, himself tripping on the harness and rolling at random in the welter, his snapping hoofs flashing in every direction. The wheel team, in the mean-

time, was doing what Packard later described as
" a vaudeville turn of its own." The near wheeler
was bucking as though there were no other horse
within a hundred miles; the off wheeler had broken
his single-tree and was facing the coach, delivering
kicks at the mêlée behind him with whole-hearted
abandon and rigid impartiality.

"It was exactly the kind of situation," Packard
remarked later, "that George Myers would have
called 'a gol-darned panorama.'"

But the horses were not to have matters altogether
their own way, for the helpers were experienced
"horse-wranglers." By main strength they pulled
the off leader to his place and blindfolded him,
delegating one of their number to sit on his head
until the snarl might be untangled. The process
was repeated with the other horses. The damage
proved to be negligible. A few small harness straps
had snapped, and a single-tree was broken. A
second trial resulted no better than the first. After
the half-crazy animals had been a second time
disentangled and a third time harnessed, quivering,
to the coach, the driver had his way with them.
The horses jumped forward into a wild run, thrash-
ing the heavy coach about as a small boy might be
thrashed about as the tail in "crack the whip."
It was a wild ride, but they reached Spearfish with
no bones broken.

"Our entrance into Deadwood was spectacular,"
said Packard later, "and ended in an invitation
ride to Lead City with Mayor Seth Bullock at the

head of the local dignitaries, riding in state inside the coach."

On the 8th of October, Packard offered the dubious joys of his stage-line for the first time to the public; and began to see a faint prospect of return on his rather extravagant investment of energy and time. But his satisfaction died still-born. The Marquis's sanguine temperament had once more proved the undoing of what might have been a profitable venture. The mail contract, which the easy-going Frenchman had thought that he had secured, proved illusory. Packard, who had been glad to leave that part of the business to his principal, discovered, as soon as he began to inquire for the mail-bags, that what his principal had actually secured from the Postmaster-General was not a contract at all, but merely a chance to bid when the annual offers for star routes came up for bidding the following May. It was a body blow to the putative owner of a stage-line.

Long after the last of his Deadwood coaches had been rattled to kindlings in Buffalo Bill's Wild West Show, Packard told the last chapter of his connection with the Medora and Black Hills Forwarding and Transportation Company.

" No mail contract; hardly a month of earnings before winter, when there was no chance of paying operating expenses; responsible for the pay-roll, but not on it; with a private pay-roll and expenses equal to or greater than my private income; with all my cash savings gone in the preliminary expenses of putting on the line, and finally with no chance, under my contract, of getting a cent from the stage-line before that nebulous time when it had paid for itself. The Marquis soon returned and I told him I could not consider myself bound by the contract. The delay in providing funds I had condoned by staying with the proposition, but a mail contract which was essential in helping to pay expenses was not even a possibility for seven or more months in the future. I stayed until another man was hired and left my duties with a grunt of relief." [1]

For Packard the failure of his venture was not a serious matter. The *Cowboy* was flourishing and there was enough in all conscience to keep him occupied in his duties as Chief of Police. But for the Marquis it was bad business. He had, as it was, few enough honest men at his side.

[1] It was Packard's stage-line which brought Scipio le Moyne (in Owen Wister's novel) from the Black Hills to Medora to become the substitute cook of the Virginian's mutinous "outfit." The cook whom the Virginian kicked off the train at Medora, because he was too anxious to buy a bottle of whiskey, is said to have been a man named Macdonald. He remained in the Bad Lands as cook for one of the ranches, but he was such an inveterate drinker that "Nitch" Kendley was forced to take drastic measures. Finding him unconscious one day, just outside of Medora, he tied him hand and foot to the sagebrush. The cook struggled twelve hours in the broiling sun before he could free himself. Tradition has it that he did not touch another drop of liquor for three years.

XIII

Oh, we're up in the morning ere breaking of day,
The chuck-wagon's busy, the flapjacks in play;
The herd is astir o'er hillside and vale,
With the night riders rounding them into the trail.
Oh, come take up your cinches, come shake out your reins;
Come, wake your old bronco and break for the plains;
Come, roust out your steers from the long chaparral,
For the outfit is off to the railroad corral.

The Railroad Corral

ROOSEVELT returned to the Bad Lands on the 16th
of November and was greeted with enthusiasm by
Merrifield and Sylvane. The next day he started
for the new ranch. He had intended to get under
way by noon, but Sylvane and Merrifield wanted
to drive a small beef herd, which they were shipping
to Chicago, to the shipping corrals near the Cantonment, and it was mid-afternoon before he was
able to put spurs to his smart little cowpony and
start on the long ride to Elkhorn. The day was
bitterly cold, with the mercury well down toward
zero, and the pony, fresh and impatient, went
along at a good rate. Roosevelt had not gone many
miles before he became conscious that darkness was
falling. The trail followed along the bottom for a
half-dozen miles and then turned off into the bad
lands, leading up and down through the ravines
and over the ridge crests of a rough and broken
country. He crossed a wide plateau where the
wind blew savagely, sweeping the powdery snow
into his face, then dipped again into the valley

where the trail led along the bottoms between the rows of high bluffs, continually crossing and re-crossing the river. The ice was too thin to bear the horse, for the cold had come suddenly and had not yet frozen it solid, and again and again, as the pony cautiously advanced, the white surface would suddenly break and let horse and rider down into the chilling water.

Roosevelt had made up his mind that he could under no circumstances reach the new ranch that night and had determined to spend the night with Robins, the seafaring man, whose hut was three or four miles nearer. But the sun set while he was still several miles from his goal, and the darkness, which had been closing round him where he rode in the narrow valley, crept over the tops of the high bluffs and shut out from his vision everything but a dim track in the snow faintly illuminated by the stars. Roosevelt hurried his pony. Clouds were gathering overhead, and soon, Roosevelt knew, even the light that the stars gave would be with-drawn. The night was very cold and the silence was profound. A light snow rendered even the hoof-beats of his horse muffled and indistinct, and the only sound that came out of the black world about him was the long-drawn, melancholy howling of a wolf.

Captain Robins's shack stood in the midst of a large clump of cottonwoods thickly grown up with underbrush. It was hard enough to find in the day-time, but in the darkness of that wintry night it proved tantalizingly elusive. There was no light in it to guide him, which depressed him.

He found the cabin at last, but it was empty and chill. He lit a fire and hunted about among the stores of the old seafaring man for something of which to make supper. The place was stripped bare. He went down to the river with an axe and a pail and brought up some water; in his pocket he had a paper of tea. It was not an altogether satisfying supper for a tired and hungry man.

He was out with his rifle at break of day. Outside the hut the prairie fowl were crowing and calling to one another in the tall trees, evidently attracted by the thick growth of choke-cherries and wild plums. As the dawn deepened, the sharp-tails began to fly down from their roosts to the berry bushes. Up among the bare limbs of the trees, sharply outlined against the sky, they offered as good a target as any hungry man might ask. He shot off the necks of five in succession, and it was not long before two of the birds, plucked and cleaned, were split open and roasting before the fire.

He found that Sewall and Dow had cut all the timber for the house, and were beginning work on the walls. It was a roomy place they were building, a palace as houses went in the Bad Lands. Roosevelt worked with them for two days. Both men were excellent company, Dow a delightful spinner of yarns, witty and imaginative, Sewall full of horse sense and quiet philosophizing. Roosevelt himself was much depressed. His virtual elimination from politics, together with the tragic breaking-up of his home life, had left him for the moment aimless and without ambition. There is a wistful note in a letter he wrote, that week to Lodge. " The statesman (?) of the past has been merged, alas, I fear for good, in the cowboy of the present." He was not in the habit of talking of himself or of asking others to share his negations; but there was something avuncular about Sewall that impelled confidences. He told the backwoodsman that he did not care what became of himself; he had nothing to live for, he said. Sewall " went for him bow-legged," as he himself described it in later years.

" You ought not to allow yourself to feel that way," he insisted. " You have your child to live for."

" Her aunt can take care of her a good deal better than I can," Roosevelt responded. " She never would know anything about me, anyway. She would be just as well off without me."

" You won't always feel that way," said Sewall. " You will get over this after a while. I know how such things are; but time heals them over. You won't always feel as you do now, and you won't always be willing to stay here and drive cattle, because, when you get to feeling differently, you will want to get back among your friends where you can do more and be more benefit to the world than you can driving cattle. If you can't think of anything else to do, you can go home and start a reform. You would make a good reformer. You always want to make things better instead of worse."

Roosevelt laughed at that, and said no more concerning the uselessness of his existence. An amusing angle of the whole matter was that "starting a reform" was actually in the back of his head at the time.

The reform in question was fundamental. It concerned the creation of an organization, ostensibly, in the absence of constituted government, for the purpose of making and enforcing certain sorely needed laws for the regulation of the cattle industry; but actually with the higher aim in view of furnishing a rallying point for the scattered forces of law and order. Montana had such an organization in the Montana Live Stock Association and more than one ranchman with large interests in the valley of the Little Missouri had appealed to that body for help. But the Montana Association found that it had no authority in Dakota. Roosevelt determined, therefore, to form a separate organization.

The need unquestionably was great. To an unusual extent the cattle industry depended upon coöperation. Each ranchman "claimed" a certain range, but no mark showed the boundaries of that range and no fence held the cattle and horses within it. On every "claim" the brands of twenty different herds might have been found. No ranchman by himself, or with the aid only of his own employees, would ever have been able to collect his widely scattered property. It was only by the coöperative effort known as " the round-up " that it was possible once or twice a year for every man to gather his own. The very persistence of the range as a feeding-ground and the vitality and very life of the cattle depended upon the honest coöperation of the stock-owners. If one man overstocked his range, it was not only his cattle which suffered, but in an equal measure the cattle of every other ranchman along the river.

Regulating this industry, which depended so largely on a self-interest looking beyond the immediate gain, was a body of tradition brought from the cattle ranges of the South, but no code of regulations. There were certain unwritten laws which you were supposed to obey; but if you were personally formidable and your " outfit " was impressive, there was nothing in heaven or earth to force you to obey them. It was comparatively simple, moreover, to conduct a private round-up and ship to Chicago cattle whose brands were not your own. If ever an industry needed " regulation" for the benefit of the honest men engaged in it, it was the cattle industry in Dakota in 1884.

But the need of a law of the range which the stockmen would respect, because it was to their own interests to respect it, was only a phase of a greater need for the presence in that wild and sparsely settled country of some sort of authority which men would recognize and accept because it was an outgrowth of the life of which they were a part. Sheriffs and marshals were imposed from without, and an independent person might have argued that in a territory under a Federal governor, they constituted government without the consent of the governed. Such a person would look with entirely different eyes on a body created from among the men with whom he was in daily association.

Medora was blest with a deputy United States Marshal, and much good did law and order derive from his presence. He happened to be the same Joe Morrill who had gained notoriety the preceding winter in the Stoneville fight, and who had long been suspected, by law-abiding folk between Medora and the Black Hills, of being " in cahoots " with everything that was sinister in the region. He had for years been stationed at Deadwood for the purpose mainly of running down deserting soldiers, and one of the rumors that followed him to Medora was to the effect that he had made himself the confidant of deserters only to betray them for thirty dollars a head. The figure was unfortunate. It stuck in the memory with its echoes of Judas.

The law-abiding element did not receive any noticeable support from Joe Morrill. He was a " gun-toting " swashbuckler, not of the " bad man " type at all, but, as Packard pointed out, altogether too noisy in denouncing the wicked when they were not present and too effusive in greeting them when they were. He gravitated naturally toward Maunders and Bill Williams and Jess Hogue, and if law and order derived any benefits from that association, history has neglected to record them. Thievery went on as before.

Roosevelt, no doubt, realized that the hope of the righteous lay not in Joe Morrill or in any other individual whom the Federal authorities might impose on the Bad Lands, but only in an organization which was the expression of a real desire for coöperation. He set about promptly to form such an organization.

After two days of house-building at Elkhorn, Roosevelt, who was evidently restless, was again under way, riding south through a snowstorm all day to the Maltese Cross, bringing Sewall and Dow with him.

It was late at night when we reached Merrifield's [he wrote " Bamie " on November 23d], and the thermometer was twenty degrees below zero. As you may imagine, my fur coat and buffalo bag have come in very handily.

I am now trying to get up a stockman's association, and in a day or two, unless the weather is too bad, I shall start up the river with Sewall to see about it.

At one ranch after another, Roosevelt, riding south through the biting cold with his philosophic backwoodsman, stopped during the week that followed, to persuade fifteen or twenty stockmen along the valley of the Little Missouri of the benefits of coöperation. It was an arduous journey, taking him well south of Lang's; but it was evidently successful.

Theodore Roosevelt, who used to was a great reformer

in the New York Legislature, but who is now a cowboy, pure and simple [remarked the Bismarck *Weekly Tribune* in an editorial on December 12th], calls a meeting of the stockmen of the West Dakota region to meet at Medora, December 19th, to discuss topics of interest, become better acquainted, and provide for a more efficient organization. Mr. Roosevelt likes the West.

Winter now settled down on the Bad Lands in earnest. There was little snow, but the cold was fierce in its intensity. By day, the plains and buttes were dazzling to the eye under the clear weather; by night, the trees cracked and groaned from the strain of the biting frost. Even the stars seemed to snap and glitter. The river lay fixed in its shining bed of glistening white, "like a huge bent bar of blue steel." Wolves and lynxes traveled up and down it at night as though it were a highway.

Winter was the ranchman's "slack season"; but Roosevelt found, nevertheless, that there was work to be done even at that time of year to test a man's fiber. Activities, which in the ordinary Eastern winter would have been merely the casual incidents of the day's work, took on some of the character of Arctic exploration in a country where the thermometer had a way of going fifty degrees below zero, and for two weeks on end never rose above a point of ten below. It was not always altogether pleasant to be out of doors; but wood had to be chopped, and coal had to be brought in by the wagon-load. Roosevelt had a mine on his own ranch some three or four miles south of Chimney

Butte. It was a vein of soft lignite laid bare in the side of a clay bluff by the corrosive action of the water, carving, through the centuries, the bed of the Little Missouri. He and his men brought the coal in the ranch-wagon over the frozen bed of the river. The wheels of the wagon creaked and sang in the bitter cold, as they ground through the powdery snow.

The cattle, moreover, had to be carefully watched, for many of them were slow in learning to " rustle for themselves," as the phrase went. A part of every day at least was spent in the saddle by one or the other or all of the men who constituted the Chimney Butte outfit. In spite of their great fur coats and caps and gauntlets, in spite of heavy underclothing and flannel-lined boots, it was not often that one or the other of them, returning from a ride, did not have a touch of the frost somewhere about him. When the wind was at his back, Roosevelt found it was not bad to gallop along through the white weather, but when he had to face it, riding over a plain or a plateau, it was a different matter, for the blast cut through him like a keen knife, and the thickest furs seemed only so much paper. The cattle were obviously unhappy, standing humped up under the bushes, except for an hour or two at midday when they ventured out to feed. A very weak animal they would bring into the cow-shed and feed with hay; but they did this only in cases of the direst necessity, as such an animal had then to be fed for the rest of the winter, and the quantity of hay was limited. As long as the cattle could be held within the narrow strip of Bad Lands, they were safe enough, for the deep ravines afforded them ample refuge from the icy gales. But if by any accident a herd was caught by a blizzard on the open prairie, it might drift before it a hundred miles.

Soon after Roosevelt's return from the East, he had sent Sylvane Ferris to Spearfish to purchase some horses for the ranch. About the first week in December his genial foreman returned, bringing fifty-two head. They were wild, unbroken " cayuses," and had to be broken then and there. Day after day, in the icy cold, Roosevelt labored with the men in the corral over the refractory animals making up in patience what he lacked in physical address.

Bill Sewall, who with Dow was on hand to drive a number of the ponies north to Elkhorn Ranch, did not feel under the same compulsion as " the boss " to risk his neck in the subjugation of the frantic animals. Will Dow had become an excellent horseman, but Sewall had come to the conclusion that you could not teach an old dog new tricks, and refused to be bulldozed into attempting what he knew he could not accomplish. There was something impressive in the firmness with which he refused to allow the cowboys to make him look foolish.

The night the horses arrived, Sewall overheard a number of the cowboys remark that they would get the men from Maine " on those wild horses and have some fun with them." " I was fore-warned," said Sewall, years after, telling about it, " and so I was forearmed."

One of the men came up to Sewall, and with malice aforethought led the subject to Sewall's participation in the breaking of the horses.

" I am not going to ride any of those horses," said Sewall.

" You will have to," said the cowboy.

" I don't know so much about that."

" If you don't," remarked the cowboy, " you will have the contempt of everybody."

" That won't affect me very much," Sewall answered quietly. " If I were younger, it might, but it won't now."

" Oh, well," said the other lightly, " you will have to ride them."

" No," remarked Sewall, " I didn't come out here to make a fool of myself trying to do what I know I can't do. I don't want to be pounded on the frozen ground."

The cowboy made a sharp reply, but Sewall, feeling his blood rise to his head, became only more firm in refusing to be bulldozed.

" I suppose you fellows can ride broncos," he said, " but you cannot ride me, and if you get on, your feet will drag."

There the conversation ended. The next morning Sewall heard the cowboy remark, not too pleas-antly, " I suppose it is no use to saddle any bad ones for Sewall, for he said he wouldn't ride them."

Sewall paid no attention to the thrust. The whole affair had a comic conclusion, for it happened that, quite by accident, Sewall, in attempting to pick out a gentle horse, picked one who ultimately proved to be one of the worst in the herd. For all the time that Sewall was on his back, he acted like a model of the virtues. It was only when Dow subsequently mounted him that he began to reveal his true character, bucking Dow within an inch of his life. The cowboy, however, made no more efforts at intimidation.

To Roosevelt — to whom difficulty and peril were always a challenge, and pain itself was a visitant to be wrestled with and never released until a blessing had been wrung from the mysterious lips — the hardships and exertions of those wintry day were a source of boyish delight. It partook of the nature of adventure to rise at five (three hours ahead of the sun) and ride under the starlight to bring in the saddle-band; and it gave a sense of quiet satisfaction to manly pride later to crowd around the fire where the cowboys were stamping and beating their numbed hands together and know that you had borne yourself as well as they. After a day of bronco-busting in the corral, or of riding hour after hour, head on into the driven snow-dust, there was a sense of real achievement when night fell, and a consciousness of strength. The cabin was small, but it was storm-proof and homelike, and the men with whom Roosevelt shared it were

brave. and true and full of humor and good yarns.
They played checkers and chess and " casino " and
" Old Sledge " through the long evenings, and read
everything in type that came under their hands.
Roosevelt was not the only one, it seemed, who
enjoyed solid literature.

Did I tell you about my cowboys reading and in
large part comprehending, your " Studies in Literature " ? [Roosevelt wrote to Lodge]. My foreman
handed the book back to me to-day, after reading the
" Puritan Pepys," remarking meditatively, and with,
certainly, very great justice, that early Puritanism
" must have been darned rough on the kids." He
evidently sympathized keenly with the feelings of the
poor little " examples of original sin."

Roosevelt spent all his time at the Maltese Cross
and went to Medora only for his mail. The quiet
of winter had descended upon the wild little town.
The abattoir was closed for the season, the butchers
(who did their part in enlivening the neighborhood)
had gone East, the squad of carpenters was silent.
There was nothing for anybody to do except to
drink, which the citizens of Medora did to the
satisfaction of even the saloon-keepers.

Roosevelt had planned all the autumn to go on
a hunting trip with Merrifield after mountain sheep,
but his departure had been delayed by Sylvane's
return with the horses, and the need for all hands
in the " outfit " in the arduous undertaking of preparing their free spirits for the obligations of civilization. It was well toward the middle of December

before they were able to make a start. Roosevelt sent George Myers ahead with the buckboard and himself followed on horseback with Merrifield. It was a savage piece of country through which their course took them.

There were tracts of varying size [Roosevelt wrote later describing that trip], each covered with a tangled mass of chains and peaks, the buttes in places reaching a height that would in the East entitle them to be called mountains. Every such tract was riven in all directions by deep chasms and narrow ravines, whose sides sometimes rolled off in gentle slopes, but far more often rose as sheer cliffs, with narrow ledges along their fronts. A sparse growth of grass covered certain portions of these lands, and on some of the steep hillsides, or in the canyons, were scanty groves of coniferous evergreens, so stunted by the thin soil and bleak weather that many of them were bushes rather than trees. Most of the peaks and ridges, and many of the valleys, were entirely bare of vegetation, and these had been cut by wind and water into the strangest and most fantastic shapes. Indeed, it is difficult, in looking at such formations, to get rid of the feeling that their curiously twisted and contorted forms are due to some vast volcanic upheavals or other subterranean forces; yet they are merely caused by the action of the various weathering forces of the dry climate on the different strata of sandstones, clays, and marls. Isolated columns shoot up into the air, bearing on their summits flat rocks like tables; square buttes tower high above surrounding depressions, which are so cut up by twisting gullies and low ridges as to be almost impassable; shelving masses of sandstone jut out over the sides of the cliffs; some of the ridges, with perfectly perpendicular sides, are so worn away that they stand up like gigantic knife-blades; and gulches, wash-outs, and canyons dig out the sides of each butte, while between them are thrust out long spurs, with sharp, ragged tops.

They hunted through the broken country on foot. Up the slippery, ice-covered buttes they climbed, working their way across the faces of the cliffs or cautiously groping along narrow ledges, peering long and carefully over every crest. But they found no sheep. The cold was intense and they were glad when, at sunset, they reached the cabin, which was to be their headquarters. George Myers had already arrived.

It was a bitter night, and through the chinks of the crazy old hut it invaded their shelter, defying any fire which they could build.

By the time the first streak of dawn had dimmed the brilliancy of the stars, the hunters were under way. Their horses had proved a bother the day before, and they were afoot, striding briskly through the bitter cold to where the great bulk of Middle Butte loomed against the sunrise. They hunted carefully through the outlying foothills and toiled laboriously up the steep sides to the level top. It was a difficult piece of mountaineering, for the edges of the cliffs had become round and slippery with the ice, and it was no easy task to move up and along them, clutching the gun in one hand and grasping each little projection with the other. That day again they found no sheep.

Hour by hour the cold grew more intense. All signs indicated a blizzard.

The air was thick and hazy as Roosevelt and Merrifield early next morning reached the distant hills where they intended that day to make their hunt. Off in the northwest a towering mass of grayish-white clouds hung, threatening trouble. The region was, if anything, even wilder and more difficult than the country they had hunted through on the two previous days. The ice made the footing perilous, and in the cold thin air every quick burst they made up a steep hill caused them to pant for breath. But they were not unrewarded. Crawling cautiously over a sharp ledge they came suddenly upon two mountain rams not a hundred yards away. Roosevelt dropped on his knee, raising his rifle. At the report, the largest of the rams staggered and pitched forward, but recovered himself and disappeared over another ridge. The hunters jumped and slid down into a ravine, clambering up the opposite side as fast as their lungs and the slippery ice would let them. They had not far to go. Two hundred yards beyond the ridge they found their quarry, dead. They took the head for a trophy.

It was still early in the day, and Roosevelt and Merrifield made up their minds to push for home. The lowering sky was already overcast by a mass of leaden-gray clouds; they had no time to lose. They hurried back to the cabin, packed up their bedding and provisions, and started northward. Roosevelt rode ahead with Merrifield, not sparing the horses; but before they had reached the ranch-house the storm had burst, and a furious blizzard

was blowing in their teeth as they galloped along
the last mile of the river bottom.

George Myers celebrated the successful conclusion of the hunt in his own fashion. In one of his
unaccountable culinary lapses, he baked the beans
that night in rosin. With the first mouthful Roosevelt dropped his knife and fork and made for the
door.

" George," he remarked as he returned to the
table with his eye fixed on the offender, " I can eat
green biscuits and most of your other infernal
concoctions, but I am hanged if I can eat rosined
beans."

He did not eat them, but he did not let the
memory of them die either, to George's deep
chagrin.

I have just returned from a three days' trip in the
Bad Lands after mountain sheep [Roosevelt wrote to
" Bamie " on December 14th], and after tramping over
the most awful country that can be imagined, I finally
shot one ram with a fine head. I have now killed every
kind of plains game.

I have to stay here till after next Friday to attend a
meeting of the Little Missouri Stockmen; on Saturday,
December 20th, I start home and shall be in New York
the evening of December 23d. I have just had fifty-two
horses brought in by Ferris, and Sewall and Dow started
down the river with their share yesterday. The latter
have lost two horses; I am afraid they have been stolen.

The meeting of the stockmen was held in Medora
on the day appointed, and it is notable that it was
Roosevelt who called it to order and who directed

its deliberations. He was one of the youngest of
the dozen stockmen present, and in the ways of
cattle no doubt one of the least experienced. Most
of the men he greeted that day had probably been
discussing the problems he was undertaking to
solve long before he himself had ever heard of the
Bad Lands. It was Roosevelt's distinction that
having observed the problems he determined to
solve them, and having made this determination he
sought a solution in the principles and methods of
democratic government. The ʹstockmen had confidence in him. He was direct, he was fearless; he
was a good talker, sure of his ground, and, in the
language of the Bad Lands, " he didn't take back-
water from any one." He was self-reliant and he
minded his own business; he was honest and he had
no axe to grind. The ranchmen no doubt felt that
in view of these qualities you might forget a man's
youth and forgive his spectacles. They evidently
did both, for, after adopting a resolution that it
was the sense of the meeting " that an Association
of the Stockmen along the Little Missouri and its
tributaries be forthwith formed," they promptly
elected Theodore Roosevelt chairman of it.

Lurid tales have been told of what went on at
that meeting. There is a dramatic story of Joe
Morrill's sudden appearance, backed by a score of
ruffians; of defiance and counter-defiance; of revolvers and " blood on the moonlight "; and of a
corrupt deputy marshal cowering with ashen face
before the awful denunciations of a bespectacled

" tenderfoot "; but unhappily, the authenticity of the story is dubious. The meeting, so far as the cold eye of the historian can discern, was dramatic only in its implications and no more exciting than a sewing-circle. The Marquis de Mores was present; so also was Gregor Lang, his most merciless critic; but whatever drama was inherent in that situation remained beneath the surface. By-laws were adopted, the Marquis was appointed " as a Committee of One to work with the committee appointed by the Eastern Montana Live Stock Association in the endeavor to procure legislation from the Territorial Legislature of Dakota favorable to the interests of the cattlemen "; and the meeting was over. It was all most amiable and commonplace. There was no oratory and no defiance of anybody. What had been accomplished, however, was that, in the absence of organized government, the conservative elements in the county had formed an offensive and defensive league for mutual protection, as the by-laws ran, " against frauds and swindlers, and to prevent the stealing, taking, and driving away of horned cattle, sheep, horses, and other stock from the rightful owners thereof."

It meant the beginning of the end of lawlessness in the Bad Lands.

XIV

I 'll never come North again.
  My home is the sunny South,
Where it's never mo' than forty below
  An' the beans don't freeze in your mouth;
An' the snow ain't like white smoke,
  An' the ground ain't like white iron;
An' the wind don't stray from Baffin's Bay
  To join you on retirin'.

From *Medora Nights*

ROOSEVELT arrived in New York a day or two before Christmas with the trophies of his hunt about him and his hunting costume in his " grip." He settled down at his sister's house, at 422 Madison Avenue, where his little girl Alice was living, and, with his characteristic energy in utilizing every experience to the full, promptly began work on a series of hunting sketches which should combine the thrill of adventure with the precise observation of scientific natural history. It is worth noting that, in order to provide a frontispiece for his work, he solemnly dressed himself up in the buckskin shirt and the rest of the elaborate costume he had described with such obvious delight to his sister; and had himself photographed. There is something hilariously funny in the visible records of that performance. The imitation grass, not quite concealing the rug beneath, the painted background, the theatrical (slightly patched) rocks against which the cowboy leans gazing dreamily across an imaginary prairie, the pose of the hunter with rifle ready and finger on the trigger, grimly facing dangerous game which is not there — all reveal a boyish delight in play-acting. For once his sense of humor was in abeyance, but posterity is the richer for this glimpse of the solemn boy in the heart of a powerful man.

Winter closed over the Bad Lands, bringing Arctic hardships. Even Bill Sewall, who had been born and bred in the Maine woods, declared that he had never known such cold. There was a theory, fostered by the real estate agents, that you did not feel the cold which the thermometer registered; and the Marquis, who never missed an opportunity to " boom " his new town in the newspapers, insisted stoutly not only that he habitually " walked and rode about comfortably without an overcoat "; but also that he " felt the cold much more severely in New York, and in Washington even." Other landowners maintained the same delusion, and it was considered almost treason to speak of the tragedies of the cold. The fact remained, however, that a snowfall, which elsewhere might scarcely make good sleighing, in the Bad Lands became a foe to human life of inconceivable fury. For with it generally came a wind so fierce that the stoutest wayfarer could make no progress against it. The small, dry flakes, driven vertically before it, cut the flesh like a razor, blinding the vision and stifling the breath and shutting out the world with an impenetrable icy curtain. A half-hour after the storm had broken, the traveler, lost in it, might wonder whether there were one foot of snow or five, and whether the greater part of it were on the ground or whirling about him in the air. With the snow came extreme cold that pierced the thickest garments.

The horses, running free on the range, seemed to feel the cold comparatively little, eating the snow for water, and pawing through it to the stem-cured prairie-grass for food. But the cattle suffered intensely, especially the Southern stock which had not yet learnt that they must eat their way through the snow to the sustenance beneath. They stood huddled together at every wind-break, and in the first biting storm of the new year even sought the shelter of the towns, taking possession of the streets. The cows, curiously enough, seemed to bear the hardship better than the bulls. The male, left to his own resources, had a tendency to " give up " and creep into the brush and die, while the females, reduced to skin and bones, struggled on, gnawing at the frozen stumps of sagebrush, battling to the last.

Western newspapers, " booming " the cattle business, insisted that every blizzard was followed by a warm wind known as a " chinook " which brought a prompt return of comfort and sleekness to the most unhappy steer; but wise men knew better. For the cattle, seeking a livelihood on the snowy, wind-swept wastes, the winter was one long-protracted misery.

It was in fact not an unalloyed delight for human beings, especially for those whose business it was to guard the cattle. The hardest and the bitterest work was what was called "line riding." The ranchmen cared little if their cattle grazed westward toward the Yellowstone; it was a different matter, however, if they drifted east and southeast to the granger country and the Sioux Reservation, where there were flat, bare plains which offered neither food nor shelter, and where thieves were many and difficult to apprehend. Along the line where the broken ground of the Bad Lands met the prairie east of the Little Missouri, the ranchmen, therefore, established a series of camps, from each of which two cowboys, starting in opposite directions, patrolled the invisible line halfway to the adjoining camps.

Bill Sewall gazed out over the bleak country with a homesick and apprehensive heart.

As for our coming back [he wrote his brother in January], you need not worry about that. As soon as I serve out my time and my sentence expires I shall return. Am having a good time and enjoy myself, should anywhere if I knew I could not do any better and was obliged to, but this is just about like being transported to Siberia, just about as cold, barren and desolate and most as far out of the way. It was hotter here last summer than it ever was at home and it has been colder here this winter than it ever was at home, 50 and 65 below all one week. Don't see how the cattle live at all and there is lots of them dieing. You can find them all around where they lay nights in the bushes. The poor ones will all go, I guess. They say they will die worse in the spring. The fat strong ones will get through, I guess. Don't know that any of our hundred have died yet, but I don't believe this is a good country to raise cattle in.

Am afraid Theodore will not make so much as he has been led to think he would. There are lots of bleeders here, but we mean to fend them off from him as well as we can.

Roosevelt spent the coldest months in New York, working steadily on his new book which was to be called " Hunting Trips of a Ranchman." On the 8th of March he wrote Lodge, " I have just sent my last roll of manuscript to the printers "; adding, " in a fortnight I shall go out West." But he postponed his departure, held possibly by the lure of the hunting-field; for on the 29th he rode with the Meadowbrook hounds and was " in at the death." It was presumably in the first days of April that he arrived at Medora. If tradition may be trusted, he came in all the glory of what were known as " store clothes." The Pittsburgh *Despatch*, which sent out a reporter to the train to interview him as he passed through that city, westward-bound, refers to " the high expanse of white linen which enclosed his neck to the ears," which sounds like a slight exaggeration. Tradition does insist, however, that he wore a derby hat when he arrived, which was considered highly venturesome. Derby hats as a rule were knocked off on sight and then bombarded with six-shooters beyond recognition. Roosevelt informed his fellow citizens early in his career as a cowpuncher that he intended to wear any hat he pleased. Evidently it was deemed expedient to suspend the rule in his case, for he was not molested.

After a brief sojourn at the Maltese Cross, Roosevelt made his way north to Elkhorn Ranch. The house was nearing completion. It was a one-story log structure, with a covered porch on the side facing the river; a spacious house of many rooms divided by a corridor running straight through from north to south. Roosevelt's bedroom, on the southeast corner, adjoined a large room containing a fireplace, which was to be Roosevelt's study by day and the general living-room by night. The fireplace, which had been built by an itinerant Swedish mason whom Sewall looked upon with disapproval as a dollar-chaser, had been designed under the influence of a Dakota winter and was enormous. Will Dow, who was somewhat of a blacksmith, had made a pair of andirons out of a steel rail, which he had discovered floating down the river loosely attached to a beam of yellow pine.[1]

The cattle, Roosevelt found, were looking well. " Bill," he said to Sewall, remembering the backwoodsman's pessimism, " you were mistaken about those cows. Cows and calves are all looking fine."

But Sewall was not to be convinced. " You wait until next spring," he answered, " and see how they look."

Roosevelt was himself physically in rather bad shape, suffering from that affliction which has, by common consent, been deemed of all of Job's troubles the one hardest to bear with equanimity.

---

[1] The andirons are still doing service at the ranch of Howard Eaton and his brothers in Wolf, Wyoming.

Douglas Robinson wrote Sewall telling him that Theodore's sisters were worried about him and asking him for news of Roosevelt's health. Roosevelt heard of the request and was indignant, " flaring up," as Sewall described it.

" They had no business to write to you," he exclaimed. " They should have written to me."

" I guess," remarked Sewall quietly, " they knew you wouldn't write about how you were getting on. You'd just say you were all right."

Roosevelt fumed and said no more about it. But the crisp air of the Bad Lands gradually put all questions of his health out of mind. All day long he lived in the open. He was not an enthusiast over the hammer or the axe, and, while Sewall and Dow were completing the house and building the corrals and the stables a hundred yards or more westward, he renewed his acquaintance with the bizarre but fascinating country. The horses which the men from Maine had missed the previous autumn, and which Roosevelt had feared had been stolen, had been reported " running wild " forty or fifty miles to the west. Sewall and Dow had made one or two trips after them without success, for the animals had come to enjoy their liberty and proved elusive. Roosevelt determined to find them and bring them back. He went on three solitary expeditions, but they proved barren of result. Incidentally, however, they furnished him experiences which were worth many horses.

On one of these expeditions night overtook him

not far from Mingusville. That hot little community, under the inspiration of a Frenchman named Pierre Wibaux, was rapidly becoming an important cattle center. As a shipping point it had, by the close of 1884, already attained notable proportions on the freight records of the Northern Pacific. Medora, in all its glory, could not compete with it, for the cattle trails through the Bad Lands were difficult, and space was lacking on the small bottoms near the railroad to hold herds of any size preparatory to shipping. About Mingusville all creation stretched undulating to the hazy horizon. The great southern cattle companies which had recently established themselves on the northern range, Simpson's " Hash-Knife " brand, Towers and Gudgell's O. X. Ranch, and the Berry, Boyce Company's " Three-Seven outfit," all drove their cattle along the Beaver to Mingusville, and even Merrifield and Sylvane preferred shipping their stock from there to driving it to the more accessible, but also more congested, yards at Medora.

Civilization had not kept pace with commerce in the development of the prairie " town." It was a lurid little place. Medora, in comparison to it, might have appeared almost sober and New-Englandish. It had no " steady " residents save a half-dozen railroad employees, the landlord of the terrible hotel south of the tracks, where Roosevelt had had his encounter with the drunken bully, and a certain Mrs. Nolan and her daughters, who kept an eminently respectable boarding-house on the opposite side of the railroad; but its " floating population " was large. Every herd driven into the shipping-yards from one of the great ranches in the upper Little Missouri country brought with it a dozen or more parched cowboys hungering and thirsting for excitement as no saint ever hungered and thirsted for righteousness; and celebrations had a way of lasting for days. The men were Texans, most of them, extraordinary riders, born to the saddle, but reckless, given to heavy drinking, and utterly wild and irresponsible when drunk. It was their particular delight to make life hideous for the station agent and the telegraph operator. For some weeks Mingusville, it was said, had a new telegraph operator every night. About ten o'clock the cowboys, celebrating at the " hotel," would drift over to the board shack which was the railroad station, and " shoot it full of holes." They had no particular reason for doing this; they had no grudge against either the railroad or the particular operator who happened to be in charge. They were children, and it was fun to hear the bullets pop, and excruciating fun to see the operator run out of the shack with a yell and go scampering off into the darkness. One operator entered into negotiations with the enemy. Recognizing their perfect right to shoot up the station if they wanted to, he merely stipulated that they allow him to send off the night's dispatches before they began. This request seemed to the cowboys altogether reasonable. They waited until the operator said that his work was done. Then, as

he faded away in the darkness, the night's bombardment began.

Into this tempestuous little " town," Roosevelt
rode one day as night was falling. No doubt because Mrs. Nolan's beds were filled, he was forced
to take a room at the nefarious hotel where he had
chastised the bully a year previous. Possibly to
prevent the recurrence of that experience, he retired
early to the small room with one bed which had
been assigned him and sat until late reading the
book he had brought along in his saddle-pocket.

The house was quiet and every one was asleep,
when a cowboy arrived from God knows whence,
yelling and shooting as he came galloping through
the darkness. He was evidently very drunk. He
thumped loudly on the door, and after some delay
the host opened it. The stranger showed no appreciation; on the contrary, he seized the hotel-
keeper, half in play, it seemed, and half in enmity,
jammed the mouth of his six-shooter against his
stomach and began to dance about the room with
him.

In the room above, Roosevelt heard the host's
agonized appeals. " Jim, don't! Don't, Jim! It'll
go off! Jim, it'll go off! "

Jim's response was not reassuring. " Yes, damn
you, it'll go off! I'll learn you! Who in hell cares if
it does go off! Oh, I'll learn you! "

But the gun, after all, did not go off. The cowboy
subsided, then burst into vociferous demands for a
bed. A minute later Roosevelt heard steps in the

hall, followed by a knock at his door. Roosevelt opened it.

" I'm sorry," said the host, " but there's a man I'll have to put in with you for the night."

" You're not as sorry as I am," Roosevelt answered coolly, " and I'm not going to have him come in here."

The host was full of apologies. " He's drunk and he's on the shoot," he said unhappily, " and he's got to come in."

This appeal was not of a character to weaken Roosevelt's resolution. " I'm going to lock my door," he remarked firmly, " and put out my light. And I'll shoot anybody who tries to break in."

The host departed. Roosevelt never knew where the unwelcome guest was lodged that night; but he himself was left undisturbed.

On another occasion that spring, when Roosevelt was out on the prairie hunting the lost horses, he was overtaken by darkness. Mingusville was the only place within thirty miles or more that offered a chance of a night's lodging, and he again rode there, knocking at the door of Mrs. Nolan's boarding-house late in the evening. Mrs. Nolan, who greeted him, was a tough, wiry Irishwoman of the type of Mrs. Maddox, with a fighting jaw and a look in her eye that had been known to be as potent as a " six-shooter " in clearing a room of undesirable occupants. She disciplined her husband (who evidently needed it) and brought up her daughters with a calm good sense that won them and her the respect of the roughest of the cowpunchers who came under her roof.

Roosevelt, having stabled his horse in an empty out-building, asked for a bed. Mrs. Nolan answered that he could have the last one that was left, since there was only one other man in it.

He accepted the dubious privilege and was shown to a room containing two double beds. One contained two men fast asleep, the other only one man, also asleep. He recognized his bedfellow. It was " Three-Seven " Bill Jones, an excellent cowman belonging to the " Three-Seven outfit " who had recently acquired fame by playfully holding up the Overland Express in order to make the conductor dance. He put his trousers, boots, shaps, and gun down beside the bed, and turned in.

He was awakened an hour or two later by a crash as the door was rudely flung open. A lantern was flashed in his face, and, as he came to full consciousness, he found himself, in the light of a dingy lantern, staring into the mouth of a " six-shooter."

Another man said to the lantern-bearer, " It ain't him." The next moment his bedfellow was " covered " with two " guns." " Now, Bill," said a gruff voice, " don't make a fuss, but come along quiet."

" All right, don't sweat yourself," responded Bill. " I'm not thinking of making a fuss."

" That's right," was the answer, " we're your friends. We don't want to hurt you; we just want you to come along. You know why."

Bill pulled on his trousers and boots and walked out with them.

All the while there had been no sound from the other bed. Now a match was scratched and a candle was lit, and one of the men looked round the room.

" I wonder why they took Bill," Roosevelt remarked.

There was no answer, and Roosevelt, not knowing that there was what he later termed an " alkali etiquette in such matters," repeated the question. " I wonder why they took Bill."

" Well," said the man with the candle, dryly, " I reckon they wanted him," and blew out the candle. That night there was no more conversation; but Roosevelt's education had again been extended.

XV

When did we long for the sheltered gloom
   Of the older game with its cautious odds?
Gloried we always in sun and room,
   Spending our strength like the younger gods.
By the wild, sweet ardor that ran in us,
By the pain that tested the man in us,
   By the shadowy springs and the glaring sand,
   You were our true-love, young, young land.
                                    BADGER CLARK

SPRING came to the Bad Lands in fits and numerous
false starts, first the "chinook," uncovering the
butte-tops between dawn and dusk, then the rushing of many waters, the flooding of low bottom-
lands, the agony of a world of gumbo, and, after
a dozen boreal setbacks, the awakening of green
things and the return of a temperature fit for
human beings to live in. Snow buntings came in
March, flocking familiarly round the cow-shed at
the Maltese Cross, now chittering on the ridge-pole,
now hovering in the air with quivering wings,
warbling their loud, merry song. Before the snow
was off the ground, the grouse cocks could be heard
uttering their hollow booming. At the break of
morning, their deep, resonant calls came from far
and near through the clear air like the vibrant
sound of some wind instrument. Now and again,
at dawn or in the early evening, Roosevelt would
stop and listen for many minutes to the weird,
strange music, or steal upon the cocks where they
were gathered holding their dancing rings, and

watch them posturing and strutting about as they paced through their minuet.

The opening of the ground — and it was occasionally not unlike the opening of a trap-door — brought work in plenty to Roosevelt and his friends at the Maltese Cross. The glades about the water-holes where the cattle congregated became bogs that seemed to have no bottom. Cattle sank in them and perished unless a saving rope was thrown in time about their horns and a gasping pony pulled them clear. The ponies themselves became mired and had to be rescued. It was a period of wallowing for everything on four feet or on two. The mud stuck like plaster.[1]

Travel of every sort was hazardous during early spring, for no one ever knew when the ground would open and engulf him. Ten thousand wash-outs, a dozen feet deep or thirty, ran " bank-high " with swirling, merciless waters, and the Little Missouri, which was a shallow trickle in August, was a torrent in April. There were no bridges. If you wanted to get to the other side, you swam your horse across, hoping for the best.

At Medora it was customary, when the Little Missouri was high, to ride to the western side on the narrow footpath between the tracks on the trestle; and after the Marquis built a dam nearby for the purpose of securing ice of the necessary

---

[1] " I never was bothered by gumbo in the Bad Lands. There wasn't a sufficient proportion of clay in the soil. But out on the prairie, oh, my martyred Aunt Jane's black and white striped cat!" — *A. T. Packard.*

thickness for use in his refrigerating plant, a venturesome spirit now and then guided his horse across
its slippery surface. It happened one day early in
April that Fisher was at the river's edge, with a
number of men, collecting certain tools and lumber
which had been used in the cutting and hauling of
the ice, when Roosevelt, riding Manitou, drew up,
with the evident intention of making his way over
the river on the dam. The dam, however, had
disappeared. The ice had broken up, far up the
river, and large cakes were floating past, accumulating at the bend below the town and raising the
water level well above the top of the Marquis's
dam. The river was what Joe Ferris had a way of
calling " swimmin' deep for a giraffe."

" Where does the dam start? " asked Roosevelt.

" You surely won't try to cross on the dam,"
exclaimed Fisher, " when you can go and cross on
the trestle the way the others do? "

" If Manitou gets his feet on that dam," Roosevelt replied, " he'll keep them there and we can
make it finely."

" Well, it's more than likely," said Fisher, " that
there's not much of the dam left."

" It doesn't matter, anyway. Manitou's a good
swimmer and we're going across."

Fisher, with grave misgivings, indicated where
the dam began. Roosevelt turned his horse into
the river; Manitou did not hesitate.

Fisher shouted, hoping to attract the attention
of some cowboy on the farther bank who might

stand ready with a rope to rescue the venturesome rider. There was no response.

On the steps of the store, however, which he had inherited from the unstable Johnny Nelson, Joe Ferris was watching the amazing performance. He saw a rider coming from the direction of the Maltese Cross, and it seemed to him that the rider looked like Roosevelt. Anxiously he watched him pick his way out on the submerged dam.

Manitou, meanwhile, was living up to his reputation. Fearlessly, yet with infinite caution, he kept his course along the unseen path. Suddenly the watchers on the east bank and the west saw horse and rider disappear, swallowed up by the brown waters. An instant later they came in sight again. Roosevelt flung himself from his horse " on the down-stream side," and with one hand on the horn of the saddle fended off the larger blocks of ice from before his faithful horse.

Fisher said to himself that if Manitou drifted even a little with the stream, Roosevelt would never get ashore. The next landing was a mile down the river, and that might be blocked by the ice.

The horse struck bottom at the extreme lower edge of the ford and struggled up the bank. Roosevelt had not even lost his glasses. He laughed and waved his hand to Fisher, mounted and rode to Joe's store. Having just risked his life in the wildest sort of adventure, it was entirely characteristic of him that he should exercise the caution of putting on a pair of dry socks.

Joe received him with mingled devotion and amazement. "Landsake, man!" he cried, "were n't you afraid?"

" I was riding Manitou," Roosevelt responded quietly. " Just," exclaimed Joe later, " as though Manitou was a steam engine." He bought a new pair of socks, put them on, and proceeded on his journey.

Fisher saw him shortly after and accused him of being reckless.

" I suppose it might be considered reckless," Roosevelt admitted. " But it was lots of fun."

Roosevelt spent his time alternately at the two ranches, writing somewhat and correcting the proofs of his new book, but spending most of his time in the saddle. The headquarters of his cattle business was at the Maltese Cross where Sylvane Ferris and Merrifield were in command. Elkhorn was, for the time being, merely a refuge and a hunting-lodge where Sewall and Dow " ran " a few hundred cattle under the general direction of the more experienced men of the other " outfit."

At the Maltese Cross there were now a half-dozen hands, Sylvane and " our friend with the beaver-slide," as Merrifield, who was bald, was known; George Myers, warm-hearted and honest as the day; Jack Reuter, known as " Wannigan," with his stupendous memory and his Teutonic appetite; and at intervals " old man " Thompson who was a teamster, and a huge being named Hank

Bennett. Roosevelt liked them all immensely. They possessed to an extraordinary degree the qualities of manhood which he deemed fundamental, — courage, integrity, hardiness, self-reliance,— combining with those qualities a warmth, a humor, and a humanness that opened his understanding to many things. He had come in contact before with men whose opportunities in life had been less than his, and who in the eyes of the world belonged to that great mass of " common people " of whom Lincoln said that " the Lord surely loved them since he made so many of them." But he had never lived with them, day in, day out, slept with them, eaten out of the same dish with them. The men of the cattle country, he found, as daily companions, wore well.

They called him " Mr. Roosevelt, " not " Theodore" nor "Teddy." For, though he was comrade and friend to all, he was also the "boss," and they showed him the respect his position and his instinctive leadership merited. More than once a man who attempted to be unduly familiar with Roosevelt found himself swiftly and effectively squelched. He himself entered with enthusiasm into the work of administration. He regarded the ranch as a most promising business venture, and felt assured that, with ordinary luck, he should make his livelihood from it. On every side he received support for this assurance. The oldest cattleman as well as the youngest joined in the chorus that there never had been such a country for turning cattle into dollars.

In the Territorial Governor's Report for 1885, Packard is quoted, waxing lyric about it:

Bunch and buffalo-grass cover almost every inch of the ground. The raw sides of buttes are the only places where splendid grazing cannot be found. On many of the buttes, however, the grass grows clear to the summit, the slopes being the favorite pasture-lands of the cattle. Generally no hay need be cut, as the grass cures standing, and keeps the cattle in as good condition all winter as if they were stall-fed. The only reason for putting up hay is to avoid a scarcity of feed in case of heavy snow. This very seldom happens, however, as very little snow falls in the Bad Lands. A curious fact with cattle is that the ones that have been here a year or two, and know how to rustle, will turn away from a stack of hay, paw away the snow from the grass, and feed on that exclusively. Even in the dead of winter a meadow has a very perceptible tinge of green.

A realist might have remarked that very little snow fell in the Bad Lands mainly because the wind would not let it. The *Cowboy* editor's exultant optimism has an aspect of terrible irony in the light of the tragedy that was even then building itself out of the over-confidence of a hundred enthusiasts.

Bill Sewall and Will Dow alone remained skeptical.

Perhaps we are wrong [Sewall wrote his brother], but we think it is too cold and barren for a good cattle country. Nobody has made anything at it yet. *All expect to.* Guess it's very much like going into the woods in fall. All are happy, *but the drive is not in yet.* When it does get in, am afraid there will be a shortness somewhere. The men that furnish the money are not many of them here themselves and the fellows that run the business and are supposed to know, all look for a very prosperous future, consider the troubles and discouragements, losses, etc., *temporary*. They are like us — *getting good and sure pay.*

Roosevelt recognized the possibility of great losses; but he would have been less than human if in that youthful atmosphere of gorgeous expectation he had not seen the possibilities of failure less vividly than the possibilities of success. Sylvane and Merrifield were confident that they were about to make their everlasting fortunes; George Myers invested every cent of his savings in cattle, " throwing them in," as the phrase went, with the herd of the Maltese Cross. In their first year the Maltese Cross " outfit " had branded well over a hundred calves; the losses, in what had been a severe winter, had been slight. It was a season of bright hopes. Late in April, Roosevelt sent Merrifield to Minnesota with Sewall and Dow and a check for twelve thousand five hundred dollars to purchase as many more head of stock as the money would buy.

Roosevelt, meanwhile, was proving himself as capable as a ranchman as he was courageous as an investor. The men who worked with him noted with satisfaction that he learned quickly and worked hard; that he was naturally progressive; that he cared little for money, and yet was thrifty; that, although conferring in all matters affecting the stock with Sylvane and Merrifield, and deferring to their experience even at times against his own judgment, he was very much the leader. He was never " bossy," they noted, but he was insistent on discipline, on regularity of habits, on prompt obedience, on absolute integrity.

He was riding over the range one day with one of his ablest cowpunchers, when they came upon a " maverick," a two-year-old steer, which had never been branded. They lassoed him promptly and built a fire to heat the branding-irons.

It was the rule of the cattlemen that a " maverick " belonged to the ranchman on whose range it was found. This particular steer, therefore, belonged, not to Roosevelt, but to Gregor Lang, who " claimed " the land over which Roosevelt and his cowboy were riding. The Texan started to apply the red-hot iron.

" It is Lang's brand — a thistle," said Roosevelt.

"That's all right, boss," answered the cowboy. " I know my business."

"Hold on!" Roosevelt exclaimed an instant later, "you are putting on my brand."

"That's all right. I always put on the boss's brand."

" Drop that iron," said Roosevelt quietly, " and go to the ranch and get your time. I don't need you any longer."

The cowpuncher was amazed. " Say, what have I done? Didn't I put on your brand?"

" A man who will steal *for* me will steal *from* me. You're fired."

The man rode away. A day or so later the story was all over the Bad Lands.

Roosevelt was scarcely more tolerant of ineffectiveness than he was of dishonesty. When a man was sent to do a piece of work, he was expected to do it promptly and thoroughly. He brooked no slack work and he had no ear for what were known as " hard-luck stories." He gave his orders, knowing why he gave them; and expected results. If, on the other hand, a man " did his turn " without complaint or default, Roosevelt showed himself eager and prompt to reward him.

His companions saw these things, and other things. They saw that " the boss " was quick-tempered and impatient of restraint; but they saw also that in times of stress the hot-headed boy seemed instantly to grow into a cautious and level-headed man, dependable in hardship and cool in the face of danger. He was, as one of them put it, " courageous without recklessness, firm without being stubborn, resolute without being obstinate. There was no element of the spectacular in his make-up, but an honest naturalness that won him friends instantly."

" Roosevelt out in Dakota was full of life and spirit, always pleasant," said Bill Sewall in after years. " He was hot-tempered and quick, but he kept his temper in good control. As a rule, when he had anything to say, he'd spit it out. His temper would show itself in the first flash in some exclamation. In connection with Roosevelt I always think of that verse in the Bible, ' He that ruleth his spirit is greater than he that taketh a city.' "

"He struck me like a sort of rough-an'-ready, all-around frontiersman," said "Dutch Wannigan." "Wasn't a bit stuck up — just the same as one of the rest of us."

Joe Ferris, who frankly adored Roosevelt, declared to a crowd at his store one day, "I wouldn't be surprised if Roosevelt would be President."

His hearers scoffed at him. "That fool Joe Ferris," remarked one of them at his own ranch that night, "says that Roosevelt will be President some day."

But Joe held his ground.[1]

The neighbors up and down the river were warm-hearted and friendly. Mrs. Roberts had decided that she wanted a home of her own, and had persuaded her husband to build her a cabin some three miles north of the Maltese Cross, where a long green slope met a huge semi-circle of gray buttes. The cabin was primitive, being built of logs stuck, stockade-fashion, in the ground, and the roof was only dirt until Mrs. Roberts planted sunflowers there and made it a garden; but for Mrs. Roberts, with her flock of babies, it was "home," and for many a cowboy, passing the time of day with the genial Irishwoman, it was the nearest approach to "home" that he knew from one year's end to another.

[1] Joe Ferris was made aware of this scornful reference to his judgment through a cowboy, Carl Hollenberg, who overheard it, and sixteen years later came into Joe's store one September day shouting, "That fool, Joe Ferris, says that Roosevelt will be President some day!" The point was that Roosevelt had that week succeeded McKinley in the White House.

Shortly after Mrs. Roberts had moved to her new house, Roosevelt and Merrifield paid her a call. Mrs. Roberts, who had the only milch cow in the Bad Lands, had been churning, and offered Roosevelt a glass of buttermilk. He drank it with an appreciation worthy of a rare occasion. But as he rode off again, he turned to Merrifield with his teeth set.

"Heavens, Merrifield!" he exclaimed, "don't you ever do that again!"

Merrifield was amazed. "Do what?"

"Put me in a position where I have to drink buttermilk. I loathe the stuff!"

"But why did you drink it?"

"She brought it out!" he exclaimed, "And it would have hurt her feelings if I hadn't. But look out! I don't want to have to do it again!"

Mrs. Roberts spared him thenceforward, and there was nothing, therefore, to spoil for Roosevelt the merriment of the Irishwoman's talk and the stimulus of her determination and courage. There were frequent occasions consequently when "the boys from the Maltese Cross" foregathered in the Roberts cabin, and other occasions, notably Sundays (when Sylvane and Merrifield and George Myers had picked up partners in Medora) when they all called for "Lady Roberts" as chaperon and rode up the valley together. They used to take peculiar delight in descending upon Mrs. Cummins and making her miserable.

It was not difficult to make that poor lady unhappy. She had a fixed notion of what life should be for people who were " nice " and " refined," and her days were a succession of regrets at the shortcomings of her neighbors. She was in many ways an admirable woman, but she seemed incapable of extending the conception of gentility which a little Pennsylvania town had given her, and she never caught a gleam of the real meaning of the life of which she was a part. She wanted everything in the Bad Lands exactly as she had had it at home. " Well," as Mrs. Roberts subsequently remarked, " she had one time of it, I'm telling you, in those old rough days."

Mrs. Cummins was not the only neighbor who furnished amusement during those spring days of 1885 to the boys at the Maltese Cross. The Eatons' " dude ranch " had developed in a totally unexpected direction. From being a headquarters for Easterners who wanted to hunt in a wild country, it had become a kind of refuge to which wealthy and distracted parents sent such of their offspring as were over-addicted to strong drink. Why any parent should send a son to the Bad Lands with the idea of putting him out of reach of temptation is beyond comprehension. The Eatons did their part nobly and withheld intoxicating drinks from their guests, but Bill Williams and the dozen or more other saloon-keepers in Medora were under no compulsion to follow their example. The " dudes " regularly came " back from town " with all they could carry without and within; and the cowboys

round about swore solemnly that you couldn't put
your hand in the crotch of any tree within a hundred
yards of the Eatons' ranch-house without coming
upon a bottle concealed by a dude being cured of
" the drink."

The neighbors who were most remote from Roosevelt in point of space continued to be closest in
point of intimacy. The Langs were now well established and Roosevelt missed no opportunity to
visit with them for an hour or a day, thinking
nothing apparently of the eighty-mile ride there
and back in comparison with the prospect of an
evening in good company. The Langs were, in
fact, excellent company. They knew books and
they knew also the graces of cultivated society.
To visit with them was to live for an hour or two
in the quietude of an Old World home, with all
the Old World's refinements and the added tang
of bizarre surroundings; and even to one who
was exuberantly glad to be a cowboy, this had
its moments of comfort after weeks of the rough
frontier existence. Cultivated Englishmen were
constantly appearing at the Langs', sent over by
their fathers, for reasons sometimes mysterious, to
stay for a week or a year. Some of them proved
very bad cowboys, but all of them were delightful
conversationalists. Their efforts to enter into the
life of the Bad Lands were not always successful,
and Hell-Roaring Bill Jones on one notable occasion, when the son of a Scotch baronet undertook
to criticize him for misconduct, expressed his

opinion of the scions of British aristocracy that drifted into Medora, in terms that hovered and poised and struck like birds of prey. Lincoln Lang, who was present, described Bill Jones's discourse as " outside the pale of the worst I have ever heard uttered by human mouth," which meant something in that particular place. But Bill Jones was an Irishman, and he was not naturally tolerant of idiosyncrasies of speech and manner. Roosevelt, on the whole, liked the " younger sons," and they in turn regarded him with a kind of awe. He was of their own class, and yet there was something in him which stretched beyond the barriers which confined them, into regions where they were lost and bewildered, but he was completely at home.

They all had delightful evenings together at Yule, with charades and punning contests, and music on the piano which Lincoln Lang had brought out through the gumbo against all the protests of nature. Mrs. Lang was an admirable cook and a liberal and hospitable hostess, which was an added reason for riding eighty miles.

To the Scotch family, exiled far up the Little Missouri, Roosevelt's visits were notable events. " We enjoyed having him," said Lincoln Lang long afterward, " more than anything else in the world."

To Gregor Lang, Roosevelt's visits brought an opportunity for an argument with an opponent worthy of his steel. The Scotchman's alert intelligence pined sometimes, in those intellectually desolate wastes, for exercise in the keen give-and-take of debate. The average cowboy was not noted for his conversational powers, and Gregor Lang clutched avidly at every possibility of talk. It was said of him that he loved a good argument so much that it did not always make much difference to him which side of the argument he took. On one occasion he was spending the night at the Eatons', when the father of the four " Eaton boys " was visiting his sons. " Old man " Eaton was a Republican; Lang was a Democrat. They began arguing at supper, and they argued all night long. To Eaton, his Republicanism was a religion (as it was to many in those middle eighties), and he wrestled with the error in Lang's soul as a saint wrestles with a devil. As the day dawned, Gregor Lang gave an exclamation of satisfaction. " It's been a fine talk we've had, Mistur-r Eaton," he cried. " Now suppose you tak' my side and I tak' yours? " What Eaton said thereupon has not been recorded; but Gregor Lang went home happy.

With all his love for forensics as such, Lang had solid convictions. They were a Democrat's, and in consequence many of them were not Roosevelt's. Roosevelt attacked them with energy and Lang defended them with skill. Roosevelt, who loved rocking-chairs, had a way of rocking all over the room in his excitement. The debates were long, but always friendly; and neither party ever admitted defeat. The best that Gregor Lang would say was, " Well, Mr. Roosevelt, when you ar-re Pr-resident

of the United States, you may r-run the gover-rn-
ment the way you mind to." He did admit in the
bosom of his family, however, that Roosevelt made
" the best ar-rgument for the other side " he had
ever heard.

Lang's love of an argument, which to unfriendly
ears might have sounded like contentiousness, did
not serve to make the excellent Scotchman popular
with his neighbors. He had a habit, moreover,
of saying exactly what he thought, regardless of
whom he might hit. He was not politic at all. He
had, in fact, come to America and to Dakota too
late in life altogether to adapt a mind, steeped in
the manners and customs of the Old World, to the
new conditions of a country in almost every way
alien to his own. He was dogmatic in his theories
of popular government and a little stubborn in
his conviction that there was nothing which the
uneducated range-rider of the Bad Lands could teach
a thinking man like him. But his courage was fine.
Against the protests of his Southern neighbors, he
insisted on treating a negro cowboy in his outfit as
on complete equality with his white employees; and
bore the storm of criticism with equanimity. Such
a spirit was bound to appeal to Roosevelt.

At the Maltese Cross there was a steady stream
of callers. One of them, a hawk-eyed, hawk-nosed
cowpuncher named " Nitch " Kendley, who was
one of the first settlers in the region, arrived one
day when Roosevelt was alone.

" Come on in," said Roosevelt, " and we'll have

some dinner. I can't bake biscuits, but I can cook meat. If you can make the biscuits, go ahead, and I will see what I can do for the rest of the dinner."

So " Nitch " made the biscuits and put them in the oven, and Roosevelt cut what was left of a saddle of venison and put it in a pan to fry. Then the two cooks went outdoors, for the cabin was small, and the weather was hot.

Roosevelt began to talk, whereupon " Nitch," who had ideas of his own, began to talk also with a fluency which was not customary, for he was naturally a taciturn man. They both forgot the dinner. " Nitch " never knew how long they talked.

They were brought back to the world of facts by a smell of burning. The cabin was filled with smoke, and " you could not," as " Nitch " subsequently remarked, " have told your wife from your mother-in-law three feet away." On investigation it proved that " Nitch's " biscuits and Roosevelt's meat were burnt to cinders.

Merrifield and Sylvane were out after deer, and Roosevelt and his companion waited all afternoon in vain for the two men to return. At last, toward evening, Roosevelt made some coffee, which, as " Nitch " remarked, " took the rough spots off the biscuits."

" If we'd talked less," reflected " Nitch," " we'd have had more dinner."

Roosevelt laughed. He did not seem to mind the loss of a meal. " Nitch " was quite positive that he was well repaid. They went on talking as before.

XVI

He went so high above the earth,
  Lights from Jerusalem shone.
Right thar we parted company,
  And he came down alone.
I hit terra firma,
  The buckskin's heels struck free,
And brought a bunch of stars along
  To dance in front of me.

Cowboy song

EARLY in May, Roosevelt's men returned from Fergus Falls with a thousand head of cattle. In a letter to his brother, Sewall describes what he terms the "Cattle Torture," in which he had been engaged. "It will perhaps interest you," he adds. "It certainly must have been interesting to the cattle."

The cattle were driven in from the country [Sewall writes] and put in a yard. This was divided in the middle by a fence and on one side was a narrow lane where you could drive six or eight Cattle at a time. This narrowed so when you got to the fence in the middle only one could pass by the post, and beyond the post there was a strong gate which swang off from the side fence at the top so to leave it wide enough to go through. Well, they would rush them into the shoot and when they came to the gate would let it swing off at the top. The animal would make a rush but it was so narrow at the bottom it would bother his feet and there was a rope went from the top of the gate over his back to a lever on the outside of the yard. While he was trying to get through, the fellow on the lever would catch him with the gate and then the frying began.

They had two good big fires and about four irons in

each and they would put an iron on each side. One is a Triangle about four inches on a side, the other an Elkhorn about six inches long with two prongs. It smelt around there as if Coolage was burning Parkman,[1] or was it Webster? I remember hearing father read about the smell of meat burning when I was a boy, and I kept thinking of that and Indians burning Prisoners at the stake. Well, we burnt them all in less than a day and a half and then hustled them into the cars.

They of course did not get much to eat for two or three days before they started. Then we put from 50 to 57 yearlings in a carr and from 32 to 37 two year olds and started. The poor cattle would lay down, then of course as many as could stand on them would do so. The ones that got down would stay there till they were completely trod under and smothered unless you made them get up. So I would go in and shove and crowd and get them off of the down ones, then I would seize a tail and the man with me would punch from outside with a pole with a brad in it. This would invigorate the annimal as he used the pole with great energy, and with my help they would get up.

I did not dislike the work though it was very warm and the cattle were rather slippery to hold on to after they had been down, but it was lively and exciting climbing from one carr to the other when they were going, especially in the night. We went to see them every time they stopped and some times we did not have time before we started. Then we would have to go from one to the other while they were going, and after we had got through run back over the tops of the cars.

Ours were all alive when we got to Medora. How they ever lived through, I don't see. John Bean would liked to have bought me by the cord, and if he had been around Medora, think I could have sold myself for dressing.

[1] A celebrated murder case in Boston.

Roosevelt met them at Medora and set out with them to drive the cattle north to Elkhorn Ranch. It was customary to drive cattle along the river bottom, but there had been a series of freshets that spring which had turned the Little Missouri into a raging torrent and its bottom into a mass of treacherous quicksands. The river valley would consequently have been dangerous even for mature stock. For the young cattle the dangers of the crossings were too great even for a none too prudent man to hazard. Accordingly Roosevelt decided to drive the animals down along the divide west of Medora between the Little Missouri and the Beaver.

Owing to a variety of causes, the preparations for the trip had been inadequate. He had only five men to help him; Sewall and Dow and Rowe and two others. Of these, only one was a cowpuncher of experience. Roosevelt placed him in charge. It was not long, however, before he discovered that this man, who was a first-rate cowhand, was wholly incapable of acting as head. Cattle and cowpunchers, chuck-wagon and saddle-band, in some fashion which nobody could explain became so snarled up with each other that, after disentangling the situation, he was forced to relegate his expert to the ranks and take command himself.

His course lay, for the most part, through the Bad Lands, which enormously increased the difficulty of driving the cattle. A herd always travels strung out in lines, and a thousand head thus going almost in single file had a way of stretching out an appreciable distance, with the strong, speedy animals in the van and the weak and sluggish ones inevitably in the rear. Roosevelt put two of his men at the head of the column, two more at the back, and himself with another man rode constantly up and down the flanks. In the tangled mass of rugged hills and winding defiles through which the trail led, it was no easy task for six men to keep the cattle from breaking off in different directions or prevent the strong beasts that formed the vanguard from entirely outstripping the laggards. The spare saddle-ponies also made trouble, for several of them were practically unbroken.

Slowly and with infinite difficulty they drove the herd northward. To add to their troubles, the weather went through "a gamut of changes," as Roosevelt wrote subsequently, "with that extraordinary and inconsequential rapidity which characterizes atmospheric variations on the plains." The second day out, there was a light snow falling all day, with a wind blowing so furiously that early in the afternoon they were obliged to drive the cattle down into a sheltered valley to keep them overnight. The cold was so intense that even in the sun the water froze at noon. Forty-eight hours afterwards it was the heat that was causing them to suffer.

The inland trail which they were following had its disadvantages, for water for the stock was scarce there, and the third day, after watering the cattle at noon, Roosevelt and his men drove them along the very backbone of the divide through barren and forbidding country. Night came on while they were still many miles from the string of deep pools which held the nearest water. The cattle were thirsty and restless, and in the first watch, which Roosevelt shared with one of his cowboys, when the long northern spring dusk had given way at last to complete darkness, the thirsty animals of one accord rose to their feet and made a break for liberty. Roosevelt knew that the only hope of saving his herd from hopeless dispersion over a hundred hills lay in keeping the cattle close together at the very start. He rode along at their side as they charged, as he had never ridden in his life before. In the darkness he could see only dimly the shadowy outline of the herd, as with whip and spur he ran his pony along its edge, turning back the beasts at one point barely in time to wheel and keep them in at another. The ground was cut up by numerous gullies, and more than once Roosevelt's horse turned a complete somersault with his rider. Why he was not killed a half-dozen times over is a mytsery. He was dripping with sweat, and his pony was quivering like a quaking aspen when, after more than an hour of the most violent exertion, he and his companion finally succeeded in quieting the herd.

I have had hard work and a good deal of fun since I came out [Roosevelt wrote to Lodge on the fifteenth of May]. To-morrow I start for the round-up; and I have just come in from taking a thousand head of cattle up on the trail. The weather was very bad and I had my hands full, working night and day, and being able to take off my clothes but once during the week I was out.

The river has been very high recently, and I have had on two or three occasions to swim my horse across it; a new experience to me. Otherwise I have done little that is exciting in the way of horsemanship; as you know I am no horseman, and I cannot ride an unbroken horse with any comfort. The other day I lunched with the Marquis de Mores, a French cavalry officer; he has hunted all through France, but he told me he never saw in Europe such stiff jumping as we have on the Meadowbrook hunt.

Whether he was or was not a horseman is a question on which there is authority which clashes with Roosevelt's. A year's experience with broncos had taught him much, and though Sylvane remained indisputably the crack rider of the Maltese Cross outfit, Roosevelt more than held his own. " He was not a purty rider," as one of his cowpunching friends expressed it, " but a hell of a good rider."

Roosevelt was a firm believer in " gentling " rather than " breaking " horses. He had no sentimental illusions concerning the character of the animals with which he was dealing, but he never ceased his efforts to make a friend instead of a suspicious servant of a horse. Most of Roosevelt's horses became reasonably domesticated, but there was one that resisted all Roosevelt's friendly advances. He was generally regarded as a fiend incarnate. " The Devil " was his name.

" The trouble with training the Devil," said

Packard, who was present at the Maltese Cross one day when Roosevelt was undertaking to ride him, " was that he was a wild four-year-old when first ridden and this first contest was a victory for the horse. If the rider had won, Devil might have become a good saddle horse. But when the horse wins the first contest, one can look for a fight every time he is saddled. The chances favor his becoming a spoiled horse. I happened to arrive at the Chimney Butte Ranch one day just as the horse-herd was being driven into the corral. Devil knew he was due for a riding-lesson. It was positively uncanny to see him dodge the rope. On several occasions he stopped dead in his tracks and threw his head down between his front legs; the loop sliding harmlessly off his front quarters, where not even an ear projected. But Devil couldn't watch two ropes at once, and Roosevelt ' snared ' him from the corral fence while Merrifield was whirling his rope for the throw. Instantly Devil stopped and meekly followed Roosevelt to the snubbing-post, where he was tied up for a period of ' gentling.' The ordinary procedure was to throw such a horse and have one man sit on his head while another bound a handkerchief over his eyes. He was then allowed to get on his feet and often made little resistance while the saddle and bridle were being adjusted. The rider then mounted and the fireworks began as soon as he jerked the handkerchief from the horse's eyes.

" Devil had gone through this procedure so often

that he knew it by heart. He had, however, not become accustomed to being 'gentled' instead of 'busted.' As Roosevelt walked toward him, the horse's fear of man overcame his dread of the rope, and he surged back until the noose was strangling him.

" It was half an hour before he allowed Roosevelt to put a hand on his neck. All this was preliminary to an attempt to blindfolding Devil without throwing, and at last it was accomplished. He then submitted to being saddled and bridled, though he shrank from every touch as though it were a hot iron. The handkerchief was then taken from his eyes, and he began bucking the empty saddle like a spoiled horse of the worst type. Every one took a seat on top of the corral fence to await the time when he had strangled and tired himself to a standstill. Several times he threw himself heavily by tripping on the rope or by tightening it suddenly. And at last he gave it up, standing with legs braced, with heaving flanks and gasping breath.

" Roosevelt walked toward him with a pail of water and the first real sign that 'gentling' was better than 'busting' was when the wild-eyed Devil took a swallow; the first time in his life he had accepted a favor from the hand of man. It was too dangerous to attempt riding in the corral, and Devil was led out to some bottom-land which was fairly level; the end of the rope around the horn of Merrifield's saddle and Sylvane Ferris on another saddle horse ready to urge Devil into a run as soon as Roosevelt had mounted. A vain attempt at mounting was made, and finally Devil had to be blindfolded. Then came the mounting, and, almost instantly with the lifting of the blindfold, Roosevelt was sprawling in the sagebrush. Somewhat scratched he was, and his teeth glittered in the way which required a look at his eyes to tell whether it was a part of a smile or a look of deadly determination. It required no second glance to know that Devil was going to be ridden or Roosevelt was going to be hurt. There was no disgrace in being thrown. It was done in the same way that Devil had unhorsed other men whom Roosevelt would have been first to call better riders than himself. There was a sudden arching of the back which jolted the rider at least six inches from the saddle, then a whirling jump which completed a half-turn, and a landing, stiff-legged, on the fore feet while the hind hoofs kicked high in the air. In his six-inch descent the rider was met with the saddle or the flanks of the horse and catapulted into space. The only way to ' stay with the leather ' was to get the horse to running instead of making this first jump.

" About every other jump we could see twelve acres of bottom-land between Roosevelt and the saddle, but now the rider stayed with the animal a little longer than before. Four times that beast threw him, but the fifth time Roosevelt maneuvered him into a stretch of quicksand in the Little Missouri River. This piece of strategy saved the day,

made Roosevelt a winner, and broke the record of
the Devil, for if there is any basis of operations
fatal to fancy bucking it is quicksand. After a
while Roosevelt turned the bronco around, brought
him out on dry land, and rode him until he was as
meek as a rabbit."

The round-up that spring gave Roosevelt an
opportunity to put his horsemanship to the severest
test there was.

Theodore Roosevelt is now at Medora [the Mandan
Pioneer reported on May 22d], and has been there for
some time past. He is preparing his outfit for the round-
up, and will take an active part in the business itself.

Roosevelt had, in fact, determined to work with
the round-up as an ordinary cowpuncher, and
shortly after the middle of May he started with
his " outfit " south to the appointed meeting-place
west of the mouth of Box Elder Creek in south-
eastern Montana. With him were all the regular
cowboys of the Maltese Cross, besides a half-dozen
other " riders," and Walter Watterson, a sandy-
haired and faithful being who drove Tony and
Dandy, the wheel team, and Thunder and Lightning, the leaders, hitched to the rumbling " chuck-
wagon." Watterson was also the cook, and in
both capacities was unexcelled. Each cowpuncher
attached to the " outfit," or to " the wagon " as it
was called on the round-up, had his own " string "
of ten or a dozen ponies, thrown together into a
single herd which was in charge of the " horse-
wranglers," one for the night and one for the morn-

ing, customarily the youngest (and most abused) cowboys on the ranch.

Roosevelt's "string" was not such as to make him look forward to the round-up with easy assurance. He had not felt that he had a right, even as "the boss," to pick the best horses for himself out of the saddle band of the Maltese Cross. With Sylvane, Merrifield, Myers, and himself choosing in succession, like boys picking teams for "one ol' cat," "the boss" having first choice on each round, he took what Fate and his own imperfect judgment gave him. At the conclusion of the "picking," he found that, of the nine horses he had chosen, four were broncos, broken only in the sense that each had once or twice been saddled. One of them, he discovered promptly, could not possibly be bridled or saddled single-handed; it was very difficult to get on him and very difficult to get off; he was exceedingly nervous, moreover, if his rider moved his hands or feet; "but he had," Roosevelt declared, "no bad tricks," which, in view of his other qualities, must have been a real comfort. The second allowed himself to be tamed and was soon quiet. The third, on the other hand, turned out to be one of the worst buckers Roosevelt possessed; and the fourth had a habit which was even worse, for he would balk and throw himself over backward. It struck Roosevelt that there was something about this refractory animal's disposition, to say nothing of his Roman nose, which greatly reminded him of the eminent Democrat, General Ben Butler, and " Ben Butler " became that bronco's name. Roosevelt had occasion to remember it.

The encampment where the round-up was to begin furnished a scene of bustle and turmoil. From here and there the heavy four-horse wagons one after another jolted in, the " horse-wranglers " rushing madly to and fro in the endeavor to keep the different saddle bands from mingling. Single riders, in groups of two or three, appeared, each driving his " string." The wagons found their places, the teamsters unharnessed the horses and unpacked the " cook outfit," the foreman sought out the round-up captain, the " riders " sought out their friends. Here there was larking, there there was horse-racing, elsewhere there was " a circus with a pitchin' bronc'," and foot-races and wrestling-matches. A round-up always had more than a little of the character of a county fair. For though the work was hard, and practically continuous for sixteen hours out of the twenty-four, it was full of excitement. The cowboys regarded it largely as sport, and the five weeks they spent at it very much of a holiday.[1]

---

[1] Roosevelt: *Ranch Life and the Hunting Trail.*

"Am inclined to think that this assertion of Mr. Roosevelt's would be open to criticism on the part of the real old-time cowpunchers. Much depended upon the weather, of course, but in a general way most of them regarded the work as anything but a picnic. Usually, it came closer to being 'Hell,' before we got through with it, as was the case on that particular round-up in 1885, when Mr. Roosevelt was along. Rained much of the time, and upon one occasion kept at it for a week on end. Tied the whole outfit up for several days at one point and I recall we had to wring the water out of our blankets every night be-

Roosevelt reported to the captain of the round-up, a man named Osterhaut, saying that he expected to be treated as a common cowhand and wanted to be shown no favors; and the captain took him at his word. He promptly justified his existence. He did not pretend to be a good roper, and his poor eyesight forbade any attempt to " cut " the cattle that bore his brand out of the milling herd; but he " wrestled calves " with the best of them; he rode " the long circle "; he guarded the day-herd and the night-herd and did the odd (and often perilous) jobs of the cowpuncher with the same cool unconcern that characterized the professional cowboy.

" Three-Seven " Bill Jones was on the round-up as foreman of the " Three-Seven Ranch." (" There," as Howard Eaton remarked with enthusiasm, " was a cowboy for your whiskers! ") He was a large, grave, taciturn man, capable of almost incredible feats of physical endurance. Dantz overheard him, one day, discussing Roosevelt.

" That four-eyed maverick," remarked " Three-Seven " Bill, " has sand in his craw a-plenty."

fore retiring. The boys liked to work on general round-ups, hard and all as they were, mainly because it brought them into contact with the boys from other ranges, so that they had a chance to renew old acquaintances. Generally the boys were all inclined to be a little wild at the start, or until cooled down by a few days of hard work. After that things got into a steady groove, eighteen hours per day in the saddle being nothing unusual.

"At the start, the round-up bore many of the aspects of a county fair, just as Mr. Roosevelt states, and unless the trip proved to be unusually hard there was always more or less horse-play in the air."— *Lincoln Lang.*

As with all other forms of work [Roosevelt wrote years after], so on the round-up, a man of ordinary power, who nevertheless does not shirk things merely because they are disagreeable or irksome, soon earns his place. There were crack riders and ropers, who, just because they felt such overweening pride in their own prowess, were not really very valuable men. Continually on the circles a cow or a calf would get into some thick patch of bulberry bush and refuse to come out; or when it was getting late we would pass some bad lands that would probably not contain cattle, but might; or a steer would turn fighting mad, or a calf grow tired and want to lie down. If in such a case the man steadily persists in doing the unattractive thing, and after two hours of exasperation and harassment does finally get the cow out, and keep her out, of the bulberry bushes, and drives her to the wagon, or finds some animals that have been passed by in the fourth or fifth patch of bad lands he hunts through, or gets the calf up on his saddle and takes it in anyhow, the foreman soon grows to treat him as having his uses and as being an asset of worth in the round-up, even though neither a fancy roper nor a fancy rider.[1]

It was an active life,[2] and Roosevelt had no opportunity to complain of restlessness. Breakfast came at three and dinner at eight or nine or ten in the morning, at the conclusion sometimes of fifty miles of breakneck riding. From ten to one, while the experts were " cutting out the cows," Roosevelt was " on day-herd," as the phrase went, riding slowly round and round the herd, turning back into

[1] *Autobiography.*
[2] Roosevelt gives an admirable description of a round-up in his *Ranch Life and the Hunting Trail.*

it any cattle that attempted to escape. In the afternoon he would " ride circle " again, over the hills; and at night, from ten to twelve, he would again be on guard, riding round the cattle, humming some eerie lullaby. It was always the same song that he sang, but what the words were or the melody is a secret that belongs to the wind.

When utterly tired, it was hard to have to get up for one's trick at night-herd [Roosevelt wrote in his " Auto-biography "]. Nevertheless on ordinary nights the two hours round the cattle in the still darkness were pleasant. The loneliness, under the vast empty sky, and the silence in which the breathing of the cattle sounded loud, and the alert readiness to meet any emergency which might suddenly arise out of the formless night, all combined to give one a sense of subdued interest.

As he lay on the ground near by, after his watch, he liked to listen to the wild and not unmusical calls of the cowboys as they rode round the half-slumbering steers. There was something magical in the strange sound of it under the stars. Now and then a song would float through the clear air.

> " The days that I was hard up,
>   I never shall forget.
>   The days that I was hard up —
>   I may be well off yet.
>   In days when I was hard up,
>   And wanted wood and fire,
>   I used to tie my shoes up
>   With little bits of wire."

It was a favorite song with the night-herders. One night, early in the round-up, Roosevelt failed satisfactorily to identify the direction in which he was to go in order to reach the night-herd. It was a pitch-dark night, and he wandered about in it for hours on end, finding the cattle at last only when the sun rose. He was greeted with withering scorn by the injured cowpuncher who had been obliged to stand double guard because Roosevelt had failed to relieve him.

Sixteen hours of work left little time for social diversions, but even when they were full of sleep the cowboys would draw up around the camp-fire, to smoke and sing and " swap yarns " for an hour. There were only three musical instruments in the length and breadth of the Bad Lands, the Langs' piano, a violin which " Fiddling Joe " played at the dances over Bill Williams's saloon, and Howard Eaton's banjo. The banjo traveled in state in the mess-wagon of the " Custer Trail," and hour on hour, about the camp-fire on the round-up, Eaton would play to the dreamy delight of the weary men. The leading spirit of those evenings was Bill Dantz, who knew a hundred songs by heart, and could spin an actual happening into a yarn so thrilling and so elaborate in every detail that no one could tell precisely where the foundation of fact ended and the Arabian dome and minaret of iridescent fancy began.

Roosevelt found the cowboys excellent companions. They were a picturesque crew with their broad felt hats, their flannel shirts of various colors, overlaid with an enamel of dust and perspiration, baked by the Dakota sun, their bright silk handkerchiefs knotted round the neck, their woolly " shaps," their great silver spurs, their loosely hanging cartridge-belts, their ominous revolvers. Roosevelt was struck by the rough courtesy with which the men treated each other. There was very little quarreling or fighting, due, Roosevelt suspected, to the fact that all the men were armed; for, it seemed, that when a quarrel was likely to end fatally, men rather hesitated about embarking upon it. The moral tone of the round-up camp seemed to Roosevelt rather high. There was a real regard for truthfulness, a firm insistence on the sanctity of promises, and utter contempt for meanness and cowardice and dishonesty and hypocrisy and the disposition to shirk. The cowpuncher was a potential cattle-owner and good citizen, and if he went wild on occasion it was largely because he was so exuberantly young. In years he was generally a boy, often under twenty. But he did the work of a man, and he did it with singular conscientiousness and the spirit less of an employee than of a member of an order bound by vows, unspoken but accepted. He obeyed orders without hesitation, though it were to mount a bucking bronco or " head off " a stampede. He worked without complaint in a smother of dust and cattle fumes at temperatures ranging as high as 136 degrees; or, snow-blinded and frozen, he " rode line " for hours on end when the thermometer was fifty or more below zero. He was in constant peril of his life from the horns of milling cattle or the antics of a "mean" horse. Roosevelt was immensely drawn to the sinewy, hardy, and self-reliant adventurers; and they in turn liked him.

Life in the camps was boisterous and the language beggared description.

"With some of these fellows around here," Dr. Stickney, the Bad Lands' surgeon, once remarked, "profanity ceases to be a habit and becomes an art."

"That's right," assented Sylvane. "Some strangers will get the hang of it, but others never do. There was 'Deacon' Cummins, for instance. He'd say such a thing as 'damned calf.' You could tell he didn't know anything about it."

The practical jokes, moreover, which the cowboys played on each other were not such as to make life easy for the timid. "The boys played all kinds of tricks," remarked Merrifield long after; "sometimes they'd stick things under the horses' tails and play tricks of that kind an' there'd be a lot of hilarity to see the fellow get h'isted into the air; but they never bothered Mr. Roosevelt. He commanded everybody's respect."

They did play one joke on him, however, but it did not turn out at all as they expected.

Roosevelt's hunting proclivities were well known, for he never missed an opportunity, even on the round-up, to wander up some of the countless coulees with a rifle on his shoulder after deer, or to ride away over the prairies after antelope; and the cowpunchers decided that it would be rather good fun to send him on a wild-goose chase. So they told him with great seriousness of a dozen antelope they had seen five or six miles back, suggesting that he had better go and get one.

He " bit," as they knew he would, and, in spite of the fact that he had had a hard day on the round-up, saddled a horse and rode off in the direction which they had indicated. The cowboys speculated as to the language he would use when he came back.

He was gone several hours, and he had two antelope across his saddle-bow when he rode back into camp.

" I found them all right," he cried, " just a quarter-mile from where you said."

There was a shout from the cowboys. By general consent the joke was declared as not to be on the " four-eyed tenderfoot."

Most of the men sooner or later accepted Roosevelt as an equal, in spite of his toothbrush and his habit of shaving; but there was one man, a surly Texan, who insisted on " picking on " Roosevelt as a dude. Roosevelt laughed. But the man continued, in season and out of season, to make him the butt of his gibes.

It occurred to the object of all this attention that the Texan was evidently under the impression that the " dude " was also a coward. Roosevelt decided that, for the sake of general harmony, that impression had better be corrected at once.

One evening, when the man was being particularly offensive, Roosevelt strode up to him.

" You're talking like an ass! " he said sharply. " Put up or shut up! Fight now, or be friends! "

The Texan stared, his shoulder dropped a little, and he shifted his feet. " I didn't mean no harm," he said. " Make it friends."

They made it friends.

XVII

At a round-up on the Gily,
  One sweet mornin' long ago,
Ten of us was throwed right freely
  By a hawse from Idaho.
And we thought he'd go a-beggin'
  For a man to break his pride,
Till, a-hitchin' up one leggin',
  Boastful Bill cut loose and cried —

" *I'm an on'ry proposition for to hurt;*
  I fulfill my earthly mission with a quirt;
  I kin ride the highest liver
  'Tween the Gulf and Powder River,
  And I'll break this thing as easy as I'd flirt."

So Bill climbed the Northern Fury,
  And they mangled up the air,
Till a native of Missouri
  Would have owned his brag was fair.
Though the plunges kep' him reelin'
  And the wind it flapped his shirt,
Loud above the hawse's squealin'
  We could hear our friend assert —

" *I'm the one to take such rakin's as a joke.*
  Some one hand me up the makin's of a smoke!
  If you think my fame needs bright'nin',
  W'y, I'll rope a streak of lightnin',
  And I'll cinch 'im up and spur 'im till he's broke."

Then one caper of repulsion
  Broke that hawse's back in two.
Cinches snapped in the convulsion;
  Skyward man and saddle flew.
Up he mounted, never laggin',
  While we watched him through our tears,
And his last thin bit of braggin'
  Came a-droppin' to our ears —

" *If you'd ever watched my habits very close,*
  You would know I've broke such rabbits by the gross.
  I have kep' my talent hidin';
  I'm too good for earthly ridin',
  And I'm off to bust the lightnin' — Adios! "

BADGER CLARK

IF Roosevelt anticipated that he would have trouble with his untamed broncos, he was not disappointed. " The effort," as he subsequently remarked, " both to ride them, and to look as if I enjoyed doing so, on some cool morning when my grinning cowboy friends had gathered round 'to see whether the high-headed bay could buck the boss off,' doubtless was of benefit to me, but lacked much of being enjoyable."

One morning, when the round-up " outfits " were camped on the Logging Camp Range, south of the Big Ox Bow, Roosevelt had a memorable struggle with one of his four broncos. The camp was directly behind the ranch-house (which the Eaton brothers owned), and close by was a chasm some sixty feet deep, a great gash in the valley which the torrents of successive springs had through the centuries cut there. The horse had to be blind-folded before he would allow a saddle to be put on him.

Lincoln Lang was among the cowboys who stood in an admiring circle, hoping for the worst.

" Mr. Roosevelt mounted, with the blind still on the horse," Lang said, telling the story afterward, " so that the horse stood still, although with a well-defined hump on his back, which, as we all knew very well, meant trouble to come. As soon as Mr. Roosevelt got himself fixed in the saddle, the men who were holding the horse pulled off the blind and turned him loose."

Here Bill Dantz, who was also in the " gallery," takes up the story:

" The horse did not buck. He started off quietly, in fact, until he was within a few feet of the chasm. Then he leapt in the air like a shot deer, and came down with all four feet buckled under him, jumped sideways and went in the air a second time, twisting ends."

Here Lang resumes the narrative:

" Almost any kind of a bucking horse is hard to ride, but the worst of all are the ' sunfishers ' who change end for end with each jump, maintaining the turning movement in one direction so that the effect is to get the rider dizzy. This particular horse was of that type, and almost simultaneous with the removal of the blind he was in gyroscopic action.

" I am aware that Mr. Roosevelt did not like to ' pull leather,' as the term goes, but this time at least he had to, but for the matter of that there were not many who would not have done the same thing. As nearly as I can remember, he got the horn of his saddle in one hand and the cantle in the other, then swung his weight well into the inside and hung like a leech. Of course, it took sheer grit to do it, because in thus holding himself tight to the saddle with his hands, he had to take full punishment, which can be avoided only when one has acquired the knack of balancing and riding loosely.

" As it was, his glasses and six-shooter took the count within the first few jumps, but in one way or another he hung to it himself, until some of the boys rode up and got the horse headed into a straight-away by the liberal use of their quirts. Once they got him running, it was all over, of course. If I remember right, Mr. Roosevelt rode the horse on a long circle that morning and brought him in safe, hours later, as good as gold."[1]

The horse which Roosevelt had called " Ben Butler " was not so easily subdued. It was " Ben Butler's " special antic to fall over backward. He was a sullen, evil-eyed brute, with a curve in his nose and a droop in his nostrils, which gave him a ridiculous resemblance to the presidential candi-date of the Anti-Monopoly Party. He was a great man-killing bronco, with a treacherous streak, and Roosevelt had put him in his " string " against the protests of his own men. " That horse is a plumb outlaw," Bill Dantz declared, " an' outlaws is never safe. They kinda git bad and bust out at any time. He will sure kill you, sooner or later, if you try to ride him."

One raw, chilly morning, Roosevelt, who had been ordered to ride " the outside circle," chose " Ben Butler " for his mount, because he knew the

[1] "During the course of the Barnes-Roosevelt trial at Syracuse in 1916, Roosevelt was taking dinner one evening at the house of Mr. Horace S. Wilkinson. Chancellor Day, of Syracuse University, who was present, said: 'Mr. Roosevelt, my attention was first directed to you by an account of a scene when you were with the cowboys. It told of your trying to get astride a bronco, and it was a struggle. But you finally conquered him, and away you went in a cloud of dust.'

"'Very true, very true,' said Roosevelt, 'but I rode him all the way from the tip of his ear to the end of his tail.'" — *Rev. D. B. Thompson*, Syracuse, N.Y.

horse was tireless and could stand the long, swift ride better than any other pony he had. As Roosevelt mounted him, the horse reared and fell over backward. He had done that before, but this time he fell on his rider. Roosevelt, with a sharp pain in his shoulder, extricated himself and mounted once more. But the horse now refused to go in any direction, backward or forward.

Sylvane and George Myers threw their lariats about the bronco's neck, and dragged him a few hundred yards, choking but stubborn, all four feet firmly planted and pawing the ground. When they released the ropes, " Ben Butler " lay down and refused to get up.

The round-up had started; there was no time to waste. Sylvane gave Roosevelt his horse, Baldy, which sometimes bucked, but never went over backwards, and himself mounted the now re-arisen " Ben Butler." To Roosevelt's discomfiture, the horse that had given him so much trouble started off as meekly as any farm-horse.

" Why," remarked Sylvane, not without a touch of triumph, " there's nothing the matter with this horse. He's a plumb gentle horse."

But shortly after, Roosevelt noticed that Sylvane had fallen behind. Then he heard his voice, in persuasive tones, " That's all right! Come along! " Suddenly a new note came into his entreaties. " Here you! Go on you! Hi, hi, fellows, help me out! He's laying on me! "

They dragged Sylvane from under the sprawling

steed, whereupon Sylvane promptly danced a war-dance, spurs and all, on the iniquitous " Ben." Roosevelt gave up the attempt to take that particular bronco on the round-up that day.

" By gollies," remarked " Dutch Wannigan " in later days, " he rode some bad horses, some that did quite a little bucking around for us. I don't know if he got throwed. If he did, there wouldn't have been nothin' said about it. Some of those Eastern punkin-lilies now, those goody-goody fellows, if they'd ever get throwed off you'd never hear the last of it. He didn't care a bit. By gollies, if he got throwed off, he'd get right on again. He was a dandy fellow."

The encounter with " Ben Butler " brought a new element into Roosevelt's cowpunching experience, and made what remained of the round-up somewhat of an ordeal. For he discovered that the point of his shoulder was broken. Under other circumstances he would have gone to a doctor, but in the Bad Lands you did not go to doctors, for the simple reason that there was only one physician in the whole region and he might at any given moment be anywhere from fifty to two hundred and fifty miles away. If you were totally incapacitated with a broken leg or a bullet in your lungs, you sent word to Dr. Stickney's office in Dickinson. The doctor might be north in the Killdeer Mountains or south in the Cave Hills or west in Mingusville, for the territory he covered stretched from Mandan a hundred and twenty miles east of Medora, to Glendive, the same distance westward, south to the Black Hills and north beyond the Canadian border, a stretch of country not quite as large as New England, but almost. The doctor covered it on horseback or in a buckboard; in the cab of a wild-cat engine or the caboose of a freight, or, on occasion, on a hand-car. He was as young as everybody else in that young country, utterly fearless, and, it seemed, utterly tireless. He rode out into the night careless alike of blinding sleet and drifting snow. At grilling speed he rode until his horse stood with heaving sides and nose drooping; then, at some ranch, he changed to another and rode on. Over a course of a hundred miles or more he would ride relays at a speed that seemed incredible, and at the end of the journey operate with a calm hand for a gun-shot wound or a cruelly broken bone, sometimes on the box of a mess-wagon turned upside down on the prairie.

Dr. Stickney was from Vermont, a quiet, lean man with a warm smile and friendly eyes, a sense of humor and a zest for life. He had a reputation for never refusing a call whatever the distance or the weather. Sometimes he rode with a guide; more often he rode alone. He knew the landmarks for a hundred miles in any direction. At night, when the trail grew faint, he held his course by the stars; when an unexpected blizzard swept down upon him and the snow hid the trail, he sought a brush-patch in a coulee and tramped back and forth to keep himself from freezing until the storm had spent itself. It was a life of extraordinary devotion. Stickney took it with a laugh, blushing when men spoke well of him; and called it the day's work.

God alone knew where the doctor happened to be on the day that " Ben Butler " rolled over backward with Theodore Roosevelt. It is safe to surmise that Roosevelt did not inquire. You did not send for Dr. Stickney for a break in the point of your shoulder. You let the thing heal by itself and went on with your job. Of course, it was not pleasant; but there were many things that were not pleasant. It was, in fact, Roosevelt found, excruciating. But he said nothing about that.

By the beginning of June, the round-up had worked down to Tepee Bottom, two or three miles south of the Maltese Cross, making its midday camp, one hot and sultry day, in a grove of ancient cottonwoods that stood like unlovely, weather-beaten, gnarled old men, within hailing distance of " Deacon " Cummins's ranch-house. A messenger from Mrs. Cummins arrived at the camp at noon inviting Roosevelt and three or four of his friends to dinner. A " home dinner " was not to be spurned, and they all rode over to the comfortable log cabin. The day was blistering, a storm hung in the humid air, and none of them remembered, not even Roosevelt, that " gentlemen " did not go to dinner parties in their shirt-sleeves, at least not in the world to which Mrs. Cummins liked to believe she belonged. Roosevelt was in his shirt and trousers, cowboy fashion.

As the men prepared to sit down to dinner, Mrs. Cummins was obviously perturbed. She left the room, returning a minute later with a coat over her arm.

" Mr. Roosevelt," she said, " I know you won't like to come to dinner without a coat. I have got one of Mr. Cummins's that will fit you. I am sure you will feel more comfortable."

What Roosevelt's emotions were at being thus singled out and proclaimed a " dude " among the men he wanted, above all things, to consider him their peer, Roosevelt concealed at the moment and later only fitfully revealed. He accepted the coat with as good grace as he could muster, to the suppressed delight of his friends.

But Mrs. Cummins was not yet done with her guest of honor. She had evidently been hurt, poor lady, by his failure to observe the amenities of social intercourse, for during the dinner she said to him, " I don't see why men and women of culture come out here and let the people pull them down. What they should do is to raise the people out here to their level."

What Roosevelt answered is lost to history; but Lincoln Lang, who was with him when he rode back to camp that afternoon, reported that Roosevelt's comments on the dinner party were " blistering." " He told my mother afterwards," said Lang in later times, " that Mrs. Cummins was out of place in the Bad Lands "; which was Mrs. Cummins's tragedy in a nutshell.

They moved the camp that same afternoon a mile or two north to a wide bottom that lay at the base of the peak known as Chimney Butte, north of Garner Creek and west of the Little Missouri. As evening approached, heavy black clouds began to roll up in the west, bringing rain. The rain became a downpour, through which flashes of lightning and rumblings of thunder came with increasing violence. The cattle were very restless and uneasy, running up and down and trying here and there to break out of the herd. The guards were doubled in anticipation of trouble.

At midnight, fearing a stampede, the night-herders, of whom Lincoln Lang happened to be one, sent a call of "all hands out." Roosevelt leaped on the pony he always kept picketed near him. Suddenly there was a terrific peal of thunder. The lightning struck almost into the herd itself, and with heads and tails high the panic-stricken animals plunged off into the darkness.

Will Dow was at Roosevelt's side. The tumult evidently had not affected his imperturbable gayety. "There'll be racing and chasing on Cannobie lea," Roosevelt heard him gayly quote. An instant later the night had swallowed him.

For a minute or two Roosevelt could make out nothing except the dark forms of the beasts, running on every side of him like the black waters of a roaring river. He was conscious that if his horse should stumble there would be no hope for him in the path of those panicky hoofs. The herd split, a part turning to one side, while the other part kept straight ahead. Roosevelt galloped at top speed, hoping to reach the leaders and turn them.

He heard a wild splashing ahead. One instant he was aware that the cattle in front of him and beside him were disappearing; the next, he himself was plunging over a cutbank into the Little Missouri. He bent far back in the saddle. His horse almost fell, recovered himself, plunged forward, and, struggling through water and quicksand, made the other side.

For a second he saw another cowboy beside him. The man disappeared in the darkness and the deluge, and Roosevelt galloped off through a grove of cottonwoods after the diminished herd. The ground was rough and full of pitfalls. Once his horse turned a somersault and threw him. At last the cattle came to a halt, but soon they were again away through the darkness. Thrice again he halted them, and thrice again they stampeded.

" The country was muddy and wet," said Lincoln Lang afterward. " We were having a heavy rain all night. I don't know how we ever got through. All we had was lightning flashes to go by. It was really one of the worst mix-ups I ever saw. That surely was a night."

Day broke at last, and as the light filtered through the clouds Roosevelt could dimly discern where he was. He succeeded at last in turning back what remained of the cattle in the direction of the camp, gathering in stray groups of cattle as he went, and driving them before him. He came upon a cowboy on foot carrying his saddle on his head. It was the man he had seen for a flash during the storm. His horse had run into a tree and been killed. He himself had escaped by a miracle.

The men in the camp were just starting on the "long circle" when Roosevelt returned. One of them saddled a fresh horse for him while he snatched a hasty breakfast; then he was off for the day's work.

As only about half of the night-herd had been brought back, the circle-riding was particularly heavy, and it was ten hours before Roosevelt was back at the wagon camp once more for a hasty meal and a fresh horse. He finished work as the late twilight fell. He had been in the saddle forty hours, changing horses five times. That night he slept like the dead.

The storm had raised the level of the river and filled every wash-out with swirling brown waters. The following day Roosevelt had an adventure which came within an ace of being tragedy and culminated in hilarious farce. He was riding with a young Englishman, the son of Lord Somebody or Other — the name is immaterial — who was living that spring with the Langs. Just north of the Custer Trail Ranch a bridge of loose stringers had been laid across the washout, which, except at times of heavy rains or melting snows, was completely dry. On this occasion, however, it was full to the banks, and had even flowed over the rude bridge, jumbling the light logs.

The stringers parted as their horses attempted to make their way gingerly across, and in an instant horses and riders and bridge timbers were floundering indiscriminately in the rushing torrent. Roosevelt's horse worked his way out, but the Englishman, who was a good rider according to his lights, was not altogether used to mishaps of this sort and became excited.

" I'm drowning! I'm drowning! " he called to Roosevelt.

Roosevelt snatched the lasso from his saddle. He was not famous as a roper, but on this occasion his " throw " went true. The rope descended over the shoulders of the British aristocrat, and an instant later Roosevelt had him on solid ground.

" As he was yanked unceremoniously out of that creek," Roosevelt subsequently remarked, " he did not seem to be very thankful."

Sober second thoughts, however, brought gratitude with them. The Britisher never forgot that Roosevelt had saved his life, and Roosevelt never forgot the picture that a son of a lord made, dragged through the water at the end of a lasso.

On June 5th, which must have been the day after the rescue of the Englishman, Roosevelt was writing to Lodge.

A cowboy from " down river " has just come up to the round-up, and brought me my mail, with your letter in it. I am writing on the ground; so my naturally good handwriting will not show to its usual advantage. I have been three weeks on the round-up and have worked as hard as any of the cowboys; but I have enjoyed it greatly. Yesterday I was eighteen hours in the saddle — from 4 A.M. to 10 P.M.— having a half-hour each for dinner and tea. I can now do cowboy work pretty well.

Toronto [1] must be a dandy; I wish I could pick up one as good. That is, if he is gentle. You are all off about my horsemanship; as you would say if you saw me now. Almost all of our horses on the ranch being young, I had to include in my string three that were but partially broken; and I have had some fine circuses with them. One of them had never been saddled but once before, and he proved vicious, and besides bucking, kept falling over backwards with me; finally he caught me, giving me an awful slat, from which my left arm has by no means recovered. Another bucked me off going down hill; but I think I have cured him, for I put him through a desperate course of sprouts when I got on again. The third I nearly lost in swimming him across a swollen creek, where the flood had carried down a good deal of drift timber. However, I got him through all right in the end, after a regular ducking. Twice one of my old horses turned a somersault while galloping after cattle; once in a prairie-dog town, and once while trying to prevent the herd from stampeding in a storm at night. I tell you, I like gentle and well-broken horses if I am out for pleasure, and I do not get on any other, unless, as in this case, from sheer necessity.

It is too bad that letters cannot be published with stage directions. For surely the words, " I like gentle and well-broken horses," should bear about them somewhere the suggestion of the glint of the eye, the flash of the teeth, the unctuous deliberate-

---

[1] Toronto was the name of Lodge's hunter.

ness, and the comical break in the voice with which, surely, Roosevelt whispered them to his soul before he wrote them down.

While Roosevelt was enjoying adventures and misadventures of various sorts, Sylvane Ferris was having what he might have described as " a little party " of his own. For Sylvane, most honest and guileless of men, had got into the clutches of the law. It happened this way.

Early in the spring some cowpunchers, driving in cattle which had strayed during the winter over the level country far to the east of the Little Missouri, came upon a cow marked with the maltese cross. They drove her westward with the rest of the " strays," but none of the men belonged to the " Roosevelt outfit " and their interest in this particular cow was therefore purely altruistic. She was not a particularly good cow, moreover, for she had had a calf in the winter and her udder had partially frozen. When, therefore, the necessity arose of paying board at the section-house at Gladstone after a few happy days at that metropolis, the cowboys, who did not have a cent of real money among them, hit upon the brilliant idea of offering the cow in payment.

The section boss accepted the settlement, but evidently not without a sense of the consequences that might follow the discovery in his possession of a cow for which he could not present a bill of sale. He therefore promptly passed the cow on to a Russian cobbler in payment for a pair of shoes.

The cobbler, with the European peasant's uncanny ability to make something out of nothing, doctored the cow with a care which he would not have dreamed of bestowing on his wife, and made a profitable milk-provider out of her.

Sylvane discovered her during the round-up, picketed outside the Russian's shack, and promptly proceeded to take possession of her. The Russian protested and told his story. Sylvane, pointing out that he was moved by charity and not by necessity, offered the man six dollars, which had been the price of the shoes. The Russian threw up his hands and demanded no less than forty. Sylvane shrugged his shoulders and annexed the cow.

That evening as Sylvane was sitting around the mess-wagon with a dozen other cowpunchers, a stranger came walking from the direction of Gladstone. The cow was hitched to the wagon, for she had shown a tendency to choose her own master. The stranger started to detach the rope that held her.

" Hold on! " cried Sylvane, " that is our cow."

The stranger took some papers out of his pocket and handed them to Sylvane.

" Here are replevin papers," he said.

" I don't want your papers," remarked Sylvane, who did not know a replevin paper from a dog license.

The stranger threw the papers at Sylvane's feet.

" I've come to take this cow."

" Well," remarked Sylvane, " if that's all the

business you have, you can go straight back where you came from."

The stranger strode toward the cow, Sylvane did likewise. They reached the rope at the same moment. There was a shout from the delighted audience of cowpunchers.

The stranger released his hold on the rope. " If you say I can't take her, I can't take her," the man grumbled. " There's too many of you. But I'll bring back men that can."

" Well, turn yourself loose," remarked Sylvane agreeably. " You'll need a lot of them."

There was another shout from the onlookers, and the stranger departed. Sylvane threw the papers into the mess-wagon.

Roosevelt did not happen to be present, and in his absence the sober counsel of " Deacon " Cummins made itself heard. The gist of it was that Sylvane had resisted an officer of the law, which was a criminal offense.

Sylvane, who was afraid of nothing that walked on two legs or on four, had a wholesome respect for that vague and ominous thing known as the Law.

" Say, I don't want to get in bad with any sheriff," he said, really worried. " What had I oughter do? "

The " Deacon," who possibly rejoiced at being for once taken seriously, suggested that Sylvane ride to Gladstone and see if he could not straighten the matter out. The other cowpunchers, whose acquaintance with legal procedure was as vague as Sylvane's, agreed that that plan sounded reasonable. Sylvane went, accompanied by the "Deacon" and another cowboy. If there was a gleam of wicked triumph in the stranger's eye when Sylvane rode up to him, Sylvane failed to notice it. Before a justice of the peace he agreed to appear in court on a certain date, and his two companions furnished a bond.

Next day, while they were in camp on the Heart River, an acquaintance of Sylvane's, a lawyer who rejoiced in the harmonious name of Western Starr, rode in from Dickinson to have dinner with "the boys." Sylvane showed him the papers the stranger had deposited at his feet.

The lawyer glanced over them. "What are these?" he asked.

"I don't know," answered Sylvane lightly. "That's what I handed them to you for, to find out."

"Why," exclaimed Starr, "these aren't anything. They haven't been signed by anybody."

Sylvane's jaw dropped. "Say, how about my bond?"

"Oh, that's valid, even if these are not. You've got to appear in court."

Sylvane's feelings concerning the "Deacon" and his precious advice were deep and earnest. The situation was serious. He knew well enough the chance that the "outfit" of a wealthy Easterner like Roosevelt would stand with a Gladstone jury, when it was a question of depriving a poor man of his cow.

Western Starr suggested that he arrange for a change of venue.

Sylvane approved. The change of venue cost ten dollars, but was granted. The date of the trial was set. Sylvane traveled to Dickinson and waited all day with his attorney for the trial to be called. No one appeared, not even the judge.

Starr's fee was twenty dollars. Sylvane's railroad fare was five more. The total bill was thirty-five.

Roosevelt paid the bill. If he remarked that, taking lost time into consideration, it would have been cheaper, in the first place, to pay the Russian the forty dollars he demanded, there is no record of it. But the remark would not have been characteristic. The chances are that he thought Sylvane's encounter with the law worth every cent that it cost.

XVIII

Somewhere on some faded page
I read about a Golden Age,
But gods and Caledonian hunts
Were nothing to what I knew once.
Here on these hills was hunting! Here
Antelope sprang and wary deer.
Here there were heroes! On these plains
Were drops afire from dragons' veins!
Here there was challenge, here defying,
Here was true living, here great dying!
Stormy winds and stormy souls,
Earthly wills with starry goals,
Battle — thunder — hoofs in flight —
Centaurs charging down the night!

Here there were feasts of song and story
And words of love and dreams of glory!
Here there were friends! Ah, night will fall
And clouds or the stars will cover all,
But I, when I go as a ghost again
To the gaunt, grim buttes, to the friendly plain
I know that for all that time can do
To scatter the faithful, estrange the true —
Quietly, in the lavender sage,
Will be waiting the friends of my golden age.

From *Medora Nights*

THE wild riding, the mishaps, the feverish activity, the smell of the cattle, the dust, the tumult, the physical weariness, the comradeship, the closeness to life and death — to Roosevelt it was all magical and enticing. He loved the crisp morning air, the fantastic landscape, the limitless spaces, half blue and half gold. His spirit was sensitive to beauty, especially the beauty that lay open for all in the warm light of dawn and dusk under the wide vault of heaven; and the experiences that were merely the day's work to his companions to him were edged with the shimmer of spiritual adventure.

" We knew toil and hardship and hunger and thirst," Roosevelt wrote thirty years later, " and we saw men die violent deaths as they worked among the horses and cattle, or fought in evil feuds with one another; but we felt the beat of hardy life in our veins, and ours was the glory of work and the joy of living."

" It was a wonderful thing for Roosevelt," said Dr. Stickney. " He himself realized what a splendid thing it was for him to have been here at that time and to have had sufficient strength in his character to absorb it. He started out to get the fundamental truths as they were in this country and he never lost sight of that purpose all the time he was here."

To the joy of strenuous living was added, for Roosevelt, the satisfaction of knowing that the speculation in which he had risked so large a part of his fortune was apparently prospering. The cattle were looking well. Even pessimistic Bill Sewall admitted that, though he would not admit that he had changed his opinion of the region as a place for raising cattle.

I don't think we shall lose many of our cattle this winter [he wrote his brother]. I think they have got past the worst now. Next year is the one that will try them. It is the cows that perish mostly and we had but few that had calves last spring, but this spring thare will be quite a lot of them. The calves suck them down and they don't get any chance to gain up before they have another calf and then if the weather is very cold they are pretty sure to die. It is too cold here to

raise cattle that way. Don't believe there is any money
in she cattle here and am afraid thare is not much in
any, unless it is the largest heards, and they are crowding
in cattle all the time and I think they will eat us out in a
few years.

Sewall, being a strong individualist, was more than
dubious concerning the practicality of the coöperative round-up. The cowmen were passionately devoted to the idea of the open range; to believe in
fences was treason; but it was in fences that Bill
Sewall believed.

I don't like so free a country [he wrote]. Whare one
man has as good a right as another nobody really has
any right, so when feed gets scarce in one place they
drive their cattle whare it is good without regard to
whose range they eat out. I am satisfied that by the time
we are ready to leave grass will be pretty scarce here.
    I think the Cattle business has seen its best days and
I gave my opinion to Mr. R. last fall. I hope he may not
lose but I think he stands a chance. Shall do all we can
to prevent it, but it is such a mixed business. One or
two can't do much. It is the most like driving on the
Lake when you are mixed with everybody. I don't like
it and never did. I want to controle and manage my
own affairs and have a right to what I have, but here as
on the Lake it is all common. One has as much right as
another.

Roosevelt remained with the round-up until it
disbanded not far from Elkhorn Bottom. Then, on
June 21st, he went East, accompanied by Wilmot
Dow, who was going home to get married and bring
Sewall's wife back with him when he brought back
his own.

Two reporters intercepted Roosevelt as he passed through St. Paul the day after his departure from Medora, and have left an attractive picture of the politician-turned-cowboy.

Rugged, bronzed, and in the prime of health [wrote the representative of the *Pioneer Press*], Theodore Roosevelt passed through St. Paul yesterday, returning from his Dakota ranch to New York and civilization. There was very little of the whilom dude in his rough and easy costume, with a large handkerchief tied loosely about his neck; but the eyeglasses and the flashing eyes behind them, the pleasant smile and the hearty grasp of hand remained. There was the same eagerness to hear from the world of politics, and the same frank willingness to answer all questions propounded. The slow, exasperating drawl and the unique accent that the New Yorker feels he must use when visiting a less blessed portion of civilization have disappeared, and in their place is a nervous, energetic manner of talking with the flat accent of the West. Roosevelt is changed from the New York club man to the thorough Westerner, but the change is only in surface indications, and he is the same thoroughly good fellow he has always been.

The reporter of the *Dispatch* caught him in the lobby of the Merchant's Hotel.

"I'm just in from my ranch," he said [runs the interview]. "Haven't had my dinner yet, but I think a short talk with a newspaper fellow will give me a whetted appetite. Yes, I am a regular cowboy, dress and all —" and his garb went far to prove his assertion, woolen shirt, big neck handkerchief tied loosely around his neck, etc. "I am as much of a cowboy as any of them and can hold my own with the best of them. I can shoot, ride, and drive in the round-up with the best of them. Oh, they are a jolly set of fellows, those cowboys; tiptop good fellows, too, when you know them, but they don't want any plug hat or pointed shoes foolishness around them. I get along the best way with them.

"We have just finished the spring round-up. You know what that means. The round-up covered about two hundred miles of grass territory along the river, and thousands of cattle were brought in. It is rare sport, but hard work after all. Do I like ranch life? Honestly I would not go back to New York if I had no interests there. Yes, I enjoy ranch life far more than city life. I like the hunt, the drive of cattle, and everything that is comprehended in frontier life. Make no mistake; on the frontier you find the noblest of fellows. How many cattle have I? Let's see, well, not less than 3500 at present. I will have more another year."

The man from the *Dispatch* wanted to talk politics, but beyond a few general remarks Roosevelt refused to satisfy him.

"Don't ask me to talk politics," he said. "I am out of politics. I know that this is often said by men in public life, but in this case it is true. I really am. There is more excitement in the round-up than in politics. And," he remarked with zest, "it is far more respectable. I prefer my ranch and the excitement it brings, to New York life," he repeated; then, lest he should seem to suggest the faintest hint of discontent, he hastened to add, "though I always make it a point to enjoy myself wherever I am."

Roosevelt spent two months in the East. On August 23d he was again in St. Paul on his way, as he told a reporter of the *Dispatch*, to Helena, Montana, and thence back to Medora. Once more the interviewer sought his views on political questions. Roosevelt made a few non-committal statements, refusing to prophesy. " My political life," he remarked, " has not altogether killed my desire to tell the truth." And with that happily flippant declaration he was off into the wilderness again.

The " womenfolks " from Maine were at Elkhorn when Roosevelt arrived. They were backwoodswomen, self-reliant, fearless, high-hearted; true mates to their stalwart men. Mrs. Sewall had brought her three-year-old daughter with her. Before Roosevelt knew what was happening, they had turned the new house into a new home.

And now for them all began a season of deep and quiet contentment that was to remain in the memories of all of them as a kind of idyl. It was a life of elemental toil, hardship, and danger, and of strong, elemental pleasures — rest after labor, food after hunger, warmth and shelter after bitter cold. In that life there was no room for distinctions of social position or wealth. They respected one another and cared for one another because and only because each knew that the others were brave and loyal and steadfast.

Life on the ranch proved a more joyous thing than ever after the women had taken charge. They demanded certain necessities at once. They demanded chickens, which Roosevelt supplied, to the delight of the bobcats, who promptly started to feast on them; they demanded at least one cow. No one had 'thought of a cow. No one in the length and breadth of that cattle country, except Mrs. Roberts, seemed to think it worth while to keep a cow for the milk that was in her, and all the cows were wild as antelope. Roosevelt and Sewall and Dow among them roped one on the range and threw her, and sat on her, and milked her upside down, which was not altogether satisfactory, but was, for the time being, the best thing they could do.

Meals became an altogether different matter from what they had been at the Maltese Cross where men were kings of the kitchen. "Eating was a sort of happy-go-lucky business at the Maltese Cross," remarked Bill Sewall subsequently. "You were happy if you got something, an' you were lucky too." There was now a new charm in shooting game, with women at home to cook it. And Mrs. Sewall baked bread that was not at all like the bread Bill baked. Soon she was even baking cake, which was an unheard-of luxury in the Bad Lands. Then, after a while, the buffalo berries and wild plums began to disappear from the bushes roundabout and appear on the table as jam.

"However big you build the house, it won't be big enough for two women," pessimists had remarked. But their forebodings were not realized. At Elkhorn no cross word was heard. They were, taken altogether, a very happy family. Roosevelt was "the boss" in the sense that, since he footed the bills, power of final decision was his; but only in that sense. He saddled his own horse; now and then he washed his own clothes; he fed the pigs; and once, on a rainy day, he blacked the Sunday boots of every man, woman, and child in the place. He was not encouraged to repeat that performance. The folks from Maine made it quite clear that if the boots needed blacking at all, which was doubtful, they thought some one else ought to do the blacking — not at all because it seemed to them improper that Roosevelt should black anybody's boots, but because he did it so badly. The paste came off on everything it touched. The women " mothered " him, setting his belongings to rights at stated intervals, for he was not conspicuous for orderliness. He, in turn, treated the women with the friendliness and respect he showed to the women of his own family. And the little Sewall girl was never short of toys.

Elkhorn Ranch was a joyous place those days. Cowboys, hearing of it, came from a distance for a touch of home life and the luxury of hearing a woman's voice.

Roosevelt's days were full of diverse activities, and the men who worked with him at Elkhorn were the pleasantest sort of companions. Bill Sewall, who, as Sylvane described him, was " like a trackhound on the deer-trail," had long ago given up the idea of making a cowboy of himself, constituting himself general superintendent of the house and its environs and guardian of the womenfolks. Not that the women needed protection. There was doubtless no safer place for women in the United States at that moment than the Bad Lands of the Little Missouri; and Mrs. Sewall and Mrs. Dow could have been counted on to handle firearms as fearlessly if not as accurately as Bill himself. But Bill tended the famished, unhappy-looking potato-patch for them, and with characteristic cheerfulness did the other chores, being quite content to leave to Roosevelt and Dow and another young cowpuncher named Rowe the riding of " sunfishers " and such things. He had a level head and an equable temper, and the cowpunchers all liked him. When a drunken cowboy, who had been a colonel in the Confederate army, accosted him one day in Joe Ferris's store with the object apparently of starting a fight, it was Sewall's quiet good nature that made his efforts abortive.

" You're a damned pleasant-looking man," exclaimed the Southerner.

Sewall smiled at him. " I am," he said. " You can't find a pleasanter man anywhere round." Which was the essential truth about Bill Sewall.

Of all Roosevelt's friends up and down the river, Sewall's nephew, Will Dow, was possibly the one who had the rarest qualities of intellect and spirit. He had a poise and a winsome lovableness that was not often found in that wild bit of country combined with such ruggedness of character. He had a droll and altogether original sense of humor, and an imagination which struck Roosevelt as extraordinary in its scope and power and which disported itself in the building of delightful yarns.

" He was always a companion that was sought wherever he went," said Bill Sewall. " There are men who have the faculty of pleasing and creating mirth and he was one of that kind."

Rowe was a different sort, of coarser fiber, but himself not without charm. He was a natural horseman, fearless to recklessness, an excellent worker, and a fighting man with a curious streak of gentleness in him that revolted against the cruelty of the branding-iron. Most men accepted the custom of branding cattle and horses as a matter of course. There was, in fact, nothing to do save accept it, for there was no other method of indicating the ownership of animals which could be reasonably relied on to defy the ingenuity of the thieves. Attempts to create opinion against it were regarded as sentimental and pernicious and were suppressed with vigor.

But Rowe had plenty of courage. " Branding cattle is rotten," he insisted, in season and out of season; adding on one occasion to a group of cow-punchers standing about a fire with branding-irons in their hands, " and you who do the branding are all going to hell."

" Aw," exclaimed a cowboy, " there ain't no hell! "

" You watch," Rowe retorted. " You'll get there and burn just as that there cow."

In comparison to the lower reaches of the Little

Missouri where Elkhorn Ranch was situated, the country about the Maltese Cross was densely populated. Howard Eaton, eight or ten miles away on Beaver Creek, was Elkhorn's closest neighbor to the north; "Farmer" Young, the only man in the Bad Lands who had as yet attacked the problem of agriculture in that region, was the nearest neighbor to the south. Six or eight miles beyond Farmer Young lived some people named Wadsworth.

Wadsworth was an unsocial being whom no one greatly liked. He had been the first man to bring cattle into the Bad Lands, and it was some of his cattle, held by Ferris and Merrifield on shares, which Roosevelt had bought in the autumn of 1883.

Roosevelt's first call on Mrs. Wadsworth had its serio-comic aspects. The Wadsworths had a great wolf-hound whom Roosevelt himself described as "a most ill-favored hybrid, whose mother was a Newfoundland and whose father was a large wolf," and which looked, it seemed, more like a hyena than like either of its parents. The dog both barked and howled, but it had a disconcerting habit of doing neither when it was on business bent. The first intimation Roosevelt had of its existence one day, as he was knocking at the door of the Wadsworth cabin, was a rush that the animal made for his trousers.

Pete Pellessier, a round-faced, genial cowpuncher from Texas, subsequently told about it. "It was one of those dogs that come sneaking around, never a growl or anything else — just grab a hunk of your leg to let you know they're around. That's the kind of a dog this was. Roosevelt just started to make a bow to Mrs. Wadsworth, 'way over, real nice. Well, that dog flew and grabbed him in the seat of the pants — he had on corduroy pants.

" ' Get out of here, you son-of-a-gun! ' he says; ' get out of here, I tell you! '

" Then he turns to Mrs. Wadsworth. ' I beg your pardon, Mrs. Wadsworth,' he says politely, ' that dog was grabbing me an' —'

" Just then the dog reached for another helping. ' Get out of here!' Roosevelt shouts to the dog, and then turns back, ' How do you do? ' he says to Mrs. Wadsworth. But the dog came back a third time, and that time Roosevelt gave that wolf-hound a kick that landed him about ten rods off. An' Roosevelt went on with his visiting."

It was a free and joyous life that Roosevelt lived with his warm-hearted companions at Elkhorn those late summer days of 1885. Now and then, when work was done, he would sit on the porch for an hour or two at a time, watching the cattle on the sand-bars, " while," as he wrote subsequently, " the vultures wheeled overhead, their black shadows gliding across the glaring white of the dry river-bed." Often he would sink into his rocking-chair, grimy and hot after the day's work, and read Keats and Swinburne for the contrast their sensuous music offered to the vigorous realities about him; or, forgetting books, he would just rock back and forth, looking sleepily out across the river while the scarlet crests of the buttes softened to rose and then to lavender, and lavender gave place to shadowy gray, and gray gave place to the luminous purple of night. The leaves of the cotton-wood trees before the house were never still, and often the cooing of mourning doves would come down to him from some high bough. He heard the thrush in the thicket near by, and in the distance the clanging cries of the water-fowl. He knew the note of every bird, and they were like friends calling to him.

XIX

We're the children of the open and we hate the haunts o' men,
 But we had to come to town to get the mail.
And we're ridin' home at daybreak — 'cause the air is cooler then —
 All 'cept one of us that stopped behind in jail.
Shorty's nose won't bear paradin', Bill's off eye is darkly fadin',
 All our toilets show a touch of disarray;
For we found that City life is a constant round of strife,
 And we ain't the breed for shyin' from a fray.

Chant your war-whoops, pardners dear, while the east turns pale with
 fear,
 And the chaparral is tremblin' all aroun';
For we're wicked to the marrer; we're a midnight dream of terror,
 When we're ridin' up the rocky trail from town!

BADGER CLARK

MEANWHILE, as the months passed by, Medora was growing, and stretching itself. Even the Mandan *Pioneer*, a hundred and fifty miles to the east, thought it worth its while to brag about it.

Medora is distinctively a cattle town [runs the comment], and is ambitious to be the cattle market of the Northwest. In two years it has grown from absolutely nothing to be a town which possesses a number of fine buildings, and represents a great many dollars of capital. The Black Hills freight depot is a well-built, substantial building. A number of brick houses have been built during the last year, including a very neat and attractive Catholic church, and a large hotel.

The *Pioneer* did not see fit to say that most of the " fine buildings " had been built by one man and that on the slender reed of that man's business acumen the prosperity of the whole community rested. To have done so would possibly have seemed like looking a gift-horse in the mouth. And Medora's prosperity appeared solid enough, in all conscience. Things were, in fact, humming. There was now a clothing store in town, a drug store, a hardware store, a barber shop. Backed by Roosevelt, Joe Ferris had erected a two-story structure on the eastern bank and moved his store from Little Missouri to be an active rival of the Marquis's company store. A school was built (by whom and with what funds remains mysterious) and Bill Dantz was made Superintendent of Education; and next to Joe's store, opposite the office of the *Bad Lands Cowboy*, Fisher laid the beginnings of Medora's Great White Way with a roller-skating pavilion, where the cowboys who drifted into town, drunk or sober, exhibited their skill to the hilarious delight of their friends.

But the architectural monuments in which Medora's opulence most vigorously expressed itself were the saloons. The number of these varied, according to the season. Sometimes there were a dozen, sometimes there were more, for no one bothered about a license and any one with ten dollars and a jug of rum could start his own " liquor parlor."

Among the saloons Bill Williams's stood in a class by itself. He, too, had followed civilization to Medora, establishing himself first in a small building near Joe's store, and, when that burnt down, in an imposing two-story frame structure which the

Marquis de Mores built for him. The bar-room was on the first floor and above it was a huge hall which was used for public meetings and occasionally for dances. The relation of the dance-hall to the bar-room had its disadvantages, especially when the shooting began. The bar-room itself was a sumptuous affair, for Williams had the shrewdness to know that it was not only rum that the lonely cowpuncher sought when he pushed in the swinging doors. The place was never closed, night or day, and the faro wheel was seldom silent.

The other saloons could not compete with the gorgeousness with which Bill Williams edged the cloud of robbery and ruin that hung about his iniquitous saloon; when they seemed for a night to compete, drawing to their own hospitable bars the cowpunchers whom Williams looked upon as his own legitimate prey, he had a way of standing at his door and shooting indiscriminately into the night. Out of a dozen rum-shops would pour excited cowboys eager to know " what the shooting was about," and as they crowded inquisitively about his bar, trade would once more become brisk in Bill Williams's saloon.

Bill Williams was a *bona-fide* " bad man." So also was Maunders. But they were of Medora's hundred-odd permanent inhabitants during that summer of 1885, the only ones who might with complete fidelity to facts have been so designated. Others blew in and blew out again, creating a little disturbance and drifting west. The great majority of Medora's noisy population were merely light-hearted youngsters who had not yet outgrown their love for fire-crackers.

Under the title " Styles in the Bad Lands," the Dickinson *Press* reprinted certain " fashion notes " from the columns of an enterprising contemporary:

The Estelline (Dak.) *Bell* has been at some trouble to collect the following latest fashion notes for the benefit of its Bad Lands readers: The " gun " is still worn on the right hip, slightly lower down than formerly. This makes it more convenient to get at during a dis-cussion with a friend. The regular " forty-five " still remains a favorite. Some affect a smaller caliber, but it is looked upon as slightly dudish. A " forty," for instance, may induce a more artistic opening in an ad-versary, but the general effect and mortality is impaired. The plug of tobacco is still worn in the pocket on the opposite side from the shooter, so when reaching for the former, friends will not misinterpret the move and subsequently be present at your funeral. It is no longer considered necessary to wait for introductions before proceeding to get the drop. There will be time enough for the mere outward formalities of politeness at the inquest. The trimming of the " iron " is still classic and severe, only a row of six cartridges grouped around the central barrel being admissible. Self-cockers are now the only style seen in the best circles.[1] Much of the effectiveness of the gun was formerly destroyed by having to thumb up the hammer, especially when the person with whom you were conversing wore the self-

[1] "Whoever wrote that was badly off his base. The simon-pure cowpuncher would not accept a self-cocker as a gift. They laughed at them in fact. Once, on a bet, a cowpuncher shot off all six shots with his single-action Colt. 45 while his opponent was getting off three with his self-cocker." — *Lincoln Lang.*

cocking variety. It has been found that on such occasions the old-style gun was but little used except in the way of circumstantial evidence at the inquest. Shooting from the belt without drawing is considered hardly the thing among gentlemen who do not wish to be considered as attempting to attract notice. In cases where the gentleman with whom you are holding a joint debate already has the drop, his navy six having a hair trigger, and he being bound to shoot, anyway, this style of discussion is allowable, though apt to cause a coldness to spring up. As regards the number of guns which it is admissible to wear, great latitude is allowed, from one up to four being noted on the street and at social gatherings. One or two is generally considered enough, except where a sheriff with a reputation of usually getting his man and a Winchester rifle is after you, when we cannot too strongly impress upon the mind of the reader the absolute necessity for going well heeled.

In Medora in those midsummer days of 1885, Hell-Roaring Bill Jones was the life of every party. Wherever there was deviltry, there was Bill Jones, profane and obscene beyond description, but irresistibly comical. He was as lean and muscular as John Falstaff was short and fat, but the divergences between the genial old reprobate of Eastcheap and the saturnine, but by no means unlovable, rapscallion of Medora were less striking than the qualities they had in common. He had good friends, none better than the gay, infinitely pathetic patrician's son, Van Zander, who played Prince Hal to him, light-heartedly flipping a fortune in the air as others, essentially less admirable, might have flipped a dollar.

" Deacon " Cummins thought Bill Jones dreadful, which naturally incited Bill Jones always to do the worst that was in him to do whenever the " Deacon " was within earshot. He found delight in drawing up beside him on the round-up and pouring forth every evil tale he knew.

" Jones, I don't know why you tell those stories when I'm around," the " Deacon " would exclaim, not without pathos. " You know I don't like them."

After his first encounter with Roosevelt in the office of the *Bad Lands Cowboy*, Bill Jones told him no foul stories. The contrast between Bill Jones's attitude toward a virtuous man who was strong and a virtuous man who was weak might furnish a theme for many sermons.

The antics of Saturday nights were many and some of them were explosive, but on the whole men looked more tolerantly on the shackles of civilization in Medora in 1885 than they had in 1884. The vigilantes' raid had undoubtedly chased the fear of God into the hearts of the evil-doers.

Whatever can be said against the methods adopted by the " stranglers " who came through here last fall [remarked the *Bad Lands Cowboy*], it cannot but be acknowledged that the result of their work has been very wholesome. Not a definite case of horse-stealing from a cowman has been reported since, and it seems as though a very thorough clean-up had been made.

The ranch-owners, evidently, did not find the situation as satisfactory as Packard found it, for in July the Little Missouri River Stockmen's Associa-

tion, of which Roosevelt was chairman, determined
to organize a posse to "clean up" the country north
of the railroad between the Missouri and the Little
Missouri rivers. Osterhaut, captain of the round-
up, was appointed leader and half a dozen ranchmen contributed a cowboy apiece. Roosevelt sent
Sewall as his representative.

The route was through about as wild and unsettled
a portion of the country as can be found now, so the
people here say [Sewall wrote his brother on his return],
and the oldest heads seemed to think thare might be
some danger, but we saw nothing worse than ourselves.

Once more, that August, Packard raised his·
voice in favor of the organization of the county, but
once more mysterious forces blocked his efforts.
Meanwhile, the Stockmen's Association was ex-
erting a stabilizing influence that was as quiet as
it was profound. No one talked about it, or thought
much about it. But to evil-doers, it loomed uncomfortably in the background. Sometime during
the year 1885, the Association voted to employ a
stock inspector at Medora to examine the brands
of all cattle shipped thence to Chicago. This was
a distinct check to the thieves, and might hàve
been checkmate, if the Association had not seen
fit to appoint to the position the same Joe Morrill
who as United States deputy marshal had already
exhibited a tenderness toward the lawbreakers
which was almost if not altogether criminal. What
Roosevelt's attitude was to this appointment is
not known; but he was under no illusions in regard
to Morrill.

Amid the tumult and excitement of life in Medora that summer of 1885, the consolations of organized religion were more inaccessible even than the services of an earthly physician, and there was no servant of Christ, of any creed or any denomination, who ministered to the men and women scattered through that wild region in a manner even remotely comparable to the self-sacrificing devotion with which Dr. Stickney ministered to them. That excellent disciple of the Lord doctored broken spirits even as he doctored broken bodies. The essentials of religion, which are love and service, he gave with both hands from a full heart; the " trimmings " he left to the parsons.

These " trimmings " were, it seemed, the only things which the few professional men of God who drifted into Medora were able to contribute. With the exception of the Roman Catholic chapel, erected by the Marquise de Mores as a thank-offering after the birth of her two children, there was no church of any denomination in Little Missouri or Medora, or, in fact, anywhere in Billings County; and in the chapel there were services not more than once or twice a month. Occasionally an itinerant Methodist or Baptist, whom no one knew anything about, blew in from anywhere, and blew out again; and if he was seen no more there were no lamentations.[1] Services of a sort

[1] The Dickinson *Press* burst into verse in describing the exploits of one of the preachers.

"Of a gospel preacher we now will tell
Who started from Glendive to save souls from hell.

were held in the " depot," in one of the stores or in the dance-hall over Bill Williams's saloon, but attendance was scanty.

The inhabitants of the Bad Lands did not greatly feel the need of spiritual instruction, and were inclined to seek consolation, when they needed it, in " Forty-Mile Red-Eye " rather than in theology.

" Anything or any one associated with religion or spiritual living was shunned," Bill Dantz explained in after days, " religion being looked on as an institution for old women and weaklings. Such traveling evangelists and, later, regular pastors as came to the Northwest were treated with respect, but never came within miles of the intimacy or confidence of the cowboys. Such early congregations as clustered about the pioneer churches were the newly arrived ' nesters ' or homesteaders of the towns; the cowboys never. There could be no possible community of interests between book-

> At the Little Missouri he struck a new game,
> With the unregenerate, 'Honest John' is its name.

> "He indulged too much in the flowing bowls,
> And forgot all about the saving of souls,
> But 'dropped' his three hundred, slept sweetly and well,
> And let the Little Missourians wander to ——
>   that place whose main principles of political economy are
>   brimstone and caloric."

But the verses tell only half the story. As Sylvane Ferris relates it Bill Williams, conniving with Jess Hogue to fleece the preacher, gave him the impression that he too was losing heavily; and actually shed tears. The preacher was heard to murmur, as he staggered into the night, "I don't mind losing my own money, but I am so sorry for that nice Mr. Williams."

learned men of sedentary profession and a half-tamed, open-range horseman."

The reason, of course, was that the missionaries were fundamentally less honest and virtuous than the gay-hearted argonauts to whom they attempted to bring the gospel; and their patient listeners, who had no illusions concerning their own piety, nevertheless knew it. The preachers, moreover, were less than human. They preached interminable sermons. Discourses lasting an hour and a half were common, and even lengthier ones were not unusual. The parsons were hopelessly thick-skinned, moreover, and impervious to hints. When on one occasion, at which Sylvane was present, the congregation began to consult their watches, the preacher, instead of bringing his sermon to a close, exclaimed, " See here, you don't want to be lookin' at your watches. You don't hear a sermon often."

One missionary, the representative of a certain Home Mission Society, came to Packard, saying that he wanted to start a church in Medora, and asking Packard for his moral support. Packard agreed that a church might be useful and secured the baggage-room at the " depot " for an auditorium. The man held his first services, preaching an hour and a half.

" See here," said Packard when the performance was over, " this won't do. You preach altogether too long."

" Well," asked the preacher, " how long shall it be? "

" Your whole service oughtn't to be longer than your sermon was."

The missionary it appeared, was eager to please. The following Sunday he preached three quarters of an hour.

But Packard was still dissatisfied. " Cut it to fifteen minutes," he insisted. " You can say all you have to say in that time."

The third Sunday the missionary did not appear. He had found it necessary to make a swift exit from his domicile, departing by one door as a sheriff entered by another. He had, it seems, knocked in the head of one of his parishioners with a hatchet.

Experiences of this sort were not calculated to inspire respect for the clergy in the minds of the cowpunchers.

" Them preachers," Sylvane subsequently remarked, " broke us fellows from going to church."

But though religion did not flourish in the alkaline soil of the Bad Lands, the fundamental American principle of orderly government, based on the consent of the governed, slowly and with many setbacks took root. The town of Medora itself began to sober down. Joe Ferris was a rock of defense for law and order. In disputes, instead of clutching at the six-shooter, men began to turn to Joe as an arbitrator, knowing that he was honest and fair and had a sense of humor. Packard, moreover, had established himself firmly in the respect and affection of his neighbors, and his reiterations, week after week and month after month, of certain notions of order and decency, gradually began to have their effect. The *Cowboy* became the dominant factor in Medora's struggle toward maturity.

From out of the blue ether and the whimsical generosity of Fate, meanwhile, had come an assistant for Packard who gave new zest to his adventure. His name was Johnny O'Hara, and Packard always insisted that he came as a gift from the gods.

" In all literature there was only one like him," said Packard in after days, " and that was Kim. And Kim's name was O'Hara. As chela to Teshoo Lama, Kim acquired merit. As devil in the *Bad Lands Cowboy* office, Johnny acquired a place in my estimation only to be described in the beatitudes of an inspired writer. Kim went out with his begging-bowl and he and his Lama feasted bounteously. Johnny boarded passenger trains with an armful of the *Cowboy* and returned with enough money to pay current expenses. Kim played the great game with Strickland Sahib and attained rupees sufficient for a ride on the tee-rain. Johnny took the remains of a bunch of bananas I had ordered by express from St. Paul and sold them for enough to pay for the first and even a second one. Two banana feasts for nothing, plus a profit! Kim came from the top of Zam-Zanneh to his chelaship with Teshoo Lama. Johnny came from the top of Mount Olympus or the biggest butte in the Bad Lands to become my right hand. Blessed be the name of O'Hara, be it Kim or Johnny."

They worked together, with Joe Ferris and Sylvane and Merrifield and Gregor Lang and Howard Eaton, the solid citizens, and Roosevelt, the aggressive champion of order, to establish America in a patch of sagebrush wilderness.

XX

Bill's head was full o' fire
   An' his gizzard full o' rum,
An' the things he said wuz rich an' red
   An' rattled as they come.

Dave wuz on his stummick,
   Readin' the news at his ease-like,
When Bill comes, brave, sayin' what he'll do to Dave
   In words what could walk away, cheese-like.

Ol' Bill's fist wuz man-size
   Sure as any alive —
But Dave, never squintin', turns over the printin'
   An' there wuz his Forty-five.

Bill he chokes an' swallers,
   But Dave he's gentle an' mild,
An' they talks together o' cows an' the weather,
   An' allows they is re-con-ciled.

From *Medora Nights*

WHERE, meanwhile, was the Marquis de Mores?

A casual observer, during the spring of 1885, might have remarked that physically he was never long at any one place; but that metaphorically he was on the crest of the wave. The erection of the great abattoir, which had replaced the more primitive structure built in 1883, gave an impression of great prosperity. Actually, however, it was a symptom of failure. It had, in fact, been erected only because of the irremediable inefficiency of the original smaller structure. By the end of 1884 the Marquis had discovered that the slaughtering of twenty-five head of cattle a day could not, by the most painstaking application of " business methods," be made profitable. It took more than butchers, the Marquis found, to operate a slaughter-house. An engine was needed and an engineer, a foreman, a bookkeeper, a hide-man, a tallow-man, a blood-man, a cooper, and a night-watchman. These men could easily take care of three or four hundred head a day, and they were required to take care only of twenty-five.

The Marquis was not without executive ability. He had, since the preceding autumn, sought competent advisers, moreover, and followed their suggestions. Among other things, these advisers had told him that, owing to the unusual quality of the stem-cured grass in the Bad Lands, beef fit for market could be slaughtered as early as the first of June when beef commanded a high price.

Accordingly, on June 1st the new abattoir was opened. Every precaution against waste had, it seemed, been taken, and for fear lest the branch houses in Kansas City, Bismarck, and elsewhere should be unable to absorb the output of the slaughter-house and interrupt its steady operation, the Marquis secured a building on West Jackson Street, Chicago, where the wholesale dealers in dressed beef had their stalls, with the purpose of there disposing of his surplus.

A hundred head of cattle were slaughtered daily at the new abattoir. At last the plant was efficient. The Marquis had a right to congratulate himself. But unexpectedly a fresh obstacle to success obtruded itself. The experts had been wrong; the beef proved of poor quality. The branch houses disposed of it with difficulty, and the retail dealers in Chicago refused to buy. Although dressed beef was produced there in enormous quantities for Eastern markets, the local consumer had a prejudice against cold-storage meat. He did not like grass-fed beef, moreover. It was as good or better than corn-fed beef, but he was not accustomed to it, and would not change his habits even at a saving.

It was a staggering blow, but the Marquis was a fighting man and he took it without wincing. Packard, discussing the situation with him one day, pointed out to him that the cattle could not possibly be stall-fed before they were slaughtered as no cattle feed was raised short of the corn country, hundreds of miles to the south.

The Marquis was not noticeably perturbed by this recital of an obvious fact. " I am arranging to buy up the hop crop of the Pacific coast," he answered calmly. " This I will sell to the Milwaukee and St. Louis brewers on an agreement that they shall return to me all the resultant malt after their beer is made. This I will bring to Medora in tank cars. It is the most concentrated and fattening food to be bought. I will cover the town site south of the track with individual feeding-pens; thousands of them. Not only can I hold fat cattle as long as I wish, but I will feed cattle all the year round and always have enough to keep the abattoir running."

There was something gorgeous in the Marquis's

inability to know when he was beaten. His power of self-hypnotism was in fact, amazing, and the persistence with which he pursued new bubbles, in his efforts to escape from the devils which the old ones had hatched as they burst, had its attractive side.

" The Medora Stage and Forwarding Company," the Dickinson *Press* announced on May 16th, " is a total wreck." It was; and shortly after, Van Driesche, most admirable of valets and now the Marquis's private secretary, went with " Johnny " Goodall, foreman of the Marquis's ranch, to Deadwood to salvage what they could from the rocks.

But two weeks later the Marquis had a new dream. The *Press* announced it; " The Marquis de Mores believes he has discovered kaoline, a clay from which the finest pottery is made, near the town of Medora." The inference is clear. If Medora could not rival Chicago, it might easily rival Sèvres or Copenhagen.

For all the Marquis's endeavors to outface fortune, however, and to win success somewhere, somehow, beyond this valley of a hundred failures, the Nemesis which every man creates out of his limitations was drawing her net slowly and irresistibly about him. He had no friends in Medora. His foreign ways and his alien attitude of mind kept him, no doubt against his own desires, outside the warm circle of that very human society. He was an aristocrat, and he did not understand the democratic individualism of the men about him. " The

Marquis," as one of his associates later explained, " always had the idea of being the head of something or other, and tried to run everything he had anything to do with."

The Marquis loved the Bad Lands; there was no question about that. " I like this country," he said to J. W. Foley, who became his superintendent about this time, " because there is room to turn around without stepping on the feet of others." The trouble was, however, that with a man of the Marquis's qualities and limitations, the Desert of Sahara would scarcely have been wide enough and unsettled enough to keep him content with his own corner of it. He seemed fated to step on other people's toes, possibly because at bottom he did not greatly care if he did step on them when they got in the way.

" De Mores," said Lincoln Lang, " seemed to think that some sort of divine right reposed in him to absorb the entire Little Missouri country and everything in it."

He had king's blood in him, in fact, and the genealogy which he solemnly revealed to Foley reached into an antiquity staggeringly remote, and made Bourbons and Guelphs, Hohenzollerns and Hapsburgs appear by comparison as very shoddy parvenus. He claimed descent on the maternal side from Caius Mucius, who, as Livy relates, crossed the Tiber to slay King Porsena and killed the King's secretary by mistake, a piece of business so similar to certain actions of the man who claimed him for an ancestor as to lend some color to the claim. De Mores was related more or less nearly to the Orleans family which had never renounced what it regarded as its title to the throne of France; and he himself had his eye on a crown. Behind all his activities in the Bad Lands loomed a grandiose purpose. To one or two of his associates he revealed it. He would make a great fortune in America, he declared, then return to France and, with the glitter of his dollars about him, gain control of the French army and by a *coup d'état* make himself King of France.

It was a gorgeous piece of day-dreaming; but its fulfillment was, in those middle eighties, not beyond the border of the possible.

As the only rival for leadership in the Bad Lands of this aspirant for a throne stood, by one of Fate's queerest whimsies, a man who also had his eye on one of the high places of this world. The Marquis de Mores was the leader, or if not the leader at least the protector, of the forces of reaction; Theodore Roosevelt was the leader of the forces of progress. They were both in the middle twenties, both aristocrats by birth, both fearless and adventurous; but one believed in privilege and the other believed in equality of opportunity.

"When it came to a show-down, the Marquis was always there," said Dr. Stickney, who watched the quiet struggle for supremacy with a philosophic eye, "but he had no judgment. You couldn't expect it. He was brought up in the army. He was brought up in social circles that didn't develop judgment. He didn't know how to mix with the cowboys. When he did mix with any of them, it was always with the worst element. Now, when Roosevelt came to the Bad Lands he naturally attracted the better element among the cowboys, such men as the Ferrises and Merrifield, men of high character whose principles were good."

And Packard said: " Roosevelt was the embodiment of the belief of obedience to the law and the right of the majority to change it. The Marquis was equally honest in his belief that he himself was the law and that he had a divine right to change the law as he wished."

The conflict between the two forces in the community was quiet but persistent. Roosevelt dined on occasion with the Marquis and the Marquis dined on occasion with Roosevelt; they discussed horsemanship and hunting and books; at the meeting of the Montana Stockgrowers' Association at Miles City in April, that year, the Marquis proposed Roosevelt for membership; on the surface, in fact, they got along together most amicably. But under the surface fires were burning.

On one occasion, when Roosevelt and the Marquis were both in the East, Roosevelt sent a message to his sister " Bamie," with whom he was living, telling her that he had invited the Marquis and his wife to dinner that evening. The message that came back from " Bamie " was, in substance, as follows: " By all means bring them. But please let me know beforehand whether you and the Marquis are on friendly terms at the moment or are likely to spring at each other's throat."

"Theodore did not care for the Marquis," said "Bamie" in later years, "but he was sorry for his wife and was constantly helping the Marquis out of the scrapes he was forever getting into with the other cattlemen."

There were many reasons why the relations between the two men should not have been noticeably cordial. Roosevelt had from the start thrown in his lot with the men who had been most emphatic in their denunciation of the Marquis's part in the killing of Riley Luffsey. Gregor Lang, who was the Marquis's most caustic critic, was Roosevelt's warm friend. "Dutch Wannigan," moreover, who had been saved only by a miracle in the memorable ambuscade, was one of Roosevelt's cow-hands. That summer of 1885 he was night-herder for the Maltese Cross "outfit." He was a genial soul and Roosevelt liked him. No doubt he was fascinated also by his remarkable memory, for "Wannigan," who was unable to read or write, could be sent to town with a verbal order for fifty items, and could be counted on not only to bring every article he had been sent for, but to give an exact accounting, item by item, of every penny he had spent. For the Marquis the presence of "Dutch Wannigan" in Roosevelt's "outfit" was, no doubt, convincing evidence of Roosevelt's own attitude in regard to the memorable affray of June 26th, 1883. Whatever irritation he may have felt toward Roosevelt because of it could scarcely have been mollified by the fact that " Dutch Wannigan," in his quiet way, was moving heaven and earth to bring about the indictment of the Marquis for murder.

But there was another reason why the relations between the Marquis and Roosevelt were strained. In the Marquis's business ventures he was constantly being confronted by unexpected and, in a sense, unaccountable obstacles, that rose suddenly out of what appeared a clear road, and thwarted his plans. The railroads, which gave special rates to shippers who did far less business than he, found for one reason or another that they could not give him any rebate at all. Wholesale dealers refused, for reasons which remained mysterious, to handle his meat; yard-men at important junctions delayed his cars. He could not help but be conscious that principalities and powers that he could not identify were working in the dark against him. He suspected that the meat-packers of Chicago had passed the word to their allies in Wall Street that he was to be destroyed; and assumed that Roosevelt, bound by a dozen ties to the leaders in the business life of New York, was in league with his enemies.

A totally unexpected incident brought the growing friction between the two men for a flash into the open. Roosevelt had agreed to sell the Marquis eighty or a hundred head of cattle at a price, on which they agreed, of about six cents a pound. Accompanied by two of his cowpunchers, he drove the cattle to the enclosure adjoining the abattoir of the Northern Pacific Refrigerator Car Company, had them weighed, and went to the Marquis for his check.

" I am sorry I cannot pay you as much as I agreed for those cattle," said the Marquis.

" But you bought the cattle," Roosevelt protested. " The sale was complete with the delivery."

" The Chicago price is down a half cent," answered the Marquis regretfully. " I will pay you a half cent less than we agreed."

The air was electric. Packard told about it long afterwards. " It was a ticklish situation," he said. " We all knew the price had been agreed on the day before; the sale being completed with the delivery of the cattle. Fluctuations in the market cut no figure. Roosevelt would have made delivery at the agreed price even if the Chicago price had gone up."

Roosevelt turned to the Marquis. " Did you agree to pay six cents for these cattle? "

" Yes," the Marquis admitted. " But the Chicago price — "

" Are you going to pay six cents for them? " Roosevelt broke in.

" No; I will pay five and a half cents."

Roosevelt turned abruptly to his cowpunchers. " Drive 'em out, boys," he said. The men drove out the cattle.

" There was no particular ill-feeling between them," Packard said later, " and Roosevelt gave the Marquis credit for an honest belief that a variation in the Chicago price would cut a figure in their agreed price. It was that very fact, however, which made impossible any further business relations between them."

The *Pioneer Press* of St. Paul, in its issue of August 23d, 1885, tells its own version of the story.

About a year ago the Marquis made a verbal contract with Theodore Roosevelt, the New York politician, who owns an immense cattle ranch near Medora, agreeing to purchase a number of head of cattle. Roosevelt had his stock driven down to the point agreed upon, when the Marquis declined to receive them, and declared that he had made no such contract. Roosevelt stormed a little, but finally subsided and gave orders to his men not to sell any cattle to the Marquis or transact any business with him. The relations between the Marquis and Roosevelt have since been somewhat strained.

A reporter of the Bismarck *Tribune*, a few days after this story appeared, caught Roosevelt as he was passing through the city on his return from a flying visit to the East, and evidently asked him what truth 'there was in it. His deprecation of the story is not altogether conclusive.

Theodore Roosevelt, the young reformer of New York, passed through this city yesterday [he writes], *en route* to his ranch in the Bad Lands. He was as bright and talkative as ever, and spoke of the great opportunities of the imperial Northwest with more enthusiasm than has ever been exhibited by the most sanguine old-timer. Mr. Roosevelt recently had a slight tilt with the Marquis de Mores on a cattle deal, and the story has been exaggerated until readers of Eastern papers are led to believe that these two cattle kings never speak as they pass by and are looking for each other with clubs. This is not true.

Meanwhile, during those summer months of 1885 the hot water into which the Frenchman had flung himself when he assisted in the killing of Riley Luffsey began to simmer once more. It came to a boil on August 26th, when a grand jury in Mandan indicted the Marquis de Mores for murder in the first degree.

The Marquis had not been unaware how matters were shaping themselves. When the movement to have him indicted first got under way, in fact, it was intimated to him that a little matter of fifteen hundred dollars judiciously distributed would cause the indictment to be withdrawn. He inquired whether the indictment would stay withdrawn or whether he would be subject to indictment and, in consequence, to blackmail, during the rest of his life. He was told that since he had never been acquitted by a jury, he might be indicted at any moment, the next day, or ten years hence. He declared that he preferred to clean up the matter then and there.

" I have plenty of money for defense," he said to a reporter of the New York *Times*, adapting, not without humor, a famous American war-cry to his own situation, " but not a dollar for blackmail."

Knowing the ways of courts, he removed himself from the Territory while the forces were being gathered against him at Mandan.

" I determined that I would not be put in jail,"

he explained to the *Times* interviewer, " to lie there perhaps for months waiting for a trial. Besides, a jail is not a safe place in that part of the country. Now the court seems to be ready and so will I be in a few days. I do not fear the result."

He was convinced that the same forces which had thwarted him in his business enterprises were using the Luffsey episode to push him out of the way.

" I think the charge has been kept hanging over me," he said, " for the purpose of breaking up my business. It was known that I intended to kill and ship beef to Chicago and other Eastern cities, and had expended much money in preparations. If I could have been arrested and put in jail some months ago, it might have injured my business and perhaps have put an end to my career."

The Marquis was convinced that it was Roosevelt who was financing the opposition to him and spoke of him with intense bitterness.

The indictment of the Marquis, meanwhile, was mightily agitating the western part of the Territory. Sentiment in the matter had somewhat veered since the first trials which had been held two years before. The soberer of the citizens, recognizing the real impetus which the Marquis's energy and wealth had given to the commercial activity of the West Missouri region, were inclined to sympathize with him. There was a widespread belief that in the matter of the indictment the Marquis had fallen among thieves.

The Marquis returned from the East about the

last day of August, and gave himself up to the sheriff at Mandan. He was promptly lodged in jail. The remark he had made to the interviewer in New York, that a jail was not a safe place in Dakota, proved prophetic. A mob, composed of cowboys and lumberjacks, bombarded the jail in which the Marquis was confined. At the close of the bombardment, Roosevelt, who happened to be in Mandan, on his way to the East, called on the Marquis.

In the Marquis's cell he found the Frenchman with his faithful valet and secretary. The secretary was under the bed, but the Marquis was sitting on its edge, calmly smoking a cigarette.

As the date for the trial drew near, feeling rose. The idle and vociferous elements in the town discovered that the Marquis was a plutocrat and an enemy of the people, and called thirstily for his blood. There was a large Irish population, moreover, which remembered that the slain man had borne the name of Riley and (two years after his demise) hotly demanded vengeance. The Marquis declared that, with popular sentiment as it was, he could not be given a fair trial, and demanded a change of venue. It was granted. The mob, robbed of its prey, howled in disappointment. A mass meeting was held and resolutions were passed calling for the immediate removal of the iniquitous judge who had granted the Marquis's petition.

The trial, which began on September 15th, was more nerve-racking for the lawyers than for the defendant. For the witnesses were elusive. The trial seemed to be regarded by the majority of those connected with it as a gracious act of Providence for the redistribution of some of the Marquis's wealth. Everybody, it seemed, was thrusting a finger into the Marquis's purse. One of his friends later admitted that the Frenchman's money had been freely used, " but, of course, only," he blandly explained, " to persuade the witnesses to tell the truth."

McFay, a carpenter, who had distinguished himself at the previous trial by the melodramatic quality of his testimony, proved the peskiest witness of all. He was spending his days and his nights during the trial gambling and living high. Whenever his money gave out he called at the office of one of the Marquis's supporters to " borrow " fifty dollars to continue his revelry, and the victim was too much afraid of what fiction he might tell the jury to refuse him. It was determined in solemn conclave, however, that McFay should be the first witness called, and disposed of.

The lawyers breathed a sigh of relief when the time came to put the shifty carpenter on the stand. But just as he was to be called, McFay drew aside the friend of the Marquis whom he had so successfully bled.

" Come outside a minute," he said.

The friend went.

" My memory is getting damn poor," declared the carpenter.

" How much do you want? "

" Oh, five hundred."

He got it. The trial proceeded.

One juror was, for no reason which they themselves could adequately analyze, withdrawn by the Marquis's attorneys at the last minute. He told one of them years after that, if he had been allowed to serve, he would have " hung up the jury until some one had passed him ten thousand." It was a close shave.

Two items in the testimony were notably significant. One was contributed by the Marquis: " O'Donald and Luffsey discharged all the barrels of their revolvers," he said, " and then began to shoot with their rifles." The other item was contributed by Sheriff Harmon, who arrested O'Donald and " Dutch Wannigan " immediately after the affray. He testified " that the guns and pistols of the hunters were loaded when handed to him."

The jury made no attempt to pick its way through contradictions such as this, and returned to the court room after an absence of ten minutes with a verdict of " not guilty."

The Marquis's acquittal did not, it seems, mollify his bitterness toward Roosevelt. He prided himself on his judgment, as he had once informed Howard Eaton, but his judgment had a habit of basing its conclusions on somewhat nebulous premises. Two or three bits of circumstantial evidence had served to convince the Marquis definitely that Roosevelt had been the impelling force behind the prosecution. The fact that " Dutch Wannigan " was an employee of Roosevelt's, in itself, not unnaturally, perhaps, stirred the Marquis's ire. When he was told, however, that "Dutch Wannigan," before departing for the trial at Mandan, had received money from Joe Ferris, his suspicions appeared confirmed, for Joe was known to be Roosevelt's close friend, and it was an open secret that Roosevelt was financing Joe's venture in storekeeping. If his suspicions needed further confirmation, they seemed to get it when a little, black-haired Irishman, named Jimmie McShane, otherwise known as "Dynamite Jimmie," received a sum of money from Joe Ferris and appeared at the trial as the first witness for the prosecution. On the surface the case against Roosevelt was convincing, and the Marquis evidently did not dip beneath it. If he had, he would have realized that Joe Ferris was the acknowledged banker of the Bad Lands to whom practically all the thrifty souls among the cowpunchers brought a portion of their wages for safe-keeping. When "Dutch Wannigan" and "Dynamite Jimmie," therefore, received money from Joe Ferris, they received only what was their own, and what they needed for their expenses at the trial.

But the Marquis, whose mind liked to jump goat-like from crag to crag, did not stop to examine the evidence against Roosevelt. He accepted it at its face value, and wrote Roosevelt a stinging letter, telling him that he had heard that Roosevelt had influenced witnesses against him in the murder trial. He had supposed, he said, that there was nothing but friendly feeling between himself and

Roosevelt, but since it was otherwise there was always "a way of settling differences between gentlemen."

Roosevelt, who had returned from the East early in October, received the letter at Elkhorn Ranch and read it aloud to Bill Sewall. "That's a threat," he exclaimed. "He is trying to bully me. He can't bully me. I am going to write him a letter myself. Bill," he went on, "I don't want to disgrace my family by fighting a duel. I don't believe in fighting duels. My friends don't any of them believe in it. They would be very much opposed to anything of the kind, but I won't be bullied by a Frenchman. Now, as I am the challenged party, I have the privilege of naming the weapons. I am no swordsman, and pistols are too uncertain and Frenchy for me. So what do you say if I make it rifles?"

Roosevelt sat down on a log and then and there drafted his reply. He had no unfriendly feeling for the Marquis, he wrote, "but, as the closing sentence of your letter implies a threat, I feel it my duty to say that I am ready at all times and at all places to answer for my actions."

Then he added that if the Marquis's letter was meant as a challenge, and he insisted upon having satisfaction, he would meet him with rifles at twelve paces, the adversaries to shoot and advance until one or the other dropped.

"Now," said Roosevelt, "I expect he'll challenge me. If he does, I want you for my second."

Sewall grunted. "You will never have to fight any duel of that kind with that man," he said. "He won't challenge you. He will find some way out of it."

Roosevelt was not at all sure of this. The Marquis was a bully, but he was no coward.

A day or so later the answer came by special messenger. Roosevelt brought it over to Sewall. "You were right, Bill, about the Marquis," he said.

Sewall read the Marquis's letter. The Marquis declared that Roosevelt had completely misunderstood the meaning of his message. The idea that he had meant to convey was that there was always a way of settling affairs of that sort between gentlemen — without trouble. And would not Mr. Roosevelt do him the honor of dining with him, and so forth and so on?

"The Marquis," as Roosevelt remarked long afterward, "had a streak of intelligent acceptance of facts, and as long as he did not *publicly* lose caste or incur ridicule by backing down, he did not intend to run risk without adequate object. He did not expect his bluff to be called; and when it was, he had to make up his mind to withdraw it."

There was no more trouble after that between Theodore Roosevelt and the Marquis de Mores.

XXI

I'd rather hear a rattler rattle,
I'd rather buck stampeding cattle,
I'd rather go to a greaser battle,
Than —
Than to —
Than to fight —
Than to fight the bloody In-ji-ans.

I'd rather eat a pan of dope,
I'd rather ride without a rope,
I'd rather from this country lope,
Than —
Than to —
Than to fight —
Than to fight the bloody In-ji-ans.

Cowboy song

ALL through that autumn of 1885, Roosevelt remained in the Bad Lands. With his whole being he
reveled in the wild and care-free life; but the newspapers did not seem to be able to rise above the
notion that he was in Dakota for political purposes:

Mr. Theodore Roosevelt, it is rumored [remarked the
Chicago *Tribune*] has an eye on politics in Dakota, and
is making himself popular with the natives. He is bright,
certainly, but Mr. Roosevelt will find the methods in
Dakota quite different from those which gave him sudden prominence in New York. There is a great deal
of breeziness in a Dakota convention, but it is not the
breeziness of innocence. It is high art. The number of
gentlemen who are in training for United States senator-
ships, when Dakota shall have acquired admission, is
not limited, and each and every aspirant can pull a
wire with a silent grace which is fascinating. If Mr.

Roosevelt really likes politics, he will enjoy himself in Dakota.

If Roosevelt had any notion of entering the race for the senatorship in Dakota, he has left no record of it. Howard Eaton spoke to him once about it. He was interested and even a little stirred, it appeared, at the possibility of representing the frontier in the United States Senate as, half a century previous, Thomas H. Benton, of Missouri, whom he greatly admired, had represented it. But the thought failed to take permanent hold of him. He was, moreover, thinking of himself in those days more as a writer than as a politician.

The autumn was not without excitement. A small band of Indians began here and there to set fire to the prairie grass, and before the cattlemen realized what was happening, thousands of acres of winter feed lay blackened and desolate.

This act of ruthless destruction was the climax of a war of reprisals which had been carried on relentlessly between the Indians and the white men since the first bold pioneer had entered the West Missouri country. There was endless trouble and bad blood between the races, which at intervals flared up in an outrage, the details of which were never told in print because they were as a rule unprintable. In the region between the Little Missouri and the Yellowstone, in the years 1884 and 1885, the wounds left by the wars, which had culminated in the death of Custer at the Little Big Horn, were still open and sore. In the conflict between white and red, the Indians were not always the ones who were most at fault. In many cases the robberies and other crimes which were committed were the acts of men maddened by starvation, for the ranges where they had hunted had been taken from them, and the reservations in many cases offered insufficient food. The agents of the Great White Father, moreover, were not always over-careful to give them all the cattle and the ponies which the Government was by treaty supposed to grant them. In consequence they "lifted" a cow or a calf where they could. The cattlemen, on their part, thoroughly imbued with the doctrine of *might is right*, regarded the Indians as a public enemy, and were disposed to treat their ponies and any other property which they might possess as legitimate prize of war. There was, in fact, during the middle eighties, open and undisguised warfare between red and white throughout the region whose eastern border was the Bad Lands. It was, moreover, a peculiarly atrocious warfare. Many white men shot whatever Indians they came upon like coyotes, on sight; others captured them, when they could, and, stripping off their clothes, whipped them till they bled. The Indians retaliated horribly, delivering their white captives to their squaws, who tortured them in every conceivable fashion, driving slivers up under their nails, burning them alive, and feeding them with flesh cut from their own bodies. Along the banks of the Little Missouri there were no outrages, for the Indians had been driven out of the country at the end of the seventies, and, save for occasional raids in the early eighties, had made little trouble; but at the edge of the Bad Lands there was a skirmish now and then, and in the winter of 1884 Schuyler Lebo, son of that odd Ulysses who had guided Roosevelt to the Big Horn Mountains, was shot in the leg by an Indian while he was hunting on Bullion Butte.

Roosevelt had a little adventure of his own with Indians that summer. He was traveling along the edge of the prairie on a solitary journey to the unexplored country north and east of the range on which his cattle grazed, and was crossing a narrow plateau when he suddenly saw a group of four or five Indians come up over the edge directly in front. As they saw him, they whipped their guns out of their slings, started their horses into a run, and came toward him at full speed.

He reined up instantly and dismounted.

The Indians came on, whooping and brandishing their weapons.

Roosevelt laid his gun across the saddle and waited.

It was possible [Roosevelt wrote subsequently] that the Indians were merely making a bluff and intended no mischief. But I did not like their actions, and I thought it likely that if I allowed them to get hold of me they would at least take my horse and rifle, and possibly kill me. So I waited until they were a hundred yards off and then drew a bead on the first. Indians — and, for the matter of that, white men — do not like to ride in on a man who is cool and means shooting, and in a twinkling every man was lying over the side of his horse, and all five had turned and were galloping backwards, having altered their course as quickly as so many teal ducks.

At some distance the Indians halted and gathered evidently for a conference.

Thereupon one man came forward alone, making the peace sign first with his blanket and then with his open hand. Roosevelt let him come to within fifty yards. The Indian was waving a piece of soiled paper, his reservation pass.

" How! Me good Injun," he called.

" How! " Roosevelt answered. " I'm glad you are. But don't come any closer."

The Indian asked for sugar and tobacco. Roosevelt told him that he had none. Another Indian now began almost imperceptibly to approach. Roosevelt called to him to keep back, but the Indian paid no attention.

Roosevelt whipped up his gun once more, covering the spokesman. That individual burst into a volume of perfect Anglo-Saxon profanity; but he retired, which was what he was supposed to do. Roosevelt led the faithful Manitou off toward the plains. The Indians followed him at a distance for two miles or more, but as he reached the open country at last they vanished in the radiant dust of the prairie.

Indians were a familiar sight in Medora and about the ranch-houses up and down the Little Missouri. In groups of a half-dozen or over they were formidable, but singly they were harmless and rather pathetic creatures. Roosevelt's attitude toward the Indians as a race was unequivocal. He detested them for their cruelty, and even more for their emphasis on cruelty as a virtue to be carefully developed as a white man might develop a sense of chivalry; but he recognized the fact that they had rights as human beings and as members of tribes having treaty relations with the United States, and insisted in season and out of season that those rights be respected.

I suppose I should be ashamed to say that I take the Western view of the Indian [he said in the course of a lecture which he delivered in New York, during January, 1886]. I don't go so far as to think that the only good Indians are the dead Indians, but I believe nine out of every ten are, and I shouldn't like to inquire too closely into the case of the tenth. The most vicious cowboy has more moral principle than the average Indian. Turn three hundred low families of New York into New Jersey, support them for fifty years in vicious idleness, and you will have some idea of what the Indians are. Reckless, revengeful, fiendishly cruel, they rob and murder, not the cowboys, who can take care of themselves, but the defenseless, lone settlers on the plains. As for the soldiers, an Indian chief once asked Sheridan for a cannon. "What! Do you want to kill my soldiers with it?" asked the general. "No," replied the chief, "want to kill the cowboy; kill soldier with a club."

It was characteristic of Roosevelt that, in spite of his detestation of the race, he should have been meticulously fair to the individual members of it who happened to cross his path. He made it a point, both at the Maltese Cross and at Elkhorn,

that the Indians who drifted in and out at intervals
should be treated as fairly as the whites, neither
wronging them himself nor allowing others to
wrong them.

Mrs. Maddox, the maker of the famous buckskin
shirt, who was an extraordinary woman in more
ways than one, had her own very individual notions
concerning the rights of the Indians. When Roosevelt stopped at her shack one day, he found three
Sioux Indians there, evidently trustworthy, self-
respecting men. Mrs. Maddox explained to him
that they had been resting there waiting for dinner,
when a white man had come along and tried to
run off with their horses. The Indians had caught
the man, but, after retaking their horses and depriving him of his gun, had let him go.

" I don't see why they let him go," she exclaimed.
" I don't believe in stealing Indians' horses any more
than white folks', so I told 'em they could go along
and hang him, I'd never cheep! Anyhow I won't
charge them anything for their dinner," she concluded.

The psychology of the Indians was curious, and
it took time occasionally for their better qualities
to reveal themselves. As chairman of the Little
Missouri Stock Association, Roosevelt on one occasion recovered two horses which had been stolen
from an old Indian. The Indian took them, muttering something that sounded like " Um, um," and
without a word or a gesture of gratitude rode away
with his property. Roosevelt felt cheap, as though

he had done a service which had not been appreciated; but a few days later the old Indian came to him and silently laid in his arms a hide bearing an elaborate painting of the battle of the Little Big Horn.

The depredations of the Indians in the autumn of 1885 made concerted action on the part of the cattlemen inevitable. The damage which the fires did to the cattle ranges themselves was not extensive, for the devastation was confined in the main to a strip of country about eighteen miles on either side of the railroad's right of way, and the ranches were situated from twenty-five to eighty miles from the track. The real harm which the fires did was in the destruction of the " drives " to the railroad. Driving cattle tended, under the best conditions of water and pasture, to cause loss of weight; when the " drive " lay through a burnt district for twenty or twenty-five miles the deterioration of the cattle became a serious matter.

Day after day the cowboys fought the fires. It was peculiarly harassing work.

The process we usually followed [Roosevelt wrote in his Autobiography] was to kill a steer, split it in two lengthwise, and then have two riders drag each half-steer, the rope of one running from his saddle-horn to the front leg, and that of the other to the hind leg. One of the men would spur his horse over or through the line of fire, and the two would then ride forward, dragging the steer, bloody side downward, along the line of flame, men following on foot with slickers or wet horse-blankets to beat out any flickering blaze that was still left. It was exciting work, for the fire and the twitching and plucking of the ox carcass over the uneven ground maddened the fierce little horses so that it was necessary to do some riding in order to keep them to their work. After a while it also became very exhausting, the thirst and fatigue being great, as, with parched lips and blackened from head to foot, we toiled at our task.

Work of this sort, day in, day out, did not make for magnanimity on the part of the cowboys. It was found that seventy-five Indians, who had received hunting permits from the agent at Berthold, were responsible for the devastation, and even the Eastern newspapers began to carry reports about a " serious conflict " which was likely to break out any minute " between cattlemen and Indian hunters in the Bad Lands of the Little Missouri."

Some one evidently called a meeting of the Little Missouri River Stockmen's Association to consider the situation, which was becoming dangerous, for on November 4th the New York *Herald* reported that

the Cattle Association on Thursday next will send in a party of thirty-five cowboys to order the Indians off the Bad Lands and to see that they go. The Indians, being well armed and having permits [the report concluded] are expected to resist unless they are surprised when separated in small parties.

Whether or not the party was ever sent is dark; but there was no further trouble with the Indians that year.

Roosevelt did not attend the meeting of the

Association he himself had established. Sometime after the middle of October, he had returned to the East. On October 24th he rode with the Meadowbrook Hunt Club and broke his arm, riding in at the death in spite of a dangling sleeve. A week or two later he was again in the Bad Lands.

He was a sorry sight as he arrived at Elkhorn Ranch, for his broken arm had not been the only injury he had incurred. His face was scarred and battered.

Bill Sewall regarded him with frank disapproval. "You're too valuable a man to use yourself up chasing foxes," he remarked. "There's some men that can afford to do it. There's some men that it don't make much difference if they do break their necks. But you don't belong to that class."

Roosevelt took the lecture without protest, giving his mentor the impression that it had sunk in.

Roosevelt remained in the Bad Lands until after Christmas, shooting his Christmas dinner in company with Sylvane. Before the middle of January he was back in New York, writing articles for *Outing* and the *Century*, doing some work as a publisher in partnership with a friend of his boyhood, George Haven Putnam, delivering an occasional lecture, and now and then making a political speech. Altogether, life was not dull for him.

Meanwhile, winter closed once more over the Bad Lands. The Marquis went to France, followed by rumors disquieting to those who had high hopes

for the future of what the Marquis liked to call
" my little town." J. B. Walker, who " operated
the Elk Hotel," as the phrase went, " skipped out,"
leaving behind him a thousand dollars' worth of
debts and a stock of strong drink. Nobody claimed
the debts, but Hell-Roaring Bill Jones took possession of the deserted cellar and sold drinks to his
own great financial benefit, until it occurred to some
unduly inquisitive person to inquire into his rights;
which spoiled everything.

The event of real importance was the arrival of
a new bride in Medora. For early in January, 1886,
Joe Ferris went East to New Brunswick; and when
he came back a month later he brought a wife with
him.

It was a notable event. The " boys " had planned
to give Joe and his lady a " shivaree," such as even
Medora had never encountered before, but Joe, who
was crafty and knew his neighbors, succeeded in
misleading the population of the town concerning
the exact hour of his arrival with his somewhat
apprehensive bride. There was a wild scurrying
after tin pans and bells and other objects which
were effective as producers of bedlam, but Joe
sent a friend forth with a bill of high denomination
and the suggestion that the " boys " break it at
Bill Williams's saloon, which had the desired effect.

The "boys" took the greatest interest in the
wife whom Joe (who was popular in town) had taken
to himself out in New Brunswick, and there was
real trepidation lest Joe's wife might be the wrong

sort. Other men, who had been good fellows and had run with the boys, had married and been weaned from their old companions, bringing out women who did not " fit in," who felt superior to the cowboys and did not take the trouble to hide their feelings. The great test was, whether Joe's wife would or would not like Mrs. Cummins. For Mrs. Cummins, in the minds of the cowpunchers, stood for everything that was reprehensible in the way of snobbery and lack of the human touch. If Mrs. Ferris liked Mrs. Cummins, it was all over; if she properly disliked her, she would do.

Mrs. Cummins called in due course. Merrifield was on the porch of the store when she came and in his excited way carried the news to the boys. As soon as she left by the front steps, Merrifield bounded up by the back. His eyes were gleaming.

" Well, now, Mrs. Ferris," he cried, " how did you like her? "

Mrs. Ferris laughed.

" Well, what did she say? " Merrifield pursued impatiently.

" Why," remarked Mrs. Joe, " for one thing she says I mustn't trust any of you cowboys."

Merrifield burst into a hearty laugh. " That's her! " he cried. " That's her! What else did she say? "

" She told me how I ought to ride, and the kind of horse I ought to get, and — "

" Go on, Mrs. Ferris," cried Merrifield.

" Why, she says I never want to ride any horse

that any of you cowboys give me, for you're all bad, and you haven't any consideration for a woman and you'd as lief see a woman throwed off and killed as not."

Merrifield's eyes sparkled in the attractive way they had when he was in a hilarious mood. " Say, did you ever hear the like of that? You'd think, to hear that woman talk, that we was nothing but murderers. What else did she say? "

" Well," remarked the new bride, " she said a good many things."

" You tell me, Mrs. Ferris," Merrifield urged.

" For one thing she said the cowboys was vulgar and didn't have any manners. And — oh, yes — she said that refined folks who knew the better things of life ought to stick together and not sink to the level of common people."

" Now, Mrs. Ferris," remarked Merrifield indignantly, " ain't that a ree-di-culous woman? Ain't she now? "

Mrs. Ferris laughed until the tears came to her eyes. " I think she is," she admitted.

Merrifield carried the news triumphantly to the " boys," and the new bride's standing was established. She became a sort of " honorary member-once-removed " of the friendly order of cow-punchers, associated with them by a dozen ties of human understanding, yet, by her sex, removed to a special niche apart, where the most irresponsible did not fail, drunk or sober, to do her deference. For her ears language was washed and scrubbed.

Men who appeared to have forgotten what shame was, were ashamed to have Mrs. Ferris know how unashamed they could be. Poor old Van Zander, whom every one in Billings County had seen " stewed to the gills," pleaded with Joe not to tell Mrs. Ferris that Joe had seen him drunk.

It became a custom, in anticipation of a " shivaree," to send round word to Mrs. Ferris not to be afraid, the shooting was all in fun.

A woman would have been less than human who had failed to feel at home in the midst of such evidences of warmth and friendly consideration. Joe Ferris's store became more than ever the center of life in Medora, as the wife whom Joe had brought from New Brunswick made his friends her friends and made her home theirs also.

She had been in Medora less than a month when news came from Roosevelt that he was getting ready to start West and would arrive on the Little Missouri sometime about the middle of March. Joe's wife knew how to get along with " boys " who were Joe's kind, but here was a different sort of proposition confronting her. Here was a wealthy, and, in a modest way, a noted, man coming to sleep under her roof and eat at her table. The prospect appalled her. Possibly she had visions, for all that Joe could say, of a sort of male Mrs. Cummins. " I was scairt to death," she admitted later.

Roosevelt arrived on March 18th. His " city get-up " was slightly distracting, for it had a perfection of style that Mrs. Joe was not accustomed to; but his delight at his return to the Bad Lands was so frank and so expressive that her anxiety began to dissolve in her wonder at this vehement and attractive being who treated her like a queen. He jumped in the air, clicking his heels together like a boy let unexpectedly out of school, and at odd moments clapped Joe on the back, crying, " By George! By George! " with the relish of a cannibal reaching into the pot for a second joint.

She tried to treat him like the city man that he looked, but he promptly put a stop to that.

" Just use me like one of the boys, Mrs. Ferris," he said decisively. His words sounded sincere; but, being a shrewd-minded lady, she wondered, nevertheless.

She did not know him when he came down to breakfast next morning. Vanished was the " dude," and in his place stood a typical cowpuncher in shaps and flannel shirt and knotted handkerchief. And his clothes revealed that they had not been worn only indoors.

He gave an exclamation of delight as he entered the dining-room. " A white tablecloth in the Bad Lands! Joe, did you ever expect to see it? "

There was no more ice to break after that.

XXII

"Listen, gentle stranger, I'll read my pedigree:
I'm known on handling tenderfeet and worser men than thee;
The lions on the mountains, I've drove them to their lairs;
The wild-cats are my playmates, and I've wrestled grizzly bears;

"The centipedes have tried and failed to mar my tough old hide,
And rattlesnakes have bit me, and crawled away and died.
I'm as wild as the wild horse that roams the boundless plains,
The moss grows on my teeth and wild blood flows through my veins.

"I'm wild and woolly and full of fleas,
And never been curried below the knees.
Now, little stranger, if you'll give me your address, —
How would you like to go, by fast mail or express?"
                                              BUCKSKIN JOE

THAT spring of 1886 Roosevelt had a notable adventure. He arrived at Elkhorn on March 19th.

I got out here all right [he wrote his sister " Bamie " the following day] and was met at the station by my men; I was really heartily glad to see the great, stalwart, bearded fellows again, and they were as honestly pleased to see me. Joe Ferris is married, and his wife made me most comfortable the night I spent in town. Next morning snow covered the ground; we pushed down, in a rough four-in-hand (how our rig would have made the estimable Mrs. Blank open her eyes!) to this ranch which we reached long after sunset, the full moon flooding the landscape with light.

It was like coming home from a foreign country to see the Little Missouri once more, and the strangely fascinating desolation of the Bad Lands, and the home ranch and the " folks " from Maine and the loyal friends of the Maltese Cross. He had good friends in the East, but there was a warmth and a stalwart sincerity in the comradeship of these men and women which he had scarcely found elsewhere. Through the cold evenings of that early spring he loved to lie stretched at full length on the elk-hides and wolf-skins in front of the great fireplace, while the blazing logs crackled and roared, and Sewall and Dow and the " womenfolks " recounted the happenings of the season of his absence.

Spring came early that year and about the 20th of March a great ice-jam, which had formed at a bend far up the river, came slowly past Elkhorn, roaring and crunching and piling the ice high on both banks.

There has been an ice gorge right in front of the house [he wrote " Bamie "], the swelling mass of broken fragments having been pushed almost up to our doorstep. The current then broke through the middle, leaving on each side of the stream, for some miles, a bank of huge ice-floes, tumbled over each other in the wildest confusion. No horse could by any chance get across; we men have a boat, and even thus it is most laborious carrying it out to the water; we work like arctic explorers.

Early in the spring, Sewall and Dow had crossed the river to hunt for a few days in the rough hills to the east, and had killed four deer which they had hung in a tree to keep them from the coyotes. Roosevelt determined to go with his men to bring home the deer, but when, after infinite difficulty, they reached the thicket of dwarf cedars where the deer had been hung, they found nothing save scattered pieces of their carcasses, and roundabout the deeply marked footprints of a pair of cougars, or " mountain lions." The beasts had evidently been at work for some time and had eaten almost every scrap of flesh. Roosevelt and his men followed their tracks into a tangle of rocky hills, but, before they had come in sight of the quarry, dusk obscured the footprints and they returned home resolved to renew the pursuit at dawn. They tied their boat securely to a tree high up on the bank.

The next day Roosevelt made arrangements with a companion of many hunts, " old man " Tompkins, who was living in the shack which Captain Robins had occupied, to make a determined pursuit of the cougars; but when, the following morning, he was ready to start once more for the farther shore, his boat was gone. It was Bill Sewall who made the discovery. He was not a man easily excited, and he took a certain quiet satisfaction in sitting down to breakfast and saying nothing while Roosevelt held forth concerning the fate which was awaiting the mountain lions.

" I guess we won't go to-day," said Sewall, at length, munching the last of his breakfast.

" Why not? " Roosevelt demanded.

Sewall showed him a red woolen mitten with a leather palm which he had picked up on the ice, and the end of the rope by which the boat had been tied. It had been cut with a sharp knife. " Some one has gone off with the boat," he said.

Roosevelt had no doubt who had stolen the boat, for the thief or thieves could scarcely have come by land without being detected. There was only one other boat on the Little Missouri, and that was a small flat-bottom scow owned by three hard characters who lived in a shack twenty miles above Elkhorn. They were considered suspicious persons, and Roosevelt and his men had shrewdly surmised for some time that they were considering the advisability of " skipping the country " before the vigilantes got after them. On inquiry they found that the shack which the men had occupied was deserted.

The leader of the three was a stocky, ill-looking individual named Finnegan, with fiery red hair which fell to his shoulders, gaining for him the nickname ." Redhead " Finnegan; a brick-red complexion, and an evil reputation. He was a surly, quarrelsome, unkempt creature, and when he came into a saloon with his stumbling gait (as he frequently did), self-respecting cowboys had a way of leaving him in full possession of the field, not because they feared him, but because they did not care to be seen in his presence. He boasted that he was " from Bitter Creek, where the farther up you went the worse people got," and he lived " at the fountain head." He had blown into Medora early in March and had promptly gone to Bill Williams's saloon and filled up on Bill Williams's peculiarly wicked brand of " conversation juice."

" Well, it laid him out all right enough," remarked

Lincoln Lang, telling about it in after years. " I can testify to that, since I was right there and saw the whole thing. Johnny Goodall, who was some practical joker at that time, went into the bar and saw Finnegan lying on the floor. He got some help and moved him to the billiard table. Then Goodall sent to the barber shop for a hair clipper, and proceeded to operate in the following manner: first he clipped off one side of Finnegan's beard and moustache, and after that removed his long curls on one side, being careful to leave a stair pattern all up the side of his head. He concluded operations by removing the fringes upon one side of his buckskin shirt. Next morning Finnegan sobered up and when he saw himself in the looking-glass he went bersark."

" His heart got bad," Bill Dantz remarked, taking up the narrative. " He laid down in a fringe of brush near the Marquis's store, where he could command a clear view of the town, and began to pump lead into everything in sight."

The first shot was aimed at the office of the *Bad Lands Cowboy*. Whether or not " Redhead " Finnegan had it in for the stern moralist who insisted that drunken criminals should be punished, not only for their crimes, but also for their drunkenness, is a question on which the records are dark. Fisher was shaving in Packard's office and the shot broke the mirror in front of him. Packard, who was on horseback on the bluff behind Medora, saw Fisher dash out of the shack, and rushed to the scene of con-

flict. His horse had knocked Finnegan senseless before the desperado knew that the Chief of Police was
on his trail. When Finnegan came to he was in a
box-car, under lock and seal. But a friend released
him, and the man from Bitter Creek made his way
down the river to his cabin.

The population of Medora had not relished
Finnegan's bombardment, and suggestions concerning a possible " necktie party " began to make themselves heard. Finnegan evidently decided that the
time had come for him, and the men who lived with
him in his ill-kept shack, to leave the country.
Travel by horse or foot was impossible. The boat
they owned was a miserable, leaky affair. The
Elkhorn skiff had evidently appeared to Finnegan
and Company in the nature of a godsend.

Roosevelt's anger boiled up at the theft of the
boat and he ran to saddle Manitou. But Sewall
restrained him, pointing out that if the country was
impassable for the horses of the thieves, it was no
less impassable for the horses of the pursuers. He
declared that he and Dow could build a flat-
bottomed boat in three days. Roosevelt told him
to go ahead. With the saddle band — his forty or
fifty cow-ponies — on the farther side of the river,
he could not afford to lose the boat. But the
determining motive in his mind was neither chagrin
nor anxiety to recover his property. In a country
where self-reliant hardihood and the ability to hold
one's own under all circumstances ranked as the
first of the virtues, to submit tamely to theft or to

any other injury was, he knew, to invite almost certain repetition of the offense.

A journal which he kept for a month or two that spring gives in laconic terms a vivid picture of those March days.

March 22. Tramped over to get deer; mountain lions had got them.

March 23. Shot 4 prairie chickens.

March 24. Thieves stole boat; started to build another to go after them.

March 25. Went out after deer; saw nothing. Boat being built. River very high; ice piled upon banks several feet.

March 26. Boat building.

March 27. Boat built. Too cold to start. Shot 4 chickens.

March 28. Bitter cold.

March 29. Furious blizzard.

While Sewall and Dow, who were mighty men with their hands, were building the boat, and his other cowpuncher, Rowe, was hurrying to Medora to bring out a wagon-load of supplies for their contemplated journey, Roosevelt himself was by no means idle. He had agreed to write a life of Thomas Hart Benton for the *American Statesmen Series*, and, after two or three months' work in the East gathering his material, had begun the actual writing of the book immediately after his return to the Bad Lands.

I have written the first chapter of the Benton [he wrote to Lodge on March 27th], so at any rate I have made a start. Writing is horribly hard work to me;

and I make slow progress. I have got some good ideas in the first chapter, but I am not sure they are worked up rightly; my style is very rough, and I do not like a certain lack of *sequitur* that I do not seem able to get rid of.

I thought the article on Morris admirable in every way; one of your crack pieces. Some of the sentences were so thoroughly characteristic of you that I laughed aloud when I read them. One of my men, Sewall (a descendant of the Judge's, by the way), read it with as much interest as I did, and talked it over afterwards as intelligently as any one could.

At present we are all snowed up by a blizzard; as soon as it lightens up I shall start down the river with two of my men in a boat we have built while indoors, after some horse-thieves who took our boat the other night to get out of the country with; but they have such a start we have very little chance of catching them. I shall take Matthew Arnold along; I have had no chance at all to read it as yet.

The next day he was writing to his sister " Bamie." He was evidently convinced that she would worry about him if she knew the nature of the adventure on which he was about to embark, for in his letter he protests almost too much concerning the utterly unexciting nature of his activities:

Since I wrote you life has settled down into its usual monotonous course here. It is not as rough as I had expected; I have clean sheets, the cooking is pretty good, and above all I have a sitting-room with a great fireplace and a rocking-chair, which I use as my study.

The walking is horrible; all slippery ice or else deep, sticky mud; but as we are very short of meat I generally spend three or four hours a day tramping round after prairie chickens, and one day last week I shot a deer. The rest of the time I read or else work at Benton, which is making very slow progress; writing is to me intensely irksome work.

In a day or two, when the weather gets a little milder, I expect to start down the river in a boat, to go to Mandan; the trip ought to take a week or ten days, more or less. It will be good fun. My life on the ranch this summer is not going to be an especially adventurous or exciting one; and my work will be mainly one of supervision so that there will be no especial hardship or labor.

I really enjoy being with the men out here; they could be more exactly described as my retainers than as anything else; and I am able to keep on admirable terms with them and yet avoid the familiarity which would assuredly breed contempt.

On the 30th of March the blizzard which had been raging a day or two moderated, and Roosevelt, hoping a thaw had set in, determined to set off after the thieves. They left Rowe as guard over the ranch and " the womenfolks," and with their unwieldy but water-tight craft, laden with two weeks' provision of flour, coffee, and bacon, started to drift down the river.

The region through which they passed was bare and bleak and terrible. On either side, beyond the heaped-up piles of ice, rose the scarred buttes, weather-worn into fantastic shapes and strangely blotched with spots of brown and yellow, purple and red. Here and there the black coal-veins that ran through them were aflame, gleaming weirdly through the dusk as the three men made their camp that night.

The weather was cold and an icy wind blew in their faces.

"We're like to have it in our faces all day," remarked Will Dow cheerfully, paddling at the bow.

"We can't, unless it's the crookedest wind in Dakota," answered Sewall, who was steering.

They followed the river's course hither and thither in and out among the crags, east and west, north and south.

"It *is* the crookedest wind in Dakota," muttered Sewall to himself.

The thermometer dropped to zero, but there was firewood in plenty, and they found prairie fowl and deer for their evening meals. Late the third day, rounding a bend, they saw their boat moored against the bank. Out of the bushes, a little way back, the smoke of a camp-fire curled up through the frosty air.

"There's your boat!" cried Sewall, who had, in his own phrase, been "looking sharp." "Get your guns ready. I'll handle the boat."

They flung off their heavy coats. Sewall was in the stern, steering the boat toward shore. Dow was at Roosevelt's side in the bow. Roosevelt saw the grim, eager look in their eyes, and his own eyes gleamed.

He was the first ashore, leaping out of the boat as it touched the shore ice and running up behind a clump of bushes, so as to cover the landing of the others. Dow was beside him in an instant. Sewall was fastening the boat.

It was rather funny business [Sewall wrote his brother subsequently] for one of the men was called a pretty hard ticket. He was also a shooting man. If he was in the bushes and saw us first he was liable to make it very unhealthy for us.

Roosevelt and Dow peered through the bushes. Beside a fire in a grove of young cottonwoods a solitary figure was sitting; his guns were on the ground at his side.

" Hands up! "

Roosevelt and Dow rushed in on the man, who was not slow to do as he was told. He was a half-witted German named Wharfenberger, a tool of rogues more keen than he, whom Sewall later described as " an oldish man who drank so much poor whiskey that he had lost most of the manhood he ever possessed."

They searched the old man, taking his gun and his knives from him, and telling him that if he did exactly as he was told they would use him well; but if he disobeyed or tried to signal the other men, they would kill him instantly. Knowing something of the frontier, he was ready to believe that he would be given short shrift, and was thoroughly submissive.

Finnegan and the third man, a half-breed named Bernstead, had, it seems, gone hunting, believing themselves safe. Sewall guarded the German, while Roosevelt and Dow, crouching under the lee of a cutbank, prepared to greet the others.

The ground before them was as level as a floor,

with no growth on it of any sort beside the short
dead grass which would not have given cover to a
rabbit. Beyond, to the east lay a wide stretch of
level bottom covered with sagebrush as high as a
man's waist, and beyond that was a fringe of bushes
bordering a stretch of broken butte country. The
wind had fallen. Save for the rush of the river,
there was no sound.

Will and I [Sewall wrote his brother] kept watch and
listened — our eyes are better than Roosevelt's, Will
on the right and I on the left. R. was to rise up and tell
them to hands up, Will and I both with double barrel
guns loaded with Buck shot, and we were all going to
shoot if they offered to raise a gun. It is rather savage
work but it don't do to fool with such fellows. If there
was any killing to be done we meant to do it ourselves.

About an hour before sunset they heard Finnegan
and his companion crawling through the stunted
bushes at the foot of the clay hill. The men started
to go upstream.

"We are going to lose them," Roosevelt whispered; "they are not coming to camp."

"I think," answered Sewall, "they are looking
for the camp smoke."

He was evidently right, for suddenly they saw it
and came straight through the sagebrush toward the
watchers. Roosevelt and his men watched them for
some minutes as they came nonchalantly toward
them, the barrels of their rifles glinting in the sunlight. Now they were forty yards away, now thirty,
now twenty.

" Hands up! "

The half-breed obeyed, but for an instant Finnegan hesitated, glaring at his captors with wolfish eyes. Roosevelt walked toward him, covering the center of the man's chest to avoid over-shooting him.

" You thief, put up your hands! "

Finnegan dropped his rifle with an oath and put up his hands.

They searched the thieves and took away their weapons. "If you'll keep quiet," said Roosevelt, "and not try to get away, you'll be all right. If you try anything we'll shoot you."

This was language which the thieves understood, and they accepted the situation. Sewall took an old double-barrel ten-gauge Parker shot-gun and stood guard.

Dow was a little uneasy about the gun.

" The right-hand barrel goes off very easily," he warned Sewall. " It's gone off with me several times when I did not mean it to, and if you are going to cover the men with it you better be careful."

" I'll be careful," remarked Sewall in his deliberate fashion, " but if it happens to go off, it will make more difference to them than it will to me."

They camped that night where they were. Having captured their men, they were somewhat in a quandary how to keep them. The cold was so intense that to tie them tightly hand and foot meant in all likelihood freezing both hands and feet

off during the night; there was no use tying them
at all, moreover, unless they tied them tightly
enough to stop in part the circulation. Roosevelt
took away everything from the thieves that might
have done service as a weapon, and corded his
harvest in some bedding well out of reach of the
thieves.

" Take off your boots! " he ordered.

It had occurred to him that bare feet would
make any thought of flight through that cactus
country extremely uninviting. The men surrendered
their boots. Roosevelt gave them a buffalo robe in
return and the prisoners crawled under it, thoroughly cowed.

Captors and captives started downstream in the
two boats the next morning. The cold was bitter.
Toward the end of the day they were stopped by a
small ice-jam which moved forward slowly only to
stop them again. They ran the boats ashore to
investigate, and found that the great Ox-Bow jam,
which had moved past Elkhorn a week ago, had
come to a halt and now effectually barred their way.
They could not possibly paddle upstream against
the current; they could not go on foot, for to do
so would have meant the sacrifice of all their
equipment. They determined to follow the slow-
moving mass of ice, and hope, meanwhile, for a
thaw.

They continued to hope; day after weary day
they watched in vain for signs of the thaw that
would not come, breaking camp in the morning

on one barren point, only to pitch camp again in the evening on another, guarding the prisoners every instant, for the trouble they were costing made the captors even more determined that, whatever was lost, Finnegan and Company should not be lost.

Roosevelt's journal for those days tells the story:

April 1. Captured the three boat-thieves.
April 2. Came on with our prisoners till hung up by ice-jam.
April 3. Hung up by ice.
April 4. Hung up by ice.
April 5. Worked down a couple of miles till again hung up by ice.
April 6. Worked down a couple of miles again to tail of ice-jam.

Their provisions ran short. They went after game, but there was none to be seen, no beast or bird, in that barren region. The addition to their company had made severe inroads on their larder and it was not long before they were all reduced to unleavened bread made with muddy water. The days were utterly tedious, and were made only slightly more bearable for Roosevelt by Tolstoy's " Anna Karenina " and Matthew Arnold, interlarded with " The History of the James Brothers," which the thieves quite properly carried among their belongings. And the thieves had to be watched every minute, and the wind blew and chilled them to the bone.

Roosevelt thought that it might be pleasant

under certain circumstances to be either a Dakota sheriff or an Arctic explorer. But he did not find great joy in being both at the same time.

When the flour was nearly gone, Roosevelt and his men had a consultation.

"We can't shoot them," said Roosevelt, "and we can't feed them. It looks to me as though we'd have to let them go."

Sewall disagreed. "The flour'll last a day or two more," he said, "and it's something to know that if we're punishing ourselves, we're punishing the thieves also."

"Exactly!" cried Roosevelt. "We'll hold on to them!"

The next day Sewall, on foot, searched the surrounding region far and wide for a ranch, and found none. The day after, Roosevelt and Dow covered the country on the other side of the river, and at last came on an outlying cow-camp of the Diamond C Ranch, where Roosevelt secured a horse.

It was a wiry, rebellious beast.

"The boss ain't no bronco-buster," remarked Dow, apologetically, to the cowboys.

But "the boss" managed to get on the horse and to stay on. Dow returned to Sewall and the thieves, while Roosevelt rode fifteen miles to a ranch at the edge of the Killdeer Mountains. There he secured supplies and a prairie-schooner, hiring the ranchman himself, a rugged old plainsman, to drive it to the camp by the ice-bound river. Sewall and Dow, now thoroughly provisioned, remained with the boats. Roosevelt with the thieves started for the nearest jail, which was at Dickinson.

It was a desolate two days' journey through a bleak waste of burnt, blackened prairie, and over rivers so rough with ice that they had to take the wagon apart to cross. Roosevelt did not dare abate his watch over the thieves for an instant, for they knew they were drawing close to jail and might conceivably make a desperate break any minute. He could not trust the driver. There was nothing for it but to pack the men into the wagon and to walk behind with the Winchester.

Hour after hour he trudged through the ankle-deep mud, hungry, cold, and utterly fatigued, but possessed by the dogged resolution to carry the thing through, whatever the cost. They put up at the squalid hut of a frontier granger overnight, but Roosevelt, weary as he was, did not dare to sleep. He crowded the prisoners into the upper bunk and sat against the cabin door all night, with the Winchester across his knees.

Roosevelt's journal gives the stages of his progress.

April 7. Worked down to C Diamond Ranch. Two prairie chickens.

April 8. Rode to Killdeer Mountains to arrange for a wagon which I hired.

April 9. Walked captives to Killdeer Mountains.

April 10. Drove captives in wagon to Captain Brown's ranch.

" What I can't make out," said the ranchman

from the Killdeers, with a puzzled expression on
his deeply wrinkled, tough old face, which Sewall
said " looked like the instep of an old boot that had
lain out in the weather for years," — " what I
can't make out is why you make all this fuss instead
of hanging 'em offhand."

Roosevelt grinned, and the following evening,
after a three-hundred-mile journey, deposited three
men who had defied the laws of Dakota in the jail
at Dickinson.

He was not a vision of beauty as he emerged from
the jail to find a place to scrape off two weeks'
accumulation of Dakota mud. His feet were in bad
shape from the long march through the gumbo, and
he asked the first man he met where he could find
a physician. By a curious coincidence the man he
addressed happened to be the only physician within
a hundred and fifty miles in any direction. It was
Dr. Stickney.

They had heard of each other, and Roosevelt was
glad, for more reasons than one, to follow him to
his office. For the quiet man with the twinkling
eyes, who combined the courage and the humanness
of a cowpuncher with the unselfish devotion of a
saint, was a great figure in the Bad Lands. Like
Roosevelt he was under thirty.

The doctor, in after years, told of that morning's
visit. " He did not seem worn out or unduly tired,"
he said. " He had just come from the jail, having
deposited his prisoners at last, and had had no sleep
for forty-eight hours, and he was all teeth and eyes;

but even so he seemed a man unusually wide awake. You could see he was thrilled by the adventures he had been through. He did not seem to think he had done anything particularly commendable, but he was, in his own phrase, ' pleased as Punch ' at the idea of having participated in a real adventure. He was just like a boy.

" We talked of many things that day while I was repairing his blistered feet. He impressed me and he puzzled me, and when I went home to lunch, an hour later, I told my wife that I had met the most peculiar, and at the same time the most wonderful, man I had ever come to know. I could see that he was a man of brilliant ability and I could not understand why he was out there on the frontier. I had heard his name and I had read something of his work in the New York Legislature and in the Republican Convention, two years previous, and it seemed to me that he belonged, not here on the frontier, but in the East, in the turmoil of large affairs."

I got the three horse-thieves in fine style [Roosevelt wrote to Lodge]. My two Maine men and I ran down the river three days in our boat, and then came on their camp by surprise. As they knew there was no other boat on the river but the one they had taken, and as they had not thought of our building another, they were completely taken unawares, one with his rifle on the ground, and the others with theirs on their shoulders; so there was no fight, nor any need of pluck on our part. We simply crept noiselessly up and rising, when only a few yards distant, covered them with the cocked rifles while I told them to throw up their hands. They saw that we had the drop on them completely, and I guess they also saw that we surely meant shooting if they hesitated, and so their hands went up at once. We kept them with us nearly a week, being caught in an ice-jam; then we came to a ranch where I got a wagon, and I sent my two men on downstream with the boat, while I took the three captives overland a two days' journey to a town where I could give them to the sheriff. I was pretty sleepy when I got there, as I had to keep awake at night a good deal in guarding; and we had gotten out of food and the cold had been intense.

To his sister Corinne he admitted that he was well satisfied to part from his prisoners.

I was really glad to give them up to the sheriff this morning [he writes from Dickinson], for I was pretty well done out with the work, the lack of sleep, and the constant watchfulness, but I am as brown and as tough as a pine knot and feel equal to anything.

It happened that the editor of the *Herald* of Newburyport, Massachusetts, had a friend in Dickinson who occasionally sent him news of the frontier which he printed as the " Dickinson (Dakota) Letter to the Newburyport Herald."

To illustrate what manner of men we need [he wrote during the week following the successful conclusion of Roosevelt's adventure], I will relate an incident which is to the point. I presume you are all acquainted, through the newspapers, with the Hon. Theodore Roosevelt, who is quite prominent in New York politics and society. He owns a ranch on the Little Missouri, about eighty miles northwest from here, and created quite a stir last

Sunday by bringing to town three horse-thieves whom he had captured with the help of two of his " cow men."

Thereupon follows the story of the capture and jailing of Finnegan and Company.

When I saw him [the correspondent continues], Mr. Roosevelt had been on the " trail " for three weeks, and wore a cowboy's hat, corduroy jacket, flannel shirt, and heavy shoes, but was in excellent health and spirits.

Said he, " I don't know how I look, but I feel first-rate! "

The next morning he appeared in the justice's court, saw the outlaws indicted, and a little later took the train bound west, for his " cow camp." I had never seen Mr. Roosevelt before, although I had read many articles from his pen; and when I left home I had no idea of meeting a gentleman of his standing on the frontier masquerading in the character of an impromptu sheriff. But, only such men of courage and energy can hope to succeed in this new, beautiful, but undeveloped country.

The justice of the peace who indicted the thieves was Western Starr. He turned out to be an old acquaintance of Roosevelt's, a classmate in the Columbia Law School. The coincidence gave an added flavor to the proceeding.

In Medora there seemed to be only one opinion concerning Roosevelt's adventure, though it was variously expressed.

" Roosevelt," said his friend, John Simpson, a Texan, who was owner of the " Hash-knife " brand and one of the greatest cattlemen in the region, " no one but you would have followed those men with just a couple of cow-hands. You are the only real damn fool in the county."

The rest of the population echoed the bewildered query of the teamster from the Killdeers. " Why didn't you *kill* them? " every one asked. " They would have killed you."

" I didn't come out here to kill anybody," Roosevelt answered. " All I wanted to do was to defend myself and my property. There wasn't any one around to defend them for me, so I had to do it myself."

And there the matter rested. But the people of Medora began to see a little more clearly than they had ever seen before the meaning of government by law.[1]

[1] The thieves were tried at Mandan in August, 1886. The German, known as "Dutch Chris," was acquitted, but Finnegan, and Bernstead, known as "the half-breed," were sentenced to twenty-five months in the Bismarck Penitentiary. Finnegan glared at Roosevelt as he passed him in the court room. "If I'd had any show at all," he cried, "you'd have sure had to fight!"

That was no doubt true, but his anger evidently wore off in the cool of the prison, for a little later he wrote Roosevelt a long and friendly epistle, which was intended to explain many things:

In the first place I did not take your boat Mr. Roosevelt because I wanted to steal something, no indeed, when I took that vessel I was labouring under the impression, die dog or eat the hachette. . . . When I was a couple of miles above your ranch the boat I had sprung a leak and I saw I could not make the Big Missouri in it in the shape that it was in. I thought of asking assistance of you, but I supposed you had lost some saddles and blamed me for taking them. Now there I was with a leaky boat and under the circumstances what was I two do, two ask you for help, the answer I expected two get was two look down the mouth of a Winchester. I saw your boat and made up my mind two get possession of it. I was bound two get out of that country cost what it might, when people talk lynch law and threaten a persons life, I think that it is about time to leave. I did not want to go back up river on the account that I feared a mob. . . . I have read a good many of your sketches of ranch life in the papers since I have been here, and they interested me deeply. Yours sincerely.

&c

P.S. Should you stop over at Bismarck this fall make a call to the Prison. I should be glad to meet you.

XXIII

Oh, I am a Texas cowboy, light-hearted, brave, and free,
To roam the wide, wide prairie, 'tis always joy to me.
My trusty little pony is my companion true,
O'er creeks and hills and rivers he's sure to pull me through.

When threatening clouds do gather and herded lightnings flash,
And heavy rain drops splatter, and rolling thunders crash;
What keeps the herds from running, stampeding far and wide?
The cowboy's long, low whistle and singing by their side.

Cowboy song

By a curious coincidence the culmination of Roosevelt's dramatic exposition of the meaning of government by law coincided in point of time precisely with the passing of the Bad Lands out of a state of primeval lawlessness into a condition resembling organized government.

Since the preceding summer, Packard had, in the columns of the *Cowboy*, once more been agitating for the organization of Billings County. The conditions, which in the past had militated against the proposal, were no longer potent. The lawless element was still large, but it was no longer in the majority. For a time a new and naïve objection made itself widely heard. The stock-growers protested that if the county were organized, they would be taxed! The Mandan *Pioneer* explained that, according to the laws of Dakota Territory, the nearest organized county was authorized to tax all the cattle and other stock in Billings County, and that " the only possible difference that could result in organization would be to keep the taxes at home and allow them to be expended for home improvements such as roads, bridges, schoolhouses, and public buildings." The cattlemen were not in a position to explain publicly what they probably meant, namely, that a board of county commissioners and a tax assessor sitting in Medora would have far less difficulty than a similar group sitting a hundred and fifty miles east in Mandan in following the mysterious movements of their cattle during the season when assessments were made. An active agent of the county might conceivably note that when Billings County, Dakota, was making its assessments, the herds could generally be found in Fallon County, Montana, and that when Fallon County was making its assessments, the cattle were all grazing in Billings. But even in the Bad Lands it was no longer politic to protest openly against what was palpably the public welfare, and the petition for the organization of the county received the necessary signatures, and was sent to the governor. "This is a step in the right direction," patronizingly remarked the Mandan *Pioneer*. "Billings County is rich enough and strong enough to run its own affairs."

Merrifield and Sylvane Ferris had been active in the work of organization, and were eager to "run" Bill Sewall for County commissioner. But that shrewd individual pleaded unfitness and lack of time and refused to be cajoled into becoming a candidate.

There is some doubt concerning the exact date

of the first election. Roosevelt's diary would indicate that it was held on April 12th, but the paragraph printed in the Minneapolis *Tribune* of April 15th would indicate that it was held on the 14th. Both statements are probably wrong, and the election in all likelihood was held on the 13th.

Roosevelt, having testified against the three thieves, returned to Medora late on the afternoon of election. There had been many threats that the party of disorder would import section hands from the neighboring railway stations to down the legions of the righteous. An especial watcher had been set at the polling-places. It was none other than Hell-Roaring Bill Jones. He was still on most cordial terms with his old intimates, the ruffians who congregated at Bill Williams's saloon, but he liked Roosevelt and the men who surrounded the young Easterner, and had cast in his lot with them. The effectiveness, as a guardian of the peace, of the man who had at the beginning of his career in the Bad Lands been saloon "bouncer" for Bill Williams was notable.

Roosevelt found a group of his friends at the polling-place.

" Has there been any disorder? " he asked.

" Disorder, hell! " said one of the men in the group. " Bill Jones just stood there with one hand on his gun and the other pointin' over toward the new jail whenever any man who did n't have the right to vote come near the polls. There was only one of them tried to vote, and Bill knocked him down. Lord!" he concluded meditatively, "the way that man fell!"

"Well," struck in Bill Jones, "if he hadn't fell, I'd of walked round behind him to see what was proppin' him up!"

The candidates for the various offices had been selected in a spirit of compromise between the two elements in the town, the forces of order securing every office except one. The county commissioners elected were "Johnny" Goodall, a blacksmith named Dan Mackenzie, and J. L. Truscott, who owned a large ranch south of the Big Ox Bow. Van Driesche, the best of all valets, was elected treasurer, and Bill Dantz superintendent of schools; but the forces of disorder could afford to regard the result without apprehension, for they had been allowed to elect the sheriff; and they had elected Joe Morrill.

Election night was lurid. Morrill, evidently desiring to make a good impression without serious inconvenience to his friends, served notice immediately after his election that there must be no "shooting up" of the town, but "the boys" did not take Morrill very seriously. Fisher, who had a room in Mrs. McGeeney's hotel next to Joe Ferris's store, found the place too noisy for comfort, and adjourned to the office of the *Bad Lands Cowboy*. The little shack was unoccupied, for Packard, having recently married, had moved his residence into one of the deserted cantonment buildings on the western side of the river. Truscott had neglected to secure a room in the hotel and Fisher invited him to join him in the *Cowboy* office.

The day had been strenuous, and the two men were soon sound asleep. Fisher was awakened by a sharp object striking him in the face. An instant later he heard a round of shots, followed instantly by another shower of broken glass. He discovered that one of the windows, which faced the Tamblyn Saloon, was completely shattered. He shook Truscott.

" I guess," he said, " we'd better look for some place not quite so convenient for a target."

They adjourned to Fisher's room in Mrs. McGeeney's hotel. After all, noise was preferable to bullets.

" The boys " were full of apologies the next morning, declaring that they had not realized that the place was occupied. Packard, it seemed, had been publishing certain editorials shortly before dealing with the criminal responsibility of drunkards, and they just thought they would give the *Cowboy* a " touching up."

Medora's new régime began with a call which Howard Eaton made upon Merrifield.

" Now that we're organized, we'll have some fun with Deacon Cummins," said Eaton, with a chuckle.

Eaton had apprehensions that the " Deacon " would ask for improvements, a road to his ranch, for instance, or possibly a bridge or two, so he suggested to Merrifield that they draw up a statement calculated to discourage any such aspirations. This was the statement as they finally submitted it to their fellow citizens:

We the undersigned do hereby solemnly covenant and agree to hang, burn, or drown any man that will ask for public improvements made at the expense of the County.

Eaton and Merrifield signed it, together with a dozen others; then they laid it before Mrs. Cummins's husband for his signature. "The Deacon" took it with extreme seriousness, and signed his name to it; and there was no call for improvements from the solemn couple at Tepee Bottom.

The day after the election, the Little Missouri Stock Association held its semi-annual meeting. Roosevelt presided, "preserving," as he wrote to Lodge a day or so later, "the most rigid parliamentary decorum." He was elected a representative of the Association at the meeting of the Montana Stock growers' Association in Miles City, to be held a day or two later, and, after a hurried trip to Elkhorn Ranch with Merrifield, started west for Miles City, taking Sylvane with him.

Miles City was a feverish little cow-town under ordinary circumstances, but in April of every year, when the cattlemen of Montana and western Dakota gathered there for the annual meeting of the Montana Stockgrowers' Association, it was jubilant and noisy beyond description. For a week before the convention was called to order, stockmen from near and far began to arrive, bringing in their train thirsty and hilarious cowboys who looked upon the occasion mainly as a golden opportunity for a spree. They galloped madly up and down the wide, dusty streets at every hour of the day and night, knowing no sober moment as long as the convention lasted.

Roosevelt and Sylvane arrived on April 18th, taking what quarters they could get in the Macqueen House which was crowded to the doors and was granting nobody more than half a bed. The ceremonies began early next morning with a blast from the Fifth Infantry band from Fort Keogh, the army post two miles to the west.

Promptly at 9:30 A.M. [runs the story in the Minneapolis *Tribune*] a procession was formed in front of the Macqueen House, with the Fifth Infantry band at its head, followed by carriages containing the officers of the Association and ladies; next a cavalcade of wild cowboys just brought in from the adjacent ranges, followed by about 150 cowmen marching four abreast. The procession was about two and one-half blocks long from end to end, and the line of march was through the principal streets to the skating rink, where the public meetings of the Association are held.

As the procession was nearing the rink, the horses of the foremost carriage, containing the president, vice-president, and secretary, took fright and dashed into the band. Both horses took the same side of the tongue and made things unpleasant. At this stage of the game President Bryan and others abandoned the carriage, and Secretary R. B. Harrison, with his large minute book, made a leap for life, and the subsequent proceedings interested him no more. The procession then broke up with a wild charge of cowboys, accompanied with such yells as would strike terror to the heart of the tenderfooted.

The actual meeting of the Stockgrowers' Association was, contrary to what might have been expected from its prelude, a thoroughly dignified affair. Roosevelt was, as one of the other stockmen later declared, "rather inclined to listen and take the advice of older men"; but it was significant that he was, nevertheless, elected to the Executive Committee as the successor of the Marquis de Mores as representative for Dakota Territory; and was appointed to one or two other committees of lesser importance.

"Roosevelt was of a restless, nervous, but aggressive disposition," said H. H. Hobson, of Great Falls, who was present at that meeting, "and took a keen interest in the proceedings. He was a great admirer of Granville Stuart, and was always on his side of every question."

The absorbing issues before the convention were the Texas fever and the overstocking of the range. Feeling ran high, and "the debates," as Hobson later remarked, "were more than warm. Roosevelt," he added, "was at all times eager and ready to champion his side."

At one of the sessions there was a fierce debate between two prominent cattlemen, which was renewed, after the meeting, at the Miles City Club. Each man had his hot partisans, who began to send messengers out for reënforcements. Most of the men were armed. It was clear that if hostilities once broke out, they would develop instantly into a miniature war.

Roosevelt saw that the situation was critical, and jumped to his feet. " If you can't settle your own difficulties," he cried to the two men who had started the quarrel, "why don't you fight it out? I'll referee."

The suggestion was received with favor. Roosevelt formed a ring and the two men expended their anger in a furious fist fight. Which man won, history does not record. The important point is that Roosevelt, by his resolute action, had prevented a fight with " six-shooters."

I have just returned from the Stockmen's Convention in Miles City [Roosevelt wrote " Bamie " from Elkhorn on April 22d], which raw, thriving frontier town was for three days thronged with hundreds of rough-looking, broad-hatted men, numbering among them all the great cattle and horse raisers of the Northwest. I took my position very well in the convention, and indeed these Westerners have now pretty well accepted me as one of themselves, and as a representative stockman. I am on the Executive Committee of the Association, am President of the Dakota branch, etc.— all of which directly helps me in my business relations here.

There is something almost touching in Roosevelt's efforts to persuade his sisters that his cattle venture was not the piece of wild recklessness which they evidently considered it.

This winter has certainly been a marvelously good one for cattle [he wrote in another letter]. My loss has been so trifling as hardly to be worth taking into account;

although there may be a number who have strayed off. I think my own expenses out here this summer will be very light indeed, and then we will be able to start all square with the beginning of the New Year.

In another letter he wrote, " Unless we have a big accident, I shall get through this all right, if only I can get started square with no debt! " And a little later he sent " Bamie " a clipping from a review of his " Hunting Trips of a Ranchman," which referred to him as " a man of large and various powers in public matters *as well as shrewd and enterprising in the conduct of business.*" " I send the enclosed slip," he wrote, " on account of the awful irony of the lines I have underscored; send it to Douglas when you write him."

" Douglas " was Douglas Robinson, the husband of Roosevelt's sister Corinne, and distinctly the business man of the family.

Bill Sewall was apprehensive. " There was always a cloud over me," he said long afterward, "because I never could see where he was going to get his money. I tried to make him see it. He was going to buy land. I urged him not to. I felt sure that what he was putting into those cattle he was going to lose."

Roosevelt admitted that spring that Sewall's conviction, that the cows would not be able in the long run to endure the hard winters, was not without reason. " Bill," he said, after he had made a careful study of the herd, " you're right about those cows. They're not looking well, and I think some of them will die."

But on the whole the herd was in good condition. He had every right to believe that with average luck his investment would emphatically justify itself.

> While I do not see any great fortune ahead [he wrote to his sister Corinne], yet, if things go on as they are now going, and have gone for the past three years, I think I will each year net enough money to pay a good interest on the capital, and yet be adding to my herd all the time. I think I have more than my original capital on the ground, and this year I ought to be able to sell between two and three hundred head of steer and dry stock.

Sewall as usual, was less sanguine.

> As for hard times [he wrote his brother that April] they are howling that here, and lots are leaving the country. Lots more would if they could. We are all right. Roosevelt is the same good fellow he always has been and though I don't think he expects to make much, his upper lip is stiff and he is all right.

Meanwhile, he was hammering ahead on his Life of Benton. He was a slow and rather laborious writer, but his persistence evidently atoned for his lack of speed in composition, for whereas, on April 29th, he wrote his sister that he had written only one chapter and intended to devote "the next three weeks to getting this work fairly under way," by the 7th of June he announced that the book was "nearly finished."

"Some days," Sewall related afterward, "he would write all day long; some days only a part of the day, just as he felt. He said sometimes he would get so he could not write. Sometimes he could not tell when a thing sounded right. Then he would take his gun and saunter off, sometimes alone, sometimes with me or Dow, if he was around."

Occasionally he would " try out " a passage on Sewall. " Bill," he exclaimed one morning, ".I am going to commit the unpardonable sin and make you sit down and listen to something I've written."

Bill was willing. The passage was from the first chapter of the biography of the Missouri statesman and dealt with the attitude of the frontier toward law and order and the rights of " the other fellow." Bill gave his approval and the passage stood.

Day after day Roosevelt pushed forward into his subject, writing with zest, tempered by cool judgment. He did not permit an occasional trip to Medora to interrupt his work. He had a room over Joe Ferris's store, and after Joe and his wife had gone to bed, he would throw open the doors of the kitchen and the dining-room and walk to and fro hammering out his sentences.

" Every once in a while," said Joe later, " everything would be quiet, then after fifteen minutes or so he would walk again as though he was walkin' for wages."

Mrs. Ferris, who had a maternal regard for his welfare, was always careful to see that a pitcher of milk was in his room before the night's labors commenced; for Roosevelt had a way of working into the small hours. " The eight-hour law," he remarked to Lodge, " does not apply to cowboys ";

nor, he might have added, to writers endeavoring to raise the wherewithal to pay for a hunting trip to the Cœur d'Alênes in the autumn.

I wonder if your friendship will stand a very serious strain [he wrote Lodge, early in June]. I have pretty nearly finished Benton, mainly evolving him from my inner consciousness; but when he leaves the Senate in 1850 I have nothing whatever to go by; and, being by nature both a timid, and, on occasions, by choice a truthful, man, I would prefer to have some foundation of fact, no matter how slender, on which to build the airy and arabesque superstructure of my fancy — especially as I am writing a history. Now I hesitate to give him a wholly fictitious date of death and to invent all of the work of his later years. Would it be too infernal a nuisance for you to hire some of your minions on the *Advertiser* (of course, at my expense) to look up, in a biographical dictionary or elsewhere, his life after he left the Senate in 1850? He was elected once to Congress; who beat him when he ran the second time; what was the issue; who beat him, and why, when he ran for Governor of Missouri; and the date of his death? I hate to trouble you; don't do it if it is any bother; but the Bad Lands have much fewer books than Boston has.

The Executive Committee of the Montana Stockgrowers' Association, of which Roosevelt was a member, had, in order to unify the work of the rounding-up of the cattle throughout Montana and western Dakota, issued directions at its meeting in April for the delimitation of the various round-up districts and the opening of the round-ups. The round-up for " District No. 6," which included the valley of the Little Missouri, commences [so ran the order] at Medora, May 25, 1886; works down the Little Missouri to the mouth of Big Beaver Creek; thence up the Big Beaver to its head; thence across to the Little Beaver at the crossing of the old government road (Keogh trail); thence down Little Beaver to its mouth; thence across to Northern Hashknife Camp on Little Missouri, and down to Medora. John Goodall, foreman.

Roosevelt apparently could not resist the temptation which the round-up offered, especially as its course would take him back in the direction of Elkhorn, and he deserted his study and entered once more into what was to him the most fascinating activity of the cowboy's life.

There were half a dozen wagons along [he wrote subsequently]. The saddle bands numbered about a hundred each; and the morning we started, sixty men in the saddle splashed across the shallow ford of the river that divided the plain where we had camped from the valley of the long winding creek up which we were first to work.

By the 7th of June he was back at Elkhorn Ranch again on a flying visit.

I will get a chance to send this note to-morrow [he wrote his sister " Bamie "] by an old teamster who is going to town. I have been on the round-up for a fortnight, and really enjoy the work greatly; in fact I am having a most pleasant summer, though I miss all of you very, very much. We breakfast at three and work from sixteen to eighteen hours a day counting night-guard; so I get pretty sleepy; but I feel as strong as a bear. I took along Tolstoy's " La Guerre et La Paix " which Madame de Mores had lent me; but I have had little chance to read it as yet. I am very fond of Tolstoy.

In " The Wilderness Hunter " Roosevelt, two or three years later, told of that " very pleasant summer " of 1886.

I was much at the ranch, where I had a good deal of writing to do; but every week or two I left, to ride among the line camps, or spend a few days on any round-up which happened to be in the neighborhood.

These days of vigorous work among the cattle were themselves full of pleasure. At dawn we were in the saddle, the morning air cool in our faces; the red sunrise saw us loping across the grassy reaches of prairie land, or climbing in single file among the rugged buttes. All forenoon we spent riding the long circle with the cowpunchers of the round-up; in the afternoon we worked the herd, cutting the cattle, with much breakneck galloping and dextrous halting and wheeling. Then came the excitement and hard labor of roping, throwing, and branding the wild and vigorous range calves; in a corral, if one was handy, otherwise in a ring of horsemen. Soon after nightfall we lay down, in a log hut or tent, if at a line camp; under the open sky, if with the round-up wagon.

After ten days or so of such work, in which every man had to do his full share, — for laggards and idlers, no matter who, get no mercy in the real and healthy democracy of the round-up, — I would go back to the ranch to turn to my books with added zest for a fortnight. Yet even during these weeks at the ranch there was some outdoor work; for I was breaking two or three colts. I took my time, breaking them gradually and gently, not, after the usual cowboy fashion, in a hurry, by sheer main strength and rough riding, with the attendant danger to the limbs of the man and very probable ruin to the manners of the horse. We rose early; each morning I stood on the low-roofed veranda, looking out under the line of murmuring, glossy-leaved cottonwoods, across the shallow river, to see the sun flame above the line of bluffs opposite.

Almost every day he was off among the buttes or across the prairie with a rifle in his hand, shooting now a whitetail buck within a few hundred yards of the ranch-house; now a blacktail, in the hills behind. Occasionally, rising before dawn, he would hunt in the rolling prairie country ten or fifteen miles away, coming home at dusk with a prong-buck across his saddle-bow. Now and then he would take the ranch-wagon and one of the men, driving to some good hunting ground, and spending a night or two, returning usually with two or three antelope; and not infrequently he would ride away by himself on horseback for a couple of days, lying at night, as he wrote, "under the shining and brilliant multitude of stars," and rising again in the chill dawn to crawl upon some wary goat of the high hills.

After writing his sister on the 7th of June, he evidently stayed at the ranch for ten days to work on his Life of Benton. Then he was away with the round-up again. His diary succinctly records his progress:

June 18. Rode to Medora on Sorrel Joe.
June 19. Out on round-up with Maltese Cross wagon.
June 20. Worked down to South Heart.
June 21. Worked up Rocky Ridge.
June 22. Worked to Davis Creek.

Early next morning Roosevelt was in Medora.

The round-up is swinging over from the East to the West Divide [he wrote to Lodge]. I rode in to get my mail and must leave at once. We are working pretty hard. Yesterday I was in the saddle at 2 A.M., and except for two very hearty meals, after each of which I took a fresh horse, did not stop working till 8.15 P.M.; and was up at half-past three this morning.

They worked next day down to Andrews Creek. While the round-up was camped at Andrews Creek an incident occurred which revealed Roosevelt's influence over the cowpunchers, not alone of his own " outfit." Andrews Creek was not more than a mile from Medora, and after the day's work was done, the cowboys naturally adjourned with much enthusiasm to that oasis for the thirsty. As the evening wore on, the men, as " Dutch Wannigan " remarked long afterward, " were getting kinda noisy." Roosevelt, who had also ridden to town, possibly to keep an eye on " the boys," heard the commotion, and, contrary to his usual habit, which was to keep out of such centers of trouble, entered the saloon where the revelry was in progress.

" I don't know if he took a drink or not," said " Dutch Wannigan " afterward. " I never saw him take one. But he came in and he paid for the drinks for the crowd. ' One more drink, boys,' he says. Then, as soon as they had their drinks, he says, ' Come on,' and away they went. He just took the lead and they followed him home. By gollies, I never seen anything like it! "

The round-up now worked southward. Roosevelt's diary gives its course from day to day.

June 24. To Gardiner Creek.
June 25. To Bullion's Creek.
June 26. Down Bullion's Creek.
June 27. To Chimney Butte.
June 28. Rode in to Medora.

From Medora he wrote his sister Corinne:

I have been off on the round-up for five weeks, taking a holiday of a few days when we had a cold snap, during which time I killed two elk and six antelopes, all the meat being smoke-dried and now hanging round the trees, till the ranch looks like an Indian encampment. Since June 24th, I have never once had breakfast as late as 4 o'clock. I have been in the saddle all the day and work like a beaver and am as happy and rugged as possible.

To " Bamie " he wrote:

If I did not miss all at home so much, and also my beautiful home, I would say that this free, open-air life, without any worry, was perfection.

The round-up ended in Medora, where it had begun.

You would hardly know my sunburned and windroughened face [Roosevelt wrote " Bamie "]. But I have really enjoyed it and am as tough as a hickory nut.

He evidently did not think he needed any vacation after the strenuous labors of the preceding weeks, for his diary records no interlude.

June 29. Rode back to Elkhorn Ranch with Merrifield.

June 30. Benton.

July 1. Benton; rode out with Bill Rowe to get and brand calves.

July 2. Benton; rode out with Bill Rowe after calves; got them into corral and branded them. Rode little black horse.

July 3. Rode up to Medora on Manitou.

Roosevelt had been invited to be the orator at Dickinson's first celebration of Independence Day, and, on the morning of the Fourth, accompanied by two New York friends, Lispenard Stewart and Dr. Taylor, and half the cowboys of Billings County, " jumped " an east-bound freight for the scene of the festivities.

Dickinson was in holiday mood. The West Missouri slope had never celebrated the Fourth with fitting ceremonies before and Dickinson, which, with its seven hundred inhabitants, considered itself somewhat of a metropolis, made up its mind to " spread itself." From near and far eager crowds streamed into the little town, on foot and on horseback. The *Press* reported the celebration with zest:

A BIG DAY

The First Fourth of July Celebration in Dickinson a Grand Success

An Epoch in the History of Our Town that Will Long be Remembered

Addresses by Hon. Theodore Roosevelt and Hon. John A. Rea

The first Fourth of July celebration, attempted in Dickinson, took place last Monday. It exceeded the anticipations of all and proved to be a grand success — a day that will long be remembered. The day dawned bright and cool. Early in the morning people began to arrive and by ten o'clock the largest crowd ever assembled in Stark County lined the principal streets. The train from the west brought a number of Medora people, amongst them Hon. Theodore Roosevelt, the orator of the day.

The first exercise was the parade, consisting of three divisions, under charge of Chief Marshal Auld, assisted by C. S. Langdon and Western Starr. About ten o'clock everything was in readiness and the parade began to move, headed by the Dickinson Silver Cornet Band. Following the band were the lady equestriennes, a large number of ladies being in line. They were followed by the members of Fort Sumter Post G.A.R. and Onward Lodge R.R.B. Next came a beautifully decorated wagon drawn by four white horses, containing little girls dressed in white, representing the States of the Union. This was one of the most attractive features of the parade, and was followed by a display of reaping and other farm machinery. The " Invincibles " were next in line and created considerable mirth by their fantastic and grotesque appearance. Citizens in carriages and on horseback brought up the rear. After parading through the principal streets the procession marched to the public square and were dismissed.

"The trouble with the parade," remarked Bill Dantz long after, "was that every one in town was so enthusiastic they insisted on joining the procession, and there was no one to watch except two men who were too drunk to notice anything"; which was Dantz's way of saying that the "first exercise" was eminently successful.

Western Starr [continues the *Press*] was introduced by Dr. V. H. Stickney, master of ceremonies, and read the Declaration of Independence in a clear, forcible tone, after which the entire audience joined in singing that familiar and patriotic song, "America." The people then partook of the free dinner prepared for the occasion. After dinner the people were called to order and Rev. E. C. Dayton offered up a prayer, followed by music by the band.

The speeches followed. The first speaker was a typical politician of the old school.

This is a big country [he said]. At a dinner party of Americans in Paris during the Civil War this toast was offered by a New Englander: "*Here's to the United States, bounded on the north by British America, on the south by the Gulf of Mexico, on the east by the Atlantic, and on the west by the Pacific Ocean.*"

An Ohio man followed with a larger notion of our greatness: "*Here's to the United States, bounded on the north by the North Pole, on the south by the South Pole, on the east by the rising sun, and on the west by the setting sun.*"

It took the Dakota man, however, to rise to the greatness of the subject: "*I give you the United States, bounded on the north by the Aurora Borealis, on the south by the precession of the equinoxes, on the east by primeval chaos, and on the west by the Day of Judgment.*"

The politician proceeded with the eloquence of the professional "orator," and the audience applauded him vociferously. Then Roosevelt rose and spoke. He looked very slim and young and embarrassed.

I am peculiarly glad [he said] to have an opportunity of addressing you, my fellow citizens of Dakota, on the

Fourth of July, because it always seems to me that those who dwell in a new territory, and whose actions, therefore, are peculiarly fruitful, for good and for bad alike, in shaping the future, have in consequence peculiar responsibilities. You have already been told, very truthfully and effectively, of the great gifts and blessings you enjoy; and we all of us feel, most rightly and properly, that we belong to the greatest nation that has ever existed on this earth — a feeling I like to see, for I wish every American always to keep the most intense pride in his country, and people. But as you already know your rights and privileges so well, I am going to ask you to excuse me if I say a few words to you about your duties. Much has been given to us, and so, much will be expected of us; and we must take heed to use aright the gifts entrusted to our care.

The Declaration of Independence derived its peculiar importance, not on account of what America was, but because of what she was to become; she shared with other nations the present, and she yielded to them the past, but it was felt in return that to her, and to her especially, belonged the future. It is the same with us here. We, grangers and cowboys alike, have opened a new land; and we are the pioneers, and as we shape the course of the stream near its head, our efforts have infinitely more effect, in bending it in any given direction, than they would have if they were made farther along. In other words, the first comers in a land can, by their individual efforts, do far more to channel out the course in which its history is to run than can those who come after them; and their labors, whether exercised on the side of evil or on the side of good, are far more effective than if they had remained in old settled communities.

So it is peculiarly incumbent on us here to-day so to act throughout our lives as to leave our children a heritage, for which we will receive their blessing and not their curse.

Stickney, sitting on the platform as presiding officer, was struck by the contrast which Roosevelt offered to the man who had preceded him. The first speaker had been " eloquent " in the accepted meaning of the word; Roosevelt was not consciously eloquent at all. He talked as he always talked, simply, directly, earnestly, emphatically.

We have rights [he went on], but we have correlative duties; none can escape them. We only have the right to live on as free men, governing our own lives as we will, so long as we show ourselves worthy of the privileges we enjoy. We must remember that the Republic can only be kept pure by the individual purity of its members; and that if it become once thoroughly corrupted, it will surely cease to exist. In our body politic, each man is himself a constituent portion of the sovereign, and if the sovereign is to continue in power, he must continue to do right. When you here exercise your privileges at the ballot box, you are not only exercising a right, but you are also fulfilling a duty; and a heavy responsibility rests on you to fulfill your duty well. If you fail to work in public life, as well as in private, for honesty and uprightness and virtue, if you condone vice because the vicious man is smart, or if you in any other way cast your weight into the scales in favor of evil, you are just so far corrupting and making less valuable the birthright of your children. The duties of American citizenship are very solemn as well as very precious; and each one of us here to-day owes it to himself, to his children, and to all his fellow Americans, to show that he is capable of performing them in the right spirit.

It is not what we have that will make us a great nation; it is the way in which we use it.

I do not undervalue for a moment our material

prosperity; like all Americans, I like big things; big prairies, big forests and mountains, big wheat-fields, railroads, — and herds of cattle, too, — big factories, steamboats, and everything else. But we must keep steadily in mind that no people were ever yet benefited by riches if their prosperity corrupted their virtue. It is of more importance that we should show ourselves honest, brave, truthful, and intelligent, than that we should own all the railways and grain elevators in the world. We have fallen heirs to the most glorious heritage a people ever received, and each one must do his part if we wish to show that the nation is worthy of its good fortune. Here we are not ruled over by others, as in the case of Europe; we rule ourselves. All American citizens, whether born here or elsewhere, whether of one creed or another, stand on the same footing; we welcome every honest immigrant no matter from what country he comes, provided only that he leaves off his former nationality, and remains neither Celt nor Saxon, neither Frenchman nor German, but becomes an American, desirous of fulfilling in good faith the duties of American citizenship.

When we thus rule ourselves, we have the responsibilities of sovereigns, not of subjects. We must never exercise our rights either wickedly or thoughtlessly; we can continue to preserve them in but one possible way, by making the proper use of them. In a new portion of the country, especially here in the Far West, it is peculiarly important to do so; and on this day of all others we ought soberly to realize the weight of the responsibility that rests upon us. I am, myself, at heart as much a Westerner as an Easterner; I am proud, indeed, to be considered one of yourselves, and I address you in this rather solemn strain to-day, only because of my pride in you, and because your welfare, moral as well as material, is so near my heart.

It was a hilarious party of cowpunchers who took the afternoon train back to Medora. For a part of the brief journey Packard sat with Roosevelt discussing his speech.

" It was during this talk," said Packard afterward, " that I first realized the potential bigness of the man. One could not help believing he was in deadly earnest in his consecration to the highest ideals of citizenship. He had already made his mark in the New York Legislature. He was known as a fighter who dared to come out in the open and depend upon the backing of public opinion. He was reputed to be wealthy enough to devote his life to any work he chose, and I learned, on the return journey to the Bad Lands that day, that he believed he could do better work in a public and political way than in any other. My conclusion was immediate, and I said, ' Then you will become President of the United States.'

" One would suppose that I could remember the actual words he used in reply, but I cannot. I remember distinctly that he was not in the least surprised at my statement. He gave me the impression of having thoroughly considered the matter and to have arrived at the same conclusion that I had arrived at. I remember only this of what he said, ' If your prophecy comes true, I will do my part to make a good one.' "

XXIV

The road is wide and the stars are out, and the breath of night is sweet,
And this is the time when wanderlust should seize upon my feet,
But I'm glad to turn from the open road and the starlight on my face,
And leave the splendor of out-of-doors for a human dwelling-place.
                                          JOYCE KILMER

A FEW days after the celebration in Dickinson,
Roosevelt went East. The political sirens were
calling. He was restless for something to do that
would bring into service the giant's strength of
which he was becoming increasingly conscious, and,
incidentally, would give him an opportunity to
win distinction. He had been half inclined to accept an offer from Mayor Grace of New York to
head the Board of Health, but Lodge, as Roosevelt
wrote to his sister Corinne, thought it "*infra dig*,"
and he reluctantly rejected it. There were rumors
in the air that he might have the Republican
nomination for Mayor of New York if he wanted it.
He went East, possibly for the purpose of investi-
gating them, returning to Elkhorn early in August.

Roosevelt was unquestionably restless. He loved
the wild country, but he had tasted all the various
joys and hardships it had to offer, and, although
he said again and again that if he had no ties of
affection and of business to bind him to the East,
he would make Dakota his permanent residence,
down in his heart he was hungering for a wider
field of action. The frontier had been a challenge

to his manhood; now that he had stood every test it had presented to him, its glamour faded and he looked about for a sharper challenge and more exacting labors.

For a few weeks that August he half hoped that he might find them on the field of battle. Several American citizens, among them a man named Cutting, had been arrested in Mexico, apparently illegally, and Bayard, who was President Cleveland's Secretary of State, had been forced more than once to make vigorous protests. Relations became strained. The anti-Mexican feeling on the border spread over the whole of Texas, regiments were organized, and the whole unsettled region between the Missouri and the Rockies, which was inclined to look upon Mexico as the natural next morsel in the fulfillment of the nation's " manifest destiny," began to dream of war.

Roosevelt, seeing how matters were tending, set about to organize a troop of cavalry in the Bad Lands. He notified the Secretary of War that it stood at the service of the Government.

I have written to Secretary Endicott [Roosevelt wrote to Lodge on August 10th], offering to try to raise some companies of horse-riflemen out here, in the event of trouble with Mexico. Won't you telegraph me at once if war becomes inevitable? Out here things are so much behindhand that I might not hear of things for a week. I have not the least idea there will be any trouble, but as my chances of doing anything in the future worth doing seem to grow continually smaller, I intend to grasp at every opportunity that turns up.

The cowboys were all eager for war, not caring much with whom. They were fond of adventure and to tell the truth [as Roosevelt wrote later], they were by no means averse to the prospect of plunder. News from the outside world came to us very irregularly, and often in distorted form, so that we began to think we might get involved in a conflict not only with Mexico, but with England also. One evening at my ranch the men began talking over English soldiers, so I got down " Napier " and read them several extracts from his descriptions of the fighting in the Spanish peninsula, also recounting as well as I could the great deeds of the British cavalry from Waterloo to Balaklava, and finishing up by describing from memory the fine appearance, the magnificent equipment, and the superb horses of the Household Cavalry and of a regiment of hussars I had once seen.

All of this produced much the same effect on my listeners that the sight of Marmion's cavalcade produced in the minds of the Scotch moss-troopers on the eve of Flodden; and at the end, one of them, who had been looking into the fire and rubbing his hands together, said, with regretful emphasis, " Oh, how I *would* like to kill one of them! "

Roosevelt went to Bismarck and found the Territorial Governor friendly to his project.

Hon. Theodore Roosevelt, of New York, the famous statesman, ranchman, and hunter [runs the story in the Bismarck *Tribune*], has been making inquiries since the announcement of the Mexican difficulties as to the available volunteer troops in the Northwest, and in the event of action being required, it is confidently believed Mr. Roosevelt would tender to the Government the services of an entire regiment of cowboys, under his command. At a recent visit here he was assured of two companies of Dakota cowboys to accompany him. Mr. Roosevelt has been the captain of a company of militia in New York, and no better man could be found to lead the daring cowboys to a seat of war and no commander would have more effective troops.

The war cloud blew over. Roosevelt evidently received a letter from Lodge explaining that the Mexican incident was of a trivial nature, for, on the 20th of August, he wrote him rather apologetically:

I wrote as regards Mexico *qua* cowboy, not *qua* statesman; I know little of the question, but conclude Bayard is wrong, for otherwise it would be phenomenal; he ought to be idolized by the mugwumps. If a war had come off, I would surely have had behind me as utterly reckless a set of desperadoes as ever sat in the saddle.

It is no use saying that I would like a chance at something I thought I could really do; at present I see nothing whatever ahead. However, there is the hunting in the fall, at any rate.

The season which began with Finnegan and Company was richer in varied experiences than it was in financial returns. Roosevelt recognized that there were already too many cattlemen in the business to make large profits possible.

In certain sections of the West [he told a reporter of the Mandan *Pioneer* in July] the losses this year are enormous, owing to the drought and over-stocking. Each steer needs from fifteen to twenty-five acres, but they are crowded on very much thicker, and the cattlemen this season have paid the penalty. Between the drought, the grasshoppers, and the late frosts, ice form-

ing as late as June 10th, there is not a green thing in all
the region I have been over. A stranger would think a
donkey could not live there. The drought has been very
bad throughout the region, and there is not a garden
in all of it.

Sewall was aware of that fact to his sorrow, for
the garden he himself had planted and tended with
infinite care had died between dawn and dusk on
that memorable Fourth of July on which Roosevelt
addressed the citizens of Dickinson.

They say dry years are best for cattle [he wrote his
brother]. If so, this must be a nice one and they do seem
to be doing well so far, but if we have much snow next
winter it looks to me as if they would have short picking.

The prospect was not engaging. But, though
Roosevelt was not getting much financial return
on his rather generous investment, he was getting
other things, for him at this time of far greater
value. He who had been weak in body and subject
to racking illnesses had in these three years developed a constitution as tough and robust as an
Indian's. He had achieved something beside this.
Living, talking, working, facing danger, and suffering hardships with the Sewalls and the Dows, the
Ferrises and the Langs, and Merrifield and Packard
and Bill Dantz and Hell-Roaring Bill Jones, and
countless other stalwart citizens of the Bad Lands,
he had come very close to the heart of the " plain
American." He loved the companions of his joys
and labors, and they in turn regarded him with
an admiration and devotion which was all the

deeper because of the amazing fact that he had come from the ranks of the " dudes."

They admired him for his courage and his feats of endurance, but, being tender-hearted themselves, they loved him for his tenderness, which had a way that they approved, of expressing itself, not in words, but in deeds. Bill Sewall had a little girl of three, " a forlorn little mite," as Roosevelt described her to " Bamie," and it was Roosevelt who sent the word East which transported the child, that had neither playmates nor toys, into a heaven of delight with picture blocks and letter blocks, a little horse and a rag doll.

His warm human sympathy found expression in a dramatic manner a day or two before his departure late that August for the Cœur d'Alênes. He was rounding up some cattle with his men near Sentinel Butte, twenty miles west of Medora, when word came that a cowpuncher named George Frazier had been struck by lightning and killed, and that his body had been taken to Medora. Frazier belonged to the " outfit " of the Marquis de Mores, but he had worked for Roosevelt two years previous, digging post-holes with George Myers in June, 1884. Roosevelt knew that the man had no relatives in that part of the world, to see that a fitting disposition of the body was made, and instantly expressed his determination to take charge of the arrangements for the funeral.

" We will flag the next train and go to Medora," he said.

The next train, they knew, was " No. 2," the finest train running over the road. It did not, on the surface, look probable that it would stop at a desolate spot in the prairie to permit a handful of cowboys to get on. " They won't stop here for nuthin'," one of the men insisted. " By Godfrey, they'll have to stop! " Roosevelt retorted, and sent a man down to the track to flag the train.

The engineer saw the warning signal and slowed down, but did not stop. The cowboys dashed alongside the engine, firing shots in the air. The engineer, believing that he was being held up by bandits and that the next shot might be aimed at himself, brought the train to a standstill. There was a wild scramble among the passengers; even the train crew expected the worst. Valuables were hurriedly secreted. " I don't believe," remarked George Myers afterward, " some of the passengers ever did find all the things that was hid away."

Leaving their horses in charge of one of the cowboys, Roosevelt, followed by Sylvane Ferris, Merrifield, Myers, and Johnny Goodall, boarded the train. The conductor was resigned by this time to a holdup; but when he discovered the actual nature of their mission, he flew into a rage and threatened to put them all off.

" You be good," cried Roosevelt, " or you'll be the one to get off! " His vigorous advice was supplemented by impressive injunctions from other members of the party. When they finally did get off, it was at Medora.

A salvo of profanity from the train crew followed them. "You'll hear from this!" thundered the conductor. They did not hear from it. It would not have greatly disturbed Roosevelt if they had. He opened a subscription to cover the expenses of the funeral. Everybody "chipped in," and the unfortunate received the burial that a God-fearing cowpuncher deserved.

Roosevelt went with Merrifield west to the Cœur d'Alênes, in northern Idaho, almost immediately after Frazier's funeral. He was to meet a hunter named John Willis, who was to take him and Merrifield out after white goat. He had never met Willis, but his correspondence with him had suggested possibilities of interest beside the chase. Roosevelt had written Willis in July that he had heard of his success in pursuit of the game of the high peaks. "If I come out," he concluded, "do you think it will be possible for me to get a goat?"

The answer he received was written on the back of his own letter and was quite to the point. "If you can't shoot any better than you can write, I don't think it will be."

Roosevelt's reply came by wire. "Consider yourself engaged."

It would have been strange if, after this epistolary exchange, the two men should not have been rather curious about each other's personalities. Roosevelt, descending from the train at a way-station in the mountains, found a huge, broad-shouldered man his own age, waiting for him. The man was not over-cordial. He did not, he later admitted, regard Roosevelt's corduroy knee-pants with favor.

Roosevelt, knowing how to catch a hunter, showed Willis his guns. "Will you go on a trip with me?" he asked.

" I am going to start out day after to-morrow for a three or four weeks' hunt," Willis answered. " If you want to go along as my guest, you are welcome to. But I want to tell you before we go, I won't take any booze."

"Why do you say that?" asked Roosevelt, thoroughly interested in this strange creature.

" Why, I've an idea you are some brewer's son who's made a lot of money. You look as if you'd been raised on beer."

Roosevelt roared with delight. " I want to make a contract with you," he said. " I will give you twenty-five dollars for everything that you show me in the way of game."

" I don't want it," said Willis gruffly.

" Then I will buy the grub."

" All the grub I'll take along won't amount to more than three or four dollars — a hundred pounds of flour, twenty-five pounds of bacon, dried apples, and black tea. That's all you'll get."

" By George," cried Roosevelt, " that's fine!"

" You can't stand a trip like this," Willis remarked with deadly frankness.

" You take me on the trip and I'll show you. I can train myself to walk as far as you can."

Willis doubted it and said so.

They camped far up in the mountains, hunting day after day through the deep woods just below the timber-line. Roosevelt and Merrifield were accustomed to life in the saddle, and although they had varied it with an occasional long walk after deer or sheep, they were quite unable to cope with Willis when it came to mountaineering. The climbing was hard, the footing was treacherous, and the sharp rocks tore their moccasins into ribbons. There was endless underbrush, thickets of prickly balsam or laurel — but there were no goats.

At last, one mid-afternoon, as he was supporting himself against a tree, halfway across a long landslide, Roosevelt suddenly discovered one of the beasts he was after, a short distance away, making his way down a hill, looking for all the world like a handsome tame billy. He was in a bad position for a shot, and as he twisted himself about he dislodged some pebbles. The goat, instantly alert, fled. Roosevelt fired, but the shot went low, only breaking a fore-leg.

The three men raced and scrambled after the fleeing animal. It leaped along the hillside for nearly a mile, then turned straight up the mountain. They followed the bloody trail where it went up the sharpest and steepest places, skirting the cliffs and precipices.

Roosevelt, intent on the quarry, was not what Bill Sewall would have called " over-cautious " in the pursuit.

He was running along a shelving ledge when a

piece of loose slate with which the ledge was covered slipped under his foot. He clutched at the rock wall, he tried to fling himself back, but he could not recover himself.

He went head first over the precipice.

Roosevelt's luck was with him that day. He fell forty or fifty feet into a tall pine, bounced through it, and landed finally, not uncomfortably, in a thick balsam, somewhat shaken and scratched, but with no bones broken and with his rifle still clutched in his hand.

From above came the hoarse voice of John Willis. " Are you hurt? " he asked.

" No," answered Roosevelt, a trifle breathless.

" Then come on! "

Roosevelt " came on," scrambling back up the steep height he had so swiftly descended, and raced after the guide. He came upon the goat at last, but winded as he was, and with the sweat in his eyes, he shot too high, cutting the skin above the spine. The goat plunged downhill and the hunters plunged after him, pursuing the elusive animal until darkness covered the trail.

" Now," said Willis, " I expect you are getting tired."

" By George," said Roosevelt, " how far have we gone? "

" About fifteen or twenty miles up and down the mountains."

" If we get that goat to-morrow, I will give you a hundred dollars."

"I don't want a hundred dollars. But we'll get the goat."

Roosevelt brought him down the next day at noon.

Roosevelt spent two weeks with Willis in the mountains. It was a rich experience for the Easterner, but for the tall Missourian it proved to be even more. Willis was a child of the frontier, who had knocked about between the Rio Grande and the Canadian border ever since his boyhood, doing a hundred different things upon which the law and civilized men were supposed to look with disapproval.[1]

To this odd child of nature, bred in the wilderness, Roosevelt opened the door to a world which John Willis did not know existed.

"He was a revelation to me," said Willis long afterward. "He was so well posted on everything. He was the first man that I had ever met that really knew anything. I had just been with a lot of roughnecks, cowpunchers, horse-thieves, and that sort. Roosevelt would explain things to me. He told me a lot of things."

Among other things, Roosevelt told Willis some of his experiences in the New York Assembly. Huge sums had been offered him to divert him from this course or that which certain interests regarded as dangerous to their freedom of action. To Willis it was amazing that Roosevelt should not have

[1] Willis was a great teller of tales. See *Hunting the Grizzly*, by Theodore Roosevelt (The Sagamore Series, G. P. Putnam's Sons, page 216 ff.), for the most lurid of his yarns.

accepted what was offered to him, and he began to be aware of certain standards of virtue and honor.

To Roosevelt the trip was a splendid adventure; to Willis it proved a turning-point in his life.[1]

Roosevelt returned to Elkhorn the middle of September, to find that Sewall and Dow had come to a momentous decision. Dow had, during his absence, taken a train-load of cattle to Chicago, and had found that the best price he was able to secure for the hundreds of cattle he had taken to the market there was less by ten dollars a head than the sum it had cost to raise and transport them. Sewall and Dow had " figured things over," and had come to the conclusion that the sooner they terminated their contract with Roosevelt the less money he would lose. They recognized that they themselves were safe enough, for by the " one-sided trade," as Sewall called it, which Roosevelt had made with them, they were to share in whatever profits there were, and in case there were no profits were to receive wages. But neither of them enjoyed the part he was playing in what seemed to both of them a piece of hopeless business.

Roosevelt himself had been wondering whether it was wise to allow the two backwoodsmen to continue in an enterprise in which the future was so clouded and full of the possibilities of disaster.

[1] When Roosevelt came to Helena in 1911, John Willis was one of the crowd that greeted him. Willis clapped Roosevelt on the back familiarly. " I made a man out of you," he cried. Quick as a flash, came Roosevelt's retort: " Yes. John made a man out of me, but I made a Christian out of John."

He himself might win through, and he might not. The thing was a gamble, in any event. He could afford to take the risk. Sewall and Dow could not.

He had written " Bamie," earlier in the summer, that he was " curious to see how the fall sales would come out." Dow's report completely satisfied his curiosity.

He called the two men into his room. He told them that he too had been " figuring up things." He would stand by his agreement, he said, if, facing an uncertain outcome, they wished to remain. But, if they were willing, he thought they had " better quit the business and go back."

Sewall and Dow did not hesitate. They said they would go back.

" I never wanted to fool away anybody else's money," Sewall added. " Never had any of my own to fool away."

" How soon can you go? " asked Roosevelt.

Sewall turned and went into the kitchen " to ask the womenfolks." It happened that three or four weeks previous the population of Elkhorn had been increased by two. Baby sons had arrived in the same week in the families of both Sewall and Dow. The ministrations of Dr. Stickney had not been available, and the two mothers had survived because they had the constitutions of frontierswomen rather than because they had the benefit of the nursing of the termagant who was Jerry Tompkins's wife. The babies — known to their families, and to the endless succession of cowboys who came from near

and far to inspect them, as " the Bad Lands babies "
— were just six weeks old.

" The womenfolks say they can go in three
weeks," Sewall reported.

" Three weeks from to-day," answered Roosevelt,
" we go."

And so the folks from Maine, who had made a
rough and simple house in the wilderness into a
home, began to gather together their belongings
and pack up. Wise old Bill Sewall had been right.

" You'll come to feel different," he had said, two
years before, when Roosevelt had been lonely and
despondent. " And then you won't want to stay
here."

Life, which for a while had seemed to Roosevelt
so gray and dismal, had, in fact, slowly taken on
new color. At times he had imagined that Dakota
might satisfy him for a permanent residence, but
that fancy, born of grief and disappointment, had
vanished in the radiance of a new happiness. He
had become engaged to Edith Carow, and he knew
that the world for him and for her was that busy
world where his friends were, and hers, and where
he and she had been boy and girl together.

The lure of politics, moreover, was calling him.
And yet, during those last weeks at Elkhorn, he
was not at all sure that he wished to reënter the
turmoil. He rode out into the prairie one day for a
last " session " with Bill Sewall shortly before the
three weeks were up. He told Sewall he had an idea
he ought to go into law.

"You'd be a good lawyer," said Bill, "but I think you ought to go into politics. Good men like you ought to go into politics. If you do, and if you live, I think you'll be President."

Roosevelt laughed. "That's looking a long way ahead."

"It may look a long way ahead to you," Sewall declared stoutly, "but it isn't as far ahead as it's been for some of the men who got there."

"I'm going home now," said Roosevelt, "to see about a job my friends want me to take. I don't think I want it. It will get me into a row. And I want to write."

An Easterner, whose name has slipped from the record, hearing possibly that Roosevelt was making changes in the management of his herds, offered to buy all of Roosevelt's cattle. Roosevelt refused. The man offered to buy Merrifield's share, then Sylvane's. Both rejected the offer. The herd had increased greatly in value since they had established it. The coming spring, they said, they would begin to get great returns. . . .

"September 25, 1886," runs an item in Bill Sewall's account-book, "squared accounts with Theodore Roosevelt." On the same day Roosevelt made a contract with Merrifield and Sylvane Ferris by which he agreed, as the contract runs, "to place all his cattle branded with the Maltese cross and all his she-stock and bulls branded with the elkhorn and triangle, some twenty-odd hundred head in all, valued at sixty thousand dollars," in charge of Ferris and Merrifield on shares for the term of four years; the men of the Maltese Cross agreeing on their part to take charge of the Elkhorn steer brand which was Roosevelt's exclusive property.

Then, knowing that his cattle were in good hands, Roosevelt once more turned his face to the East, conscious in his heart, no doubt, that, however soon he might return, or however often, the Dakota idyl was ended.

XXV

I may not see a hundred
  Before I see the Styx,
But coal or ember, I'll remember
  Eighteen-eighty-six.

The stiff heaps in the coulee,
  The dead eyes in the camp,
And the wind about, blowing fortunes out
  As a woman blows out a lamp.

From *Medora Nights*

ROOSEVELT accepted the Republican nomination for Mayor of New York City, " with the most genuine reluctance," as he wrote Lodge. He recognized that it was " a perfectly hopeless contest; the chance for success being so very small that it may be left out of account." It was a three-cornered fight, with Henry George as the nominee of a United Labor Party on a single-tax platform, and Abram S. Hewitt as the candidate of Tammany Hall.

The nomination gave Dakota an occasion to express its mind concerning its adopted son, and it did so, with gusto.

Theodore is a Dakota cowboy [said the *Press* of Sioux Falls], and has spent a large share of his time in the Territory for a couple of years. He is one of the finest thoroughbreds you ever met — a whole-souled, clear-headed, high-minded gentleman. When he first went on the range, the cowboys took him for a dude, but soon they realized the stuff of which the youngster was built, and there is no man now who inspires such enthusiastic regard among them as he.

Roosevelt conducted a lively campaign, for it was not in him to make anything but the best fight of which he was capable even with the odds against him. The thoughtful element of the city, on whose support against the radicalism of Henry George on the one hand and the corruption of Tammany on the other, he should have been able to count, became panic-stricken at the possibility of a labor victory, and gave their votes to Hewitt. He was emphatically defeated; in fact, he ran third. " But anyway," he remarked cheerfully, " I had a bully time."

He went abroad immediately after election, and in December, at St. George's, Hanover Square, London, he married Edith Kermit Carow.

Once more, winter descended upon the Bad Lands.

Medora [remarked the Bismarck *Tribune* in November] has pretty nearly gone into winter quarters. To be sure, the slaughter-house establishment of Marquis de Mores will not formally shut down until the end of the month, but there are many days on which there is no killing done and the workmen have to lay off. The past season has not been of the busiest, and the near approach of winter finds this about the quietest place in western Dakota. The hotel is closed. There is only one general store and its proprietor declared that the middle of December will find him, stock and all, hundreds of miles from here. The proprietor of the drug store will move early in December, as he cannot make his board in the place.

A. T. Packard, the editor of the *Bad Lands Cowboy*, which now has a circulation of 650, is evidently prospering well, and, with the managers of the Northern Pacific Refrigerator Company and the railroad agents, seems to be about the only person who expresses an intention of spending the season here.

Fortunate were those who spent that season elsewhere. Old-timers, whose wits had been sharpened by long life in the open, had all the autumn been making ominous predictions. They talked of a hard winter ahead, and the canniest of them defied the skeptics by riding into Medora trailing a pack-horse and purchasing six months' supplies of provisions at one time.

Nature, they pointed out, was busier than she had ever been, in the memory of the oldest hunter in that region, in " fixin' up her folks for hard times." The muskrats along the creeks were building their houses to twice their customary height; the walls were thicker than usual, and the muskrats' fur was longer and heavier than any old-timer had ever known it to be. The beavers were working by day as well as by night, cutting the willow brush, and observant eyes noted that they were storing twice their usual winter's supply. The birds were acting strangely. The ducks and geese, which ordinarily flew south in October, that autumn had, a month earlier, already departed. The snowbirds and the cedar birds were bunched in the thickets, fluttering about by the thousands in the cedar brakes, obviously restless and uneasy. The Arctic owls, who came only in hard winters, were about.

There was other evidence that the winds were

brewing misery. Not only the deer and the antelope, the wolves and the coyotes, but the older range cattle and the horses were growing unusually long coats.

Other signs of strange disturbances of Nature were not lacking. During October the usual Indian-summer haze seemed to have lifted to a higher altitude, interposing, as it were, a curtain between earth and sun. The light became subdued and unnatural. Halos appeared about the sun, with sundogs at opposite sides of the circle. The superstitious were startled, in the time of the full moon, at four shafts of light, which could be seen emanating from it, giving an eerie effect as of a cross over the silver disc.

There was usually a wet snowstorm in late October; this year it did not come. A weird, dull stillness was in the air. Then, one evening toward the end of the first week in November, the snow came, falling lightly and noiselessly. As the evening advanced, the wind arose; and even as it increased in violence, the spirit in the thermometer fell. The wind became a gale, and before midnight a blizzard was howling and sweeping through the Bad Lands such as no one there had ever known before. The snow was like the finest powder, driving through every crack and nail hole, and piling snowdrifts within the houses as well as without.

"Upon getting up in the morning," said Lincoln Lang long afterward, describing that storm, " the house was intensely cold, with everything that could freeze frozen solid. The light was cut off from the windows looking south. As we opened the front door, we were confronted by a solid wall of snow reaching to the eaves of the house. There was no drift over the back door, looking north, but, as I opened it, I was blown almost from my feet by the swirl of the snow, which literally filled the air, so that it was impossible to see any of the surrounding ranch-buildings or even the fence, less than fifty feet distant. It was like a tornado of pure white dust or very fine sand, icy cold, and stinging like a whip-lash."

As fast as the fine dry snow fell, it drifted and packed itself into the coulees, gulches, and depressions, filling them to a depth of a hundred feet or more. The divides and plateaus, and other exposed places, were left almost bare, except where some mound or rock or bit of sagebrush created an obstruction, about which the eddying currents piled snowdrifts which rose week after week to huge proportions. On the river bottoms where the sagebrush was thick, the snow lay level with the top of the brush, then drove on to lodge and pack about the cottonwood trees and beneath the river-banks, forming great drifts, extending here and there from bank to bank.

The blizzard abated, but the icy cold did not; another blizzard came, and another and another. Save as it was whirled by the wind, ultimately to become a part of some great drift, the snow remained where it fell. No momentary thaw came to carry away a portion of the country's icy burden, or to alleviate for a few hours the strain on the snow-bound men and women in the lonely ranch-houses. On the bottoms the snow was four feet deep.

November gave way to December, and December to January. The terrible cold persisted, and over the length and breadth of the Bad Lands the drifts grew monstrous, obliterating old landmarks and creating new, to the bewilderment of the occasional wayfarer.

Blizzard followed blizzard. For the men and women on the scattered ranches, it was a period of intense strain and privation; but for the cattle, wandering over the wind-swept world of snow and ice, those terrible months brought an affliction without parallel.

No element was lacking to make the horror of the ranges complete. The country, as Roosevelt had pointed out in July, was over-stocked. Even under favorable conditions there was not enough grass to feed the cattle grazing in the Bad Lands. And conditions throughout the summer of 1886 had been menacingly unfavorable. The drought had been intense. A plague of grasshoppers had swept over the hills. Ranchmen, who were accustomed to store large quantities of hay for use in winter, harvested little or none, and were forced to turn all their cattle out on the range to shift for themselves. The range itself was barren. The stem-cured grass which generally furnished adequate nutriment had been largely consumed by the grasshoppers. What there was of it was buried deep under successive layers of snow. The new stock, the " yearlings," driven into the Bad Lands from Texas or Iowa or Minnesota, succumbed first of all. In the coulees or the creek-beds, where they sought refuge in droves from the stinging blasts of the driven snow, they stood helpless and were literally snowed under, or imprisoned by the accumulation of ice about their feet, and frozen to death where they stood. The native stock, in their shaggier coats, faced the iron desolation with more endurance, keeping astir and feeding on sagebrush and the twigs of young cottonwoods. Gaunt and bony, they hung about the ranches or drifted into Medora, eating the tar-paper from the sides of the shacks, until at last they dropped and died. There was no help that the most sympathetic humanitarian or the most agonized cattle-owner could give them; for there was no fodder. There was nothing that any one could do, except, with aching and apprehensive heart, to watch them die.

They died by thousands and tens of thousands, piled one on the other in coulees and wash-outs and hidden from sight by the snow which seemed never to cease from falling. Only the wolves and coyotes throve that winter, for the steers, imprisoned in the heavy snow, furnished an easy " kill." Sage chickens were smothered under the drifts, rabbits were smothered in their holes.

It was a winter of continuous and unspeakable tragedy. Men rode out into the storms and never reached their destinations, wandering desperately in circles and sinking down at last, to be covered like the cattle with the merciless snow. Children lost their way between ranch-house and stable and were frozen to death within a hundred yards of their homes. The " partner " of Jack Snyder, a pleasant "Dutchman," whom Roosevelt knew well, died and could not be buried, for no pick could break through that iron soil; and Snyder laid him outside the cabin they had shared, to remain there till spring came, covered also by the unremitting snow.

Here and there a woman went off her head. One such instance was productive of a piece of unconscious humor that, in its grimness, was in key with the rest of that terrible winter:

Dear Pierre [wrote a friend to Wibaux, who had gone to France for the winter, leaving his wife in charge of the ranch],— No news, except that Dave Brown killed Dick Smith and your wife's hired girl blew her brains out in the kitchen. Everything O.K. here.

Yours truly

HENRY JACKSON

Early in March, after a final burst of icy fury, a quietness came into the air, and the sun, burning away the haze that lay over it, shone down once more out of a blue sky. Slowly the temperature rose, and then one day, never to be forgotten, there came a warm moistness into the atmosphere. Before night fell, the " Chinook" was pouring down from beyond the mountains, releasing the icy tension and softening all things.

Last Sunday [the Dickinson *Press* recorded, on March 5th] the welcome Chinook wind paid us a visit, and before noon the little rills were trickling down the hills and the brown herbage began to appear through the snow in every direction; the soft, balmy wind fanning the cheek brought memories and hopes of spring to the winter-wearied denizens of our community.

" Within a day or so," said Lincoln Lang afterward, " the snow had softened everywhere. Gullies and wash-outs started to run with constantly increasing force, until at length there was a steady roar of running water, with creeks out of bounds everywhere. Then, one day, we suddenly heard a roar above that of the rushing water, coming from the direction of the Little Missouri, and hurrying there saw a sight, once seen, never to be forgotten. The river was out of banks clear up into the cottonwoods and out on to the bottom, going down in a raging, muddy torrent, literally full of huge, grinding ice-cakes, up-ending and rolling over each other as they went, tearing down trees in their paths, ripping, smashing, tearing at each other and everything in their course in the effort to get out and away. The spectacle held us spellbound. None of us had ever seen anything to compare with it, for the spring freshets of other years had been mild affairs as compared to this. But there was something *else* that had never been seen before, and doubtless never will be seen again, for as we gazed we could see countless carcasses of cattle going down with the ice, rolling over and over as they went, so that at times all four of the stiffened legs of a carcass would point skyward as it turned under the impulsion of the swiftly moving current and the grinding ice-cakes. Now and then a carcass would become pinched between two ice-floes, and either go down entirely or else be forced out on the top of the ice, to be rafted along for a space until the cake upon which it rested suddenly up-ended or turned completely over in the maelstrom of swirling water and ice. Continuously carcasses seemed to be going down while others kept bobbing up at one point or another to replace them."

And this terrible drama continued, not for an hour or for a few hours, but for days. Only as the weeks went by and the snow retreated was it possible for the cattlemen to make any estimate of their losses. The coulees were packed with dead cattle; the sheltered places in the cottonwood trees in the bottoms along the river were packed with them. Here and there a carcass was discovered high up in a crotch of a tree where the animal had struggled over the drifts to munch the tender twigs.

" I got a saddle horse and rode over the country," said Merrifield afterward, " and I'm telling you, the first day I rode out I never saw a live animal."

The desolation of the Bad Lands was indescribable. Where hundreds of thousands of cattle had grazed the previous autumn, shambled and stumbled a few emaciated, miserable survivors. Gregor Lang, who had gone into the winter with three thousand head all told, came out of it with less than four hundred. The " Hash-Knife outfit," which had owned a hundred thousand head, lost seventy-five thousand. Not a ranchman up and down the Little Missouri lost less than half his herd.

The halcyon days of Billings County were over. What had been a flourishing cattle country was a boneyard where the agents of fertilizer factories bargained for skeletons.

XXVI

Some towns go out in a night,
  And some are swept bare in a day,
But our town like a phantom island,
  Just faded away.

Some towns die, and are dead,
  But ours, though it perished, breathes;
And, in old men and in young dreamers
  Still, glows and seethes.

From *Medora Nights*

ROOSEVELT returned from Europe on March 28th.

The loss among the cattle has been terrible [he wrote Sewall from New York early in April]. About the only comfort I have out of it is that, at any rate, you and Wilmot are all right; I would not mind the loss of a few hundred if it was the only way to benefit you and Will — but it will be much more than that.

I am going out West in a few days to look at things for myself.

Well, I must now try to worry through as best I may. Sometime I hope to get a chance to go up and see you all. Then I shall forget my troubles when we go off into the woods after caribou or moose.

There was no merriment this time when Roosevelt arrived in Medora. With Sylvane he rode over the ranges.

You cannot imagine anything more dreary than the look of the Bad Lands [he wrote Sewall]. Everything was cropped as bare as a bone. The sagebrush was just fed out by the starving cattle. The snow lay so deep that nobody could get around; it was almost impossible to get a horse a mile.

In almost every coulee there were dead cattle.

There were nearly three hundred on Wadsworth bottom.
Annie came through all right; Angus died. Only one
or two of our horses died; but the O K lost sixty head.
In one of Munro's draws I counted in a single patch of
brushwood twenty-three dead cows and calves.

You boys were lucky to get out when you did; if you
had waited until spring, I guess it would have been a
case of walking.

" I don't know how many thousand we owned at
Elkhorn and the Maltese Cross in the autumn of
1886," said Merrifield afterward. "But after that
terrible winter there wasn't a cow left, only a few
hundred sick-looking steers."

I am bluer than indigo about the cattle [Roosevelt
wrote his sister Corinne]. It is even worse than I feared;
I wish I was sure I would lose no more than half the
money I invested out here. I am planning how to get out
of it.

With Sylvane and Merrifield, with whom in other
days Roosevelt had talked of golden prospects, he
gloomily reviewed the tragic situation. The impulse
was strong in them all to start afresh and retrieve
their losses. Most of the cattlemen were completely
discouraged and were selling at ridiculously low
prices the stock which had survived the winter. But
Roosevelt resisted the temptation.

"I can't afford to take a chance by putting in any
more capital," said Roosevelt. "I haven't the right
to do it."

And there the discussion ended.

There was a matter beside the wreck of his cattle
business which required Roosevelt's immediate

attention. George Myers was under suspicion (honest George Myers, of all men!) of being a cattle-thief. Roosevelt would have jumped to George's defense in any case, but the fact that the man who brought the charges against him was Joe Morrill, whom the forces of disorder had elected sheriff the previous April, added an extra zest to the fight.

George had, for some years, "run" a few cattle of his own with the Maltese Cross herd. Of these, two steers had, through an oversight, remained un-branded and been sent to Chicago with what was known as a "hair-brand" picked on the hide. Morrill was stock inspector as well as sheriff and allowed the animals to pass, but when Myers, shortly after, went East to visit his family, Morrill swore out a warrant for his arrest and started in pursuit.

He found Myers at Wooster, Ohio, arrested him, obtained his extradition and then, to the amazement of the local judge, released him.

"You can go now, George," he said. " When will you be ready to start back? "

"Oh, in a day or two, I guess," said George.

" That's a hell of a way to use a prisoner," exclaimed the judge.

" Thanks, judge," Morrill replied coolly, " but he's my prisoner."

They returned West shortly after, living high on the way. The sheriff had his wife with him, and it dawned on George that Joe Morrill was having an extraordinarily pleasant vacation at the expense of the taxpayers and of George's own reputation, and, in addition, was making a tidy sum of money out of the trip. His transportation, reservations, and allowance *per diem* were paid, of course, by the county he represented. George, having brought a load of cattle to the stock-yards, had a pass for his return. But that was the sheriff's luck, it appeared, not the county's. Morrill treated him most affably. As they were nearing Medora, in fact, he informed his prisoner that he would appear before the justice of the peace, explain that he had discovered that the charge was baseless, and ask for a dismissal of the case without a hearing on the ground that a mistake had been made.

But the sheriff was not taking into account the fact that Medora had, during the past two or three years, emerged from barbarism, and that there was such a thing as public opinion to be confronted and satisfied. To the majority of the citizens, an accusation of cattle-thieving was almost identical with a conviction, and feeling ran high for a time against George Myers. But Packard jumped into the fight and in the columns of the *Bad Lands Cowboy* excoriated Joe Morrill.

The affair spilled over beyond the limits of Billings County, for the Bismarck *Tribune* printed Morrill's version of the case, and a day or so later published a stinging letter from Packard, who was nothing if not belligerent. It did not hurt his cause that he was able to quote a statement, made by Morrill, that " there's plenty in it if the justice of the peace and the sheriff work together."

Myers, backed by Packard, refused to have the case dismissed and it was put on the calendar at Mandan. There it rested until the following spring.

Roosevelt, arriving in Medora in April, saw at once that a larger issue was at stake than even the question of doing justice to a man wrongfully accused. To have a man like Morrill officially responsible for the detection of cattle-thieves was a travesty.

He promptly sought Joe Morrill, finding him at the "depot." In his capacity as chairman of the Little Missouri River Stockmen's Association, he was in a position to speak as Morrill's employer, and he spoke with his customary directness. Gregor Lang, who happened to be present, told Lincoln afterward that he had "never heard a man get such a scathing" as Roosevelt gave the shifty stock inspector.

"Roosevelt was taking a lot of chances," said Lincoln Lang later, "because Morrill was cornered. He was known to be a gunman and a risky man to mix with."

Roosevelt ordered Morrill to resign his inspectorship at once. Morrill refused.

The annual meeting of the Montana Stockgrower's Association was to be held in Miles City the middle of the month. Roosevelt knew that the Association would not consent to sit in judgment on the case as between Myers and Morrill. He determined, therefore, to demand that the inspectorship at Medora be abolished on the ground that the inspector was worse than useless.

Roosevelt presented his charges before the Board of Stock Commissioners on April 18th. The Board was evidently reluctant to act, and, at the suggestion of certain members of it, Roosevelt, on the following day, presented the matter before the Executive Committee of the Association. He asked that the Committee request the Board of Stock Commissioners to do away with the inspectorship at Medora, but the Committee, too, was wary of giving offense. He asked twice that the Committee hear the charges. The Committee refused, referring him back to the Board of Stock Commissioners.

That Board, meanwhile, was hearing from other cattlemen in the Bad Lands. Boyce, of the great "Three-Seven outfit," supported Roosevelt's charges, and Towers, of the Towers and Gudgell Ranch near the Big Ox Bow, supported Boyce. Morrill was sent for and made a poor showing. It was evidently with hesitant spirits that the Board finally acted. Morrill was dismissed, but the Board hastened to explain that it was because its finances were too low to allow it to continue the inspectorship at Medora and passed a vote of thanks for Morrill's "efficiency and faithful performance of duty."

What Roosevelt said about the vote of thanks is lost to history. He was, no doubt, satisfied with the general result and was ready to let Morrill derive what comfort he could out of the words with which it was adorned.

Through the records of that meeting of the

cattlemen, Roosevelt looms with singular impressiveness. At the meeting of the previous year he
had been an initiate, an effective follower of men
he regarded as better informed than himself; this
year he was himself a leader. During the three
years that had elapsed since he had last taken a
vigorous part in the work of an important deliber-
ative body, he had grown to an extraordinary extent.
In the Legislature in Albany, and in the Republican
Convention in Chicago in 1884, he had been nervous,
vociferous, hot-headed, impulsive; in Miles City,
in 1887, there was the same vigor, the same drive
but with them a poise which the younger man had
utterly lacked. On the first day of the meeting he
made a speech asking for the elimination, from a
report which had been submitted, of a passage
condemning the Interstate Commerce Law. The
house was against him almost to a man, for the
cattlemen considered the law an abominable in-
fringement of their rights.

In the midst of the discussion, a stockman named
Pat Kelly, who was incidentally the Democratic
boss of Michigan, rose in his seat. " Can any
gentleman inform me," he inquired, "why the
business of this meeting should be held up by the
talk of a broken-down New York State politician? "

There was a moment's silence. The stockmen
expected a storm. There was none. Roosevelt took
up the debate as though nothing had interrupted
it. The man from Michigan visibly " flattened
out." Meanwhile, Roosevelt won his point.

He spent most of that summer at Elkhorn Ranch.

Merrifield had, like Joe Ferris, gone East to New Brunswick for a wife, and the bride, who, like Joe's wife, was a woman of education and charm, brought new life to the deserted house on Elkhorn bottom. But something was gone out of the air of the Bad Lands; the glow that had burned in men's eyes had vanished. It had been a country of dreams and it was now a country of ruins; and the magic of the old days could not be re-created.

The cattle industry of the Bad Lands, for the time being, was dead; and the pulses of the little town at the junction of the railroad and the Little Missouri began to flutter fitfully and ominously. Only the indomitable pluck of the Marquis and his deathless fecundity in conceiving new schemes of unexampled magnitude kept it alive at all. The Marquis's ability to create artificial respiration and to make the dead take on the appearance of life never showed to better effect than in that desolate year of 1887. His plan to slaughter cattle on the range for consumption along the line of the Northern Pacific was to all intents and purposes shattered by the autumn of 1885. But no one, it appears, recognized that fact, least of all the Marquis. He changed a detail here, a detail there; then, charged with a new enthusiasm, he talked success to every reporter who came to interview him, flinging huge figures about with an ease that a Rockefeller might envy; and the newspapers from coast to coast called him one of the builders of the Northwest.

His plan to sell dressed beef along the railroad gave way to a project to sell it at the wholesale stalls in Chicago. That failed. Thereupon, he evolved an elaborate and daring scheme to sell it direct to consumers in New York and other Eastern seaboard cities.

" The Marquis actually opened his stores in Fulton Market," said Packard afterward, " and there sold range beef killed in Medora. Of course his project failed. It was shot full of fatal objections. But with his magnetic personality, with his verbalistic short-jumps over every objection, with every newspaper and magazine of the land an enthusiastic volunteer in de Mores propaganda, and with the halo of the von Hoffman millions surrounding him and all his deeds, bankers and business men fell into line at the tail of the de Mores chariot. We of the Bad Lands were the first to see the fatal weaknesses in his plans, but we were believers, partly because the Marquis seemed to overcome every difficulty by the use of money, and mainly because we wanted to believe."

Dozens of shops were in fact opened by the Marquis, but the public refused to trade, even at a saving, in stores where only one kind of meat could be bought. The Marquis had all the figures in the world to prove that the public should buy; but human nature thwarted him.

The plan failed, but the Marquis, with his customary dexterity, obscured the failure with a new and even more engaging dream.

'"Our company is to be merged into another very large cattle syndicate," he said in March, 1887, " and having abundant capital, we propose to buy up every retail dealer in this city either by cash or stock."

The National Consumers' Company was the name of the new organization.

There was a fine mixture of altruism and business in the first prospectus which the Marquis's new company issued:

Crushed, as so many others, by monopoly, we have been looking for the means of resisting it by uniting in a practical way with those who, like ourselves, try to make their future by their work. This has led to the organization of this company. The name of the company shows its aims. It must be worked by and for the people.

That sounded very impressive, and the newspapers began to speak of the Marquis as a true friend of the people. Meanwhile, the *Bad Lands Cowboy* announced:

Marquis de Mores has completed contracts with the French Government to supply its soldiers with a newly invented soup. He intends to visit Europe soon to make contracts with Western range cattle companies who have their headquarters there, for the slaughtering of their cattle.

The soup scheme evidently died stillborn, for history records nothing further of it, and less than three months after the National Consumers' Company was founded with blare of trumpets, it had collapsed. It was characteristic of von Hoffman, whose fortune was behind the undertaking, that he paid back every subscriber to the stock in full. If any one was to lose, he intimated, it was von Hoffman. But, having settled with the creditors of his expensive son-in-law, he explained to that gentleman, in words which could not be misunderstood, that he would have no more of his schemes. Von Hoffman thereupon betook himself to Europe, and the Marquis to Medora.

His optimism remained indomitable to the last. To reporters he denied vigorously that he had any intentions " of removing his business interests from Dakota."

" I like Dakota and have come to stay," he remarked. Thereupon he launched one more grandiose scheme, announcing that he had discovered a gold mine in Montana and was planning to begin working it for all it was worth as soon as his prospectors had completed their labors; and sailed for India with his intrepid Marquise to hunt tigers.

Dakota knew him no more, and under the heading, " An Ex-Dakota Dreamer," the Sioux Falls *Press* pronounced his epitaph:

The Marquis is a most accomplished dreamer, and so long as his fortune lasted, or his father-in-law, Baron von Hoffman, would put up the money, he could afford to dream. He once remarked confidentially to a friend, " I veel make ze millions and millions by ze great enterprizes in America, and zen I veel go home to France, and veel capture my comrades in ze French armee, an veel plot and plan, and directly zey veel put me in command, and zen I veel swoop down on ze government, and first zing you know I veel mount the zrone." One time his agent at Medora, his ranch on the Northern Pacific, wrote him at New York about the loss of three thousand head of sheep, the letter going into all the details of the affair. The Marquis turned the sheet over and wrote, " Please don't trouble me with trifles like these." He is a very pleasant gentleman to meet, but unfortunately his schemes are bigger than he is.

Medora was a town whose glory had departed. A pall was on all things, and the *Cowboy* was no longer present to dispel it with the cheerful optimism of old. For, one night, when the cold was most bitter, and the wind was high, a fire had started in the old cantonment building where Packard lived with his newly wedded wife, and printed the pages that had for three years brought gayety to the inhabitants of Medora, and stability to its infant institutions. The files were burned up, the presses destroyed; the *Cowboy* was a memory. It was as though the soul of Medora had gone out of its racked body. The remains lay rigid and voiceless.

One by one its leading citizens deserted it. Roosevelt came and went, making his long stays no longer in the West, but in the East, where " home " was now. Packard went, then Fisher, then Van Driesche.

[J. C. Maunders,] of Medora [runs an item in the Dickinson *Press*], is talking of moving two or three of his buildings from there to Dickinson.

It was followed by other items full of mournful import.

[J. C. Maunders,] [Joseph Morrill,] and John W. Goodall, of Medora, were here Thursday and closed contracts for several lots. They will build.

Two weeks later, the exodus began. The telling of it has a Shaksperean flavor:

Medora is coming to Dickinson. On Thursday a train came in from the west with a number of flat-cars on which were loaded the buildings of [J. C. Maunders,] who recently bought lots here.

Thus it was that the Pyramid Park Hotel, where Roosevelt had spent his first night in Little Missouri, four years previous, came to Dickinson to become a most respectable one-family dwelling. Mrs. Mc-Geeney's hotel followed it two weeks later.

In August came the final blow:

D. O. Sweet and family have moved from Medora to Dickinson. Mr. Sweet desired to reside where there was some life and prospect of growth.

Alas, for earthly greatness, when a son of the town that was to rival Omaha should desert her with such a valedictory!

XXVII

The range is empty and the trails are blind,
   And I don't seem but half myself to-day.
I wait to hear him ridin' up behind
   And feel his knee rub mine the good old way.
He's dead — and what that means no man kin tell.
   Some call it "gone before."
Where? I don't know, but, God! I know so well
   That he ain't here no more!

                             BADGER CLARK

THIS, then, is the story of Roosevelt in the Bad Lands. What remains is epilogue.

In the autumn of 1887, Roosevelt was again with the Merrifields at Elkhorn and with Sylvane at the Maltese Cross, to assist in the round-up of a train-load of cattle which he subsequently sold at Chicago (again at a loss, for the prices for beef were even lower than the previous year). He went on a brief hunt after antelope in the broken country between the Little Missouri and the Beaver; he fought a raging prairie fire with the split and bleeding carcass of a steer; he went on another hunt late in December with a new friend named Fred Herrig, and was nearly frozen to death in a blizzard, attempting (not without success) to shoot mountain sheep; whereupon, feeling very fit, he returned East to his family and his books.

He was now increasingly busy with his writing, completing that winter a volume of vigorous sketches of the frontier, called "Ranch Life and the Hunting Trail," beside his " Life of Gouverneur

Morris," and a book of "Essays on Practical Politics." In the autumn of 1888, he was again at Elkhorn and again on the chase, this time in the Selkirks in northern Idaho, camping on Kootenai Lake, and from there on foot with a pack on his back, ranging among the high peaks with his old guide John Willis and an Indian named Ammal, who was pigeon-toed and mortally afraid of hobgoblins.

In 1889 he became a member of the Civil Service Commission in Washington, and thereafter he saw the Bad Lands only once a year, fleeing from his desk to the open country every autumn for a touch of the old wild life and a glimpse of the old friends who yet lingered in that forsaken country.

Medora had all the desolation of "a busted cowtown" whose inhabitants, as one cowpuncher remarked in answer to a tenderfoot's inquiry, were "eleven, including the chickens, when they were all in town." All of the wicked men and most of the virtuous ones, who had lent picturesqueness to Medora in the old days, were gone. Sylvane Ferris still lingered as foreman of the cattle which Roosevelt still retained in the Bad Lands, and Joe Ferris still ran his store, officiated as postmaster, and kept a room for Roosevelt on his infrequent visits. Bill Williams shot a man and went to jail, and with him went the glory of his famous saloon. Of his old cronies, Hell-Roaring Bill Jones only remained. He was a man of authority now, for he had been elected sheriff when Joe Morrill moved his *lares et penates* to Dickinson. His relations with Roosevelt criss-crossed, for, as sheriff, Roosevelt was his deputy, but whenever Roosevelt went on an extended hunting trip, Hell-Roaring Bill Jones was his teamster. He was, incidentally, an extraordinarily efficient teamster. He had certain profane rituals which he repeated on suitable occasions, word for word, but with an emphasis and sincerity that made them sound each time as though he had invented them under the inspiration of the immediate necessity. He had a special torrent of obscenity for his team when they were making a difficult crossing somewhere on the Little Missouri. It was always the same succession of terrifying expletives, and it always had the desired effect. It worked better than a whip.

Meanwhile, the devotion of Bill Jones to Theodore Roosevelt was a matter of common report throughout the countryside, and it was said that he once stayed sober all summer in order to be fit to go on a hunting trip with Roosevelt in the fall.

Sylvane married, like his " partners " going for his bride to New Brunswick, whose supply of delightful young ladies seemed to be inexhaustible. They went to live in a " martin's cage," as they called it, under the bluff at Medora, and there Roosevelt visited them, after Joe moved to Montana and his store passed into other hands. The Langs remained at Yule. After the evil winter, Sir James Pender threw them upon their own resources, and the years that followed were hard. Lang had long recognized the mistake he had made in not accepting Roosevelt's offer that September of 1883, and the matter remained a sore subject for Mrs. Lang, who never ceased regretting the lapse of judgment which had made her otherwise excellent husband miss what she knew, as soon as she met Roosevelt, had been the greatest opportunity which Gregor Lang would ever have placed in his hands. Lang, as county commissioner, became an important factor in the development of the county, and his ranch flourished. Lincoln Lang turned to engineering and became an inventor. He went East to live, but his heart remained among the buttes where he had spent his adventurous boyhood.

The Eatons forsook the punching of cattle, and engaged in " dude " ranching on a grand scale, and the " Eaton Ranch " began to be famous from coast to coast even before they moved to Wolf, Wyoming, in the foothills of the Big Horn Mountains. Mrs. Cummins drifted away with her family, carrying, no doubt, her discontent with her. Lloyd Roberts disappeared, as though the earth had swallowed him, murdered, it was supposed, in Cheyenne, after he had loaned Bill Williams seven hundred dollars. Mrs. Roberts was not daunted. She kept the little ranch on Sloping Bottom and fed and clothed and educated her five daughters by her own unaided efforts. The Vines, father and son, drifted eastward. Packard and Dantz took to editing newspapers, Packard in Montana, Dantz in Pennsylvania. Edgar Haupt became a preacher, and Herman Haupt a physician. Fisher grew prosperous in the

State of Washington; Maunders throve mightily in Dickinson; Wilmot Dow died young; Bill Sewall resumed his life in Maine as a backwoodsman and guide; Foley remained custodian of the deserted de Mores property at Medora; "Redhead" Finnegan was hanged.

Poor "Dutch" Van Zander drank up his last remittance. "There," he cried, "I have blown in a hundred and twenty thousand dollars, but I've given the boys a whale of a good time!" He gave up drinking thereafter and went to work for the "Three Seven" outfit as an ordinary cowhand. He became a good worker, but when the call of gold in Alaska sounded, he responded and was seen no more in his old haunts. A few years later he appeared again for a day, saying that he was on his way to his old home in Holland. A month or two later news filtered into Medora that the brilliant and most lovable Dutch patrician's son had been found, dead by his own hand, in a cemetery in Amsterdam, lying across his mother's grave.

Twice Roosevelt's path crossed Joe Morrill's, and each time there was conflict. Morrill opened a butcher-shop in a town not far from Medora, and it devolved on Roosevelt, as chairman of the Stockmen's Association, to inform him that, unless he changed his manner of acquiring the beef he sold, he would promptly go to jail. The shifty swashbuckler closed his shop, and not long after, Roosevelt, who was at the time serving on the Civil Service Commission in Washington, heard that Morrill was endeavoring to have himself made marshal of one of the Northwestern States. The "reference" Roosevelt gave him on that occasion was effective. Morrill was not appointed; and what happened to him thereafter is lost to history.

In 1890, Roosevelt was at the ranch at Elkhorn with Mrs. Roosevelt; a year later he hunted elk with an English friend, R. H. M. Ferguson, at Two Ocean Pass in the Shoshones, in northwestern Wyoming. That autumn the Merrifields moved to the Flathead country in northwestern Montana, and Roosevelt closed the ranch-house. A year later he returned to Elkhorn for a week's hunting. The wild forces of nature had already taken possession. The bunch-grass grew tall in the yard and on the sodded roofs of the stables and sheds; the weather-beaten log walls of the house itself were one in tint with the trunks of the gnarled cottonwoods by which it was shaded. "The ranch-house is in good repair," he wrote to Bill Sewall, "but it is melancholy to see it deserted."

Early the next spring Roosevelt took Archibald D. Russell, R. H. M. Ferguson, and his brother-in-law Douglas Robinson into partnership with him and formed the Elkhorn Stock Company, transferring his equity in the Elkhorn Ranch to the new corporation.[1]

It was at the end of a wagon-trip to the Black Hills, which Roosevelt took with Sylvane and Hell-

[1] See Appendix for a statement of Roosevelt's cattle investment.

Roaring Bill Jones in 1893, that Roosevelt met Seth Bullock.

Seth was at that time sheriff in the Black Hills district [wrote Roosevelt in his " Autobiography "], and a man he had wanted — a horse-thief — I finally got, I being at the time deputy sheriff two or three hundred miles to the north. The man went by a nickname which I will call " Crazy Steve." It was some time after " Steve's " capture that I went down to Deadwood on business, Sylvane Ferris and I on horseback, while Bill Jones drove the wagon. At a little town, Spearfish, I think, after crossing the last eighty or ninety miles of gumbo prairie, we met Seth Bullock. We had had rather a rough trip, and had lain out for a fortnight, so I suppose we looked somewhat unkempt. Seth received us with rather distant courtesy at first, but unbent when he found out who we were, remarking, " You see, by your looks I thought you were some kind of a tin-horn gambling outfit, and that I might have to keep an eye on you! " He then inquired after the capture of " Steve " — with a little of the air of one sportsman when another has shot a quail that either might have claimed — " My bird, I believe? "

In a letter to John Hay, Roosevelt described that meeting.

When somebody asked Seth Bullock to meet us, he at first expressed disinclination. Then he was told that I was the Civil Service Commissioner, upon which he remarked genially, " Well, anything civil goes with me," and strolled over to be introduced.

During these years, while Roosevelt was working on the Civil Service Commission, fighting the spoilsmen and rousing the conscience of the American people with a new ideal of public service, even while he stimulated their national pride with a fresh expression of the American spirit, his old rival, the Marquis de Mores, was noticeably stirring the Old World. A year in India had been succeeded by a long stay in China, where the Marquis had conceived a scheme to secure concessions for France, which somehow went the way of all the Marquis's schemes; nothing came of it.

He returned to France. The French people were in a restless, unhappy state. More than once, war with Germany seemed imminent. The Government was shot through with intrigue and corruption. The Marquis, with all the faults of his temperament, was an idealist, with a noble vision for his country. He saw that it had fallen into the hands of base, self-seeking men, and he grasped at every means that presented itself to overthrow the powers that seemed to him to be corrupting and enfeebling France. He became an enthusiastic follower of Boulanger; when Boulanger fell, he became a violent anti-Semite, and shortly after, a radical Socialist. Meanwhile, he fought one duel after another, on one occasion killing his man. More than once he came into conflict with the law, and once was imprisoned for three months, accused of inciting the populace to violence against the army. There were rumors of plots with the royalists and plots with the anarchists. It did not apparently seem of particular importance to the Marquis by whom the Government was overthrown, so it was overthrown.

His plans did not prosper. Anti-Semitism grew beyond his control. The Dreyfus affair broke, and set the very foundations of France quivering. What the Marquis's part in it was, is obscure, but it was said that he was deeply involved.

His attention was turning in another direction. France and England were struggling for the possession of Central Africa, and the Marquis conceived the grandiose dream of uniting all the Mohammedans of the world against England. He went to Tunis in the spring of 1896, commissioned, it was said, by the French Government to lead an expedition into the Soudan to incite the Arabs to resist the English advance in Africa.

Whether the Marquis actually had the support of the Government is more than dubious. When he set out on his expedition to the wild tribes of the Tunisian desert, he set out practically alone. At the last moment, the Marquis changed his Arab escort for a number of Touaregs, who offered him their services. They were a wild, untrustworthy race, and men who knew the country pleaded with him not to trust himself to them. But the Marquis, who had prided himself on his judgment in Little Missouri in 1883, had not changed his spots in 1896. His camel-drivers led him into an ambush near the well of El Ouatia. He carried himself like the game fighting man that he had always been, and there was a ring of dead men around him when he himself finally succumbed.

Nineteen days later an Arab official, sent out by

the French military commander of the district, found his body riddled with wounds and buried in the sand near a clump of bushes close to where he had fallen. His funeral in Paris was a public event.

It was a tragic but a fitting close to a dreamer's romantic career. But the end was not yet, and the romance connected with the Marquis de Mores was not yet complete. The investigation into his death which the French Government ordered was abandoned without explanation. The Marquis's widow protested, accusing the Government of complicity in her husband's death, and charging that those who had murdered the Marquis were native agents of the French authorities and had been acting under orders.

The Marquise herself went to Tunis, determined that the assassins of her husband should be brought to justice. There is a ring in her proclamation to the Arabs which might well have made the stripped bones of the Marquis stir in their leaden coffin.

In behalf of the illustrious, distinguished, and noble lady, the Marquise of Mores, wife of the deceased object of God's pity, the Marquis of Mores, who was betrayed and murdered at El Ouatia, in the country of Ghadames, salutations, penitence, and the benediction of God!

Let it herewith be known to all faithful ones that I place myself in the hands of God and of you, because I know you to be manly, energetic, and courageous. I appeal to you to help me avenge the death of my husband by punishing his assassins. I am a woman. Vengeance cannot be wreaked by my own hand. For this reason I inform you, and swear to you, by the one Almighty God, that to whosoever shall capture and deliver to the authorities at El-Qued, at Ouargia, or at El-Goleah one of my husband's assassins I will give 1000 douros ($750), 2000 douros for two assassins, 3000 douros for three assassins. As to the principal assassins, Bechaoui and Sheik Ben Abdel Kader, I will give 2000 douros for each of them. And now, understand, make yourselves ready, and may God give you success.

MARQUISE DE MORES

The murderers were captured, convicted, and executed. Then the little American woman, with her hair of Titian red, whom the cowboys of Little Missouri had christened " The Queen of the West," quietly withdrew from the public gaze; and the curtain fell on a great romantic drama.

Theodore Roosevelt was just coming into national eminence as Police Commissioner of New York City when the Marquis de Mores died beside the well of El Ouatia. As a member of the Civil Service Commission in Washington he had caught the imagination of the American people, and a growing number of patriotic men and women, scattered over the country, began to look upon him as the leader they had been longing for. He came to Medora no more for the round-up or the chase.

In May, 1897, Roosevelt became Assistant Secretary of the Navy. Less than a year later the Spanish War broke out. The dream he had dreamed in 1886 of a regiment recruited from the wild horsemen of the plains became a reality. From the Canadian border to the Rio Grande, the men he had lived and worked with on the round-up, and thousands of others whose imaginations had been seized by the stories of his courage and endurance, which had passed from mouth to mouth and from camp-fire to camp-fire through the cattle country, offered their services. The Rough Riders were organized, and what they accomplished is history. There were unquestionably more weighty reasons why he should become Governor of New York State than that he had been the successful leader of an aggregation of untamed gunmen in Cuba. But it was that fact in his career which caught the fancy of the voters, and by a narrow margin elected him a Republican Governor of his State in what, as everybody knew, was a " Democratic year."

The men and women of the Bad Lands, scattered far and wide over the Northwest, watched his progress with a glowing feeling in their hearts that was akin to the pride that a father feels at the greatness of a son whom he himself has guided in the way that he should go. There was none of them but felt that he had had a personal share in the making of this man who was beginning to loom larger and larger on the national horizon. They had been his mentors, and inasmuch as they had shown him how to tighten a saddle cinch or quiet a restless herd, they felt that they had had a part in the building of his character. They had a great pride, moreover, in the bit of country where they had spent their ardent youth, and they felt assured that the experiences which had thrilled and deepened them, had thrilled and deepened him also. In their hearts they felt that they knew something of what had made him—"the smell, the singing prairies, the spirit that thrilled the senses there, the intoxicating exhilaration, the awful silences, the mysterious hazes, the entrancing sunsets, the great storms and blizzards, the quiet, enduring people, the great, unnoted tragedies, the cheer, the humor, the hospitality, the lure of fortunes at the end of rainbows"—all those things they felt had joined to build America's great new leader; and they, who had experienced these things with him, felt that they were forever closer to him than his other countrymen could ever possibly be.

Roosevelt was nominated for the vice-presidency in June, 1900, and in July he began a campaign tour over the country which eclipsed even Bryan's prodigious journeyings of 1896. Early in September he came to Dakota.

Joe Ferris was the first to greet him after he crossed the border at a way-station at six o'clock in the morning.[1]

"Joe, old boy," cried Roosevelt exuberantly, "will you ever forget the first time we met?"

Joe admitted that he would not.

"You nearly murdered me. It seemed as if all the ill-luck in the world pursued us."

Joe grinned.

"Do you remember too, Joe," exclaimed Roosevelt, "how I swam the swollen stream and you stood

[1] The account of Roosevelt's triumphant return to Medora is taken verbatim from contemporary newspapers.

on the bank and kept your eyes on me? The stream was very badly flooded when I came to it," said the Governor, turning to the group that had gathered about them. "I forced my horse into it and we swam for the other bank. Joe was very much distressed for fear we would not get across."

"I wouldn't have taken that swim for all of Dakota," said Joe.

At Dickinson, a gray-faced, lean man pushed his way through the crowd. It was Maunders, who had prospered, in spite of his evil ways. "Why," exclaimed Roosevelt, "it does me good to see you. You remember when I needed a hammer so badly and you loaned it to me? You loaned me a rifle also. I never shall forget how badly I needed that hammer just then."

Maunders, who had always been affable, grinned with delight and joined the Governor's party.

The train moved on to Medora. Roosevelt and Joe Ferris sat by the window, and it seemed that every twisted crag and butte reminded them of the days when they had ridden over that wild country together.

As the train neared Medora, Roosevelt was palpably moved. "The romance of my life began here," he said.

There were forty or fifty people at the station in Medora. They hung back bashfully, but he was among them in an instant.

"Why, this is Mrs. Roberts!" he exclaimed. "You have not changed a bit, have you?"

She drew his attention to George Myers, who was all smiles.

" My, my, George Myers! " exclaimed Roosevelt, " I did not even hope to see you." Roosevelt turned to the crowd. "George used to cook for me," he said, with a wry expression.

"Do you remember the time I made green biscuits for you? " asked George, with a grin.

" I do," said Roosevelt emphatically, " I do, George. And I remember the time you fried the beans with rosin instead of lard. The best proof in the world, George, that I have a good constitution is that I ate your cooking and survived."

" Well, now, Governor," exclaimed George, " I was thinking it would be a good idea to get that man Bryan up here and see what that kind of biscuit would do for him."

Roosevelt looked about him, where the familiar buttes stretched gray and bleak in every direction. " It does not seem right," he exclaimed, " that I should come here and not stay."

Some one brought a bronco for Roosevelt. A minute later he was galloping eastward toward the trail leading up to the bluff that rose a thousand feet behind Medora. " Over there is Square Butte," he cried eagerly, " and over there is Sentinel Butte. My ranch was at Chimney Butte. Just this side of it is the trail where Custer marched westward to the Yellowstone and the Rosebud to his death. There is the church especially erected for the use of the wife of the Marquis de Mores. His old house is beyond. You can see it."

For a minute he sat silent. " Looking back to my old days here," he said, " I can paraphrase Kipling and say, 'Whatever may happen, I can thank God I have lived and toiled with men.'"

Roosevelt was inaugurated as Vice-President in March, 1901. Six months later he was President of the United States. From a venturesome cowpuncher who made his way shyly into the White House, the glad tidings were spread to the Bad Lands and through the whole Northwest that Roosevelt was the same Roosevelt, and that everybody had better take a trip to Washington as soon as he could, for orders had gone forth that "the cowboy bunch can come in whenever they want to."

Occasionally one or the other had difficulty in getting past the guards. It took Sylvane two days, once, to convince the doorkeeper that the President wanted to see him. Roosevelt was indignant. " The next time they don't let you in, Sylvane," he exclaimed, " you just shoot through the windows."

No one shot through the windows. It was never necessary. The cowboys dined at the President's table with Cabinet ministers and ambassadors.

" Remember, Jim, that if you shot at the feet of the British Ambassador to make him dance," Roosevelt whispered to one of his cowboy guests on one occasion, " it would be likely to cause international complications."

" Why, Colonel, I shouldn't think of it," exclaimed Jim. " I shouldn't think of it! "

The cowpunchers were the only ones who refused

to take altogether seriously the tradition that an invitation to the White House was equivalent to a command. John Willis on one occasion came down from Montana to discuss reclamation with the President, and Roosevelt asked him to take dinner at the White House that night. Willis murmured that he did not have a dress-suit, and it would not do to dine with the President of the United States " unless he were togged out proper."

" Oh, that needn't bother you," exclaimed the President.

" It makes a heap of difference," said Willis. "I may not always do the right thing, but I know what's proper."

" You would be just as welcome at my table if you came in buckskin trousers."

" I know that's true," Willis replied, " but I guess I will have to side-step this trip. If you are taking any horseback rides out on the trail here to-morrow, I'm your man, but I guess I will get my grub downtown at the hashery where I'm bunking."

That was all there was to it. John Willis could not be persuaded.

Once more, for the last time, Roosevelt in 1903 went back to Medora. As they came into the Bad Lands, he stood on the rear platform of his car, gazing wistfully over the forbidding-looking landscape.

" I know all this country like a book," he said to John Burroughs, who was beside him. " I have ridden over it and hunted in it and tramped over it in all seasons and weather, and it looks like home to me."

As soon as I got west of the Missouri I came into my own former stamping-ground [he wrote to John Hay, describing that visit]. At every station there was somebody who remembered my riding in there when the Little Missouri round-up went down to the Indian reservation and then worked north across the Cannon Ball and up Knife and Green Rivers; or who had been an interested and possibly malevolent spectator when I had ridden east with other representatives of the cowmen to hold a solemn council with the leading grangers on the vexed subject of mavericks; or who had been hired as a train-hand when I had been taking a load of cattle to Chicago, and who remembered well how he and I at the stoppages had run frantically down the line of the cars and with our poles jabbed the unfortunate cattle who had lain down until they again stood up, and thereby gave themselves a chance for their lives; and who remembered how when the train started we had to clamber hurriedly aboard and make our way back to the caboose along the tops of the cattle cars.

At Mandan two of my old cow-hands, Sylvane and Joe Ferris, joined me. At Dickinson all of the older people had known me and the whole town turned out with wild and not entirely sober enthusiasm. It was difficult to make them much of a speech, as there were dozens of men each earnestly desirous of recalling to my mind some special incident. One man, how he helped me bring in my cattle to ship, and how a blue roan steer broke away leading a bunch which it took him and me three hours to round up and bring back; another, how seventeen years before I had come in a freight train from Medora to deliver the Fourth of July oration; another, a gray-eyed individual named [Maunders], who during my early years at Medora had shot and killed an equally objectionable individual, reminded me how, just twenty years before, when I was on my first buffalo hunt, he loaned me the hammer off his Sharp's rifle to replace the broken hammer of mine; another recalled the time when he and I worked on the round-up as partners, going with the Little Missouri " outfit " from the head of the Box Alder to the mouth of the Big Beaver, and then striking over to represent the Little Missouri brands on the Yellowstone round-up; yet another recalled the time when I, as deputy sheriff of Billings County, had brought in three cattle-thieves named Red Finnegan, Dutch Chris, and the half-breed to his keeping, he being then sheriff in Dickinson, etc., etc., etc.

At Medora, which we reached after dark, the entire population of the Bad Lands down to the smallest baby had gathered to meet me. This was formerly my home station. The older men and women I knew well; the younger ones had been wild tow-headed children when I lived and worked along the Little Missouri. I had spent nights in their ranches. I still remembered meals which the women had given me when I had come from some hard expedition, half famished and sharp-set as a wolf. I had killed buffalo and elk, deer and antelope with some of the men. With others I had worked on the trail, on the calf round-up, on the beef round-up. We had been together on occasions which we still remembered when some bold rider met his death in trying to stop a stampede, in riding a mean horse, or in the quicksands of some swollen river which he sought to swim. They all felt I was their man, their old friend; and even if they had been hostile to me in the old days, when we were divided by the sinister bickering and jealousies and hatreds of all frontier communities, they now firmly believed they had always been my staunch friends and admirers. They had all gathered in the town hall, which was draped for a dance — young children, babies, everybody being present. I shook hands with them all, and almost each one had some memory of special association with me he or she wished to discuss. I only regretted that I could not spend three hours with them.

Hell-Roaring Bill Jones was supposed to be at Gardiner, Wyoming, and Roosevelt, arriving there a few days later for a camping trip through the Yellowstone, asked eagerly for his old friend. Bill Jones was down in the world. He had had to give up his work as sheriff in Medora because he began to lose his nerve and would break down and weep like a child when he was called upon to make an arrest. He was driving a team in Gardiner outside the Park, and during the days preceding Roosevelt's arrival took so many drinks while he was telling of his intimacy with the man who had become President of the United States, that he had to be carried into the sagebrush before Roosevelt actually arrived. Roosevelt left word to keep Bill Jones sober against his return, and when Roosevelt emerged from the Park, they met for the last time. It was a sad interview, for what was left of Hell-Roaring Bill Jones was only a sodden, evil-looking shell.

" Bill Jones did not live long after that," said Howard Eaton. " The last I saw of him was two or three miles from Old Faithful. He said, 'I'm going to the trees.' We went out to look for him, but couldn't find a trace. This was in March. He wandered way up one of those ravines and the supposition is that he froze to death. Some fellow found him up there in June, lying at the edge of a creek. The coyotes had carried off one of his arms, and they planted him right there. And that was the end of old Bill Jones."

Years passed, and bitter days came to Roosevelt, but though other friends failed him, the men of the Bad Lands remained faithful.

In 1912, four of them were delegates to the Progressive Convention—Sylvane Ferris from North Dakota, where he was president of a bank; Joe Ferris, George Myers, and Merrifield from Montana. Even "Dutch Wannigan," living as a hermit in the wilderness forty miles west of Lake MacDonald, became an ardent Progressive. "I can't afford to go to Helena," he wrote in answer to an appeal from Merrifield to attend the State Progressive Convention, "but if you think there'll be a row, I'll try to make it." Packard and Dantz gave their pens to the cause.

George Myers was the last of the "cowboy bunch" to see him. They met in Billings in October, 1918. The town was filled with the crowds who had come from near and far to see the man who, everybody said, was sure again to be President of the United States.

"Have you got a room, George?" cried Roosevelt, as they met.

Myers shook his head cheerfully.

"Share mine with me," said Roosevelt, "and we'll talk about old times."

Three months later to a day, the man who had been Little Missouri's " four-eyed tenderfoot " was dead.

The Bad Lands are still the Bad Lands, except that the unfenced prairies are fenced now and on each bit of parched bottom-land a " nester " has his cabin and is struggling, generally in vain, to dig a living out of the soil in a region which God never made for farming. The treacherous Little Missouri is treacherous still; here and there a burning mine still sends a tenuous wisp toward the blue sky; the buttes have lost none of their wild magnificence; and dawn and dusk, casting long shadows across the coulees, reveal the old heart-rending loveliness.

Medora sleeps through the years and dreams of other days. Schuyler Lebo, who was shot by the Indians, delivers the mail; "Nitch" Kendley operates the pump for the water-tank at the railroad station; a nonogenarian called " Frenchy," who hunted with Roosevelt and has lost his wits, plays cribbage all day long at the "Rough Riders Hotel." These three are all that remain of the gay aggregation that made life a revel at the " depot " and at Bill Williams's saloon. And yet, even in its desolation, as the cook of the "Rough Riders Hotel" remarked, " There's something fascinating about the blinkety-blank place. I don't know why I stay here, but I do."

The ranch-house of the Maltese Cross has been moved to Bismarck, where it stands, wind-beaten and neglected, in the shadow of the capitol. The Elkhorn ranch-house is gone, used for lumber, but the great foundation stones that Bill Sewall and Will Dow laid under it remain, and the row of cottonwoods that shaded it still stand, without a gap. Near by are the ruins of the shack which Maunders claimed and Roosevelt held, in spite of threats. The river flows silently beneath a grassy bank. There is no lovelier spot in the Bad Lands.

THE END